The Other Side Of The Closet

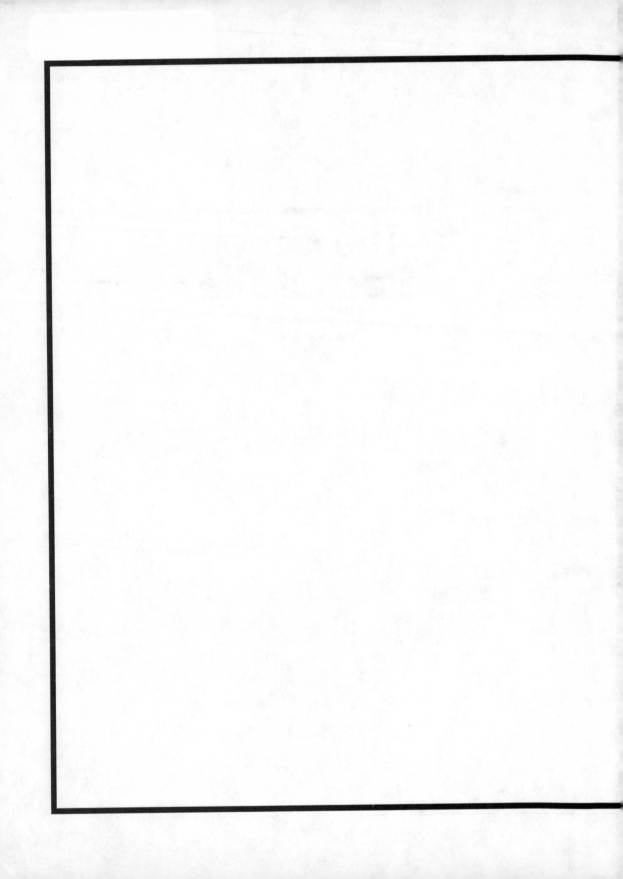

The Other Side Of The Closet

THE COMING-OUT CRISIS
FOR STRAIGHT SPOUSES

by
Amity Pierce Buxton, Ph.D.

IBS PRESS, INC.
SANTA MONICA, CALIFORNIA

Cover and book design by Melvin L. Harris and Susan Muller-Harris
Airbrushing by Debbie R. Marr
Computer Graphics by Melvin L. Harris
Type composition by Susan Muller-Harris
Editing by BettyClare Moffatt and Miriam Jacobson

IBS PRESS, Inc.
744 Pier Avenue
Santa Monica, CA 90405
(213)450-6485

IBS PRESS FIRST PRINTING, JUNE, 1991

Library of Congress Cataloging-in-Publication Data
Buxton, Amity.
The other side of the closet : the coming-out crisis for straight spouses / by Amity Pierce Buxton.
p. cm.
Includes bibliographical references.
ISBN 1-877880-07-8 : $14.95
1. Bisexuality in marriage—United States. 2. Coming out (Sexual identity)—United States. 3. Homosexuality—United States. 4. Married people—United States—Psychology. I. Title
HQ74.B89 1991
306.76'5—dc20   91-6975

Manufactured in the United States of America

dedication

To my children...
whose love sustained me in my journey
from trauma to transformation,
after my husband came out in 1983

the few friends who knew...
and dared support me,
without knowing what it really means
to be on the other side of the closet

the more than two million other straight spouses ...
whose stories aren't here,
yet who could tell similar tales of pain and
increased strength and understanding

and the readers of this book...
with hope for spouses facing a partner's coming out
and for mixed-orientation couples trying to stay together;

with compassion for homosexual and bisexual persons
coping with the intolerance of society;

with encouragement to those who view gay and lesbian
issues from extreme positions to consider the middle ground,
where the human condition common to us all plays
out its uneven course in individual lives.

<u>acknowledgments</u>

The professionals and hundreds of
spouses whose assistance was crucial to
the completion of this project are too
numerous to list. Special mention goes to
Sandra Auerback, M.S.W.,
George Deabill, Ph.D.,
Bill Jones,
Webster Lithgow,
Kathy McMahon, Psy.D.,
BettyClare Moffatt, M.A.,
Charles Moser, Ph.D.,
Sharon Nathan, Ph.D.,
Jay P. Paul, Ph.D.,
Aurele Samuels,
Riette Smith, M.S.,
Bryan Strong, Ph.D.,
Jane E. Vennard, M. Div.,
and Claire Ortalda, my editor, whose
challenging mind helped me clarify the
confounding issues straight spouses face.

contents

Part Six
BREAKING THE MOLD
Transformation of Shattered Belief System

Afterword
BEYOND THE CLOSET

introduction

COMING OUT IN MARRIAGE

THE UNTOLD STORY

So they sit and watch me
they wonder, they whisper...
and still I lay pinned under the load.

—HANNA, 35, mother of three

anna is a cheerful and capable woman who tried to hold her marriage together for two years while caring for her three children under the age of twelve and keeping secret her husband's two arrests for sex acts in public men's restrooms. The night before she finally sought therapy, she wrote the lines above.

What Hanna didn't know was that she is only one of well over two million women and men across the country who are or have been married to a homosexual or bisexual partner.[1] Only a few are aware of their partner's sexual orientation when they marry. In some cases the partner is not even sure. In time the truth comes out with painful consequences for all involved.

What happens when a husband or wife comes out of the closet has been too long hidden from public view. It is a profound crisis that cuts across race, socioeconomic class, religion, and age. Interviews with hundreds of women and men from coast to coast attest to the devastation that the three words, "I am gay," uttered by a marriage partner, can have on his or her straight spouse. The partner's coming out thrusts the straight spouse into the closet as well.

The way out is a long, wrenching struggle marked by denial, anger, grief, illness, and sometimes suicide attempts. In the end most issues can be resolved with positive results for most spouses. *The Other Side of the Closet* presents the untold story of the straight spouse's struggle—not to cast stones at the gay partner, but rather to reveal an integral chapter of gay, lesbian and bisexual history.

The Closet

Behind the married partner's coming out lies his or her own traumatic tale. Most homosexual or bisexual persons don't want to be rejected for belonging to a minority which Judeo-Christian society historically has stigmatized as unnatural, immoral or criminal. Many people therefore deny or repress feelings of attraction to the same sex. Fearing rejection or loss of job, social status or self-respect by admitting to any degree of homosexuality, some adopt a straight lifestyle entirely, and others only publicly. Because the same-sex drive is both compelling and stigmatizing, becoming comfortable with it may take a long time. Keeping it hidden consumes considerable psychic energy but the sacrifice to offset guilt or meet life goals in an anti-gay climate seems worth it.

According to most research studies homosexuality and bisexuality are not a matter of choice. Though no definitive cause has been determined, they seem to result from the interplay of many biochemical, environmental and psychosocial factors operating from conception through adolescence.

At any given time there exists a small minority of homosexual and bisexual people in society. The most commonly accepted figures for the United States come from Alfred Kinsey's studies of sexual behavior of adult white males (1948) and adult white women (1953). Using a zero-to-six point scale representing degrees of homosexual behavior on a continuum, Kinsey estimates that ten percent of men are exclusively gay for at least three years, including four percent who are gay for life. From three to seven percent of women aged twenty to thirty-five are estimated to be more or less exclusively lesbian.[2]

Bisexuality—experiencing a high degree of sexual pleasure from both sexes—forms a less definitive picture although it is a distinct orientation. Current research suggests that at least twice as many bisexual as homosexual persons exist.[3] The range includes those reporting more than incidental orgasmic experiences, those with somewhat equal homosexual and heterosexual experiences and those who report predominantly homosexual behavior. Estimates of the number of bisexual persons rise when same-sex erotic feelings, distinct from behavior, are studied.

Many homosexuals and bisexuals begin to sense that they are attracted to others of the same sex in childhood or adolescence. Others report that they didn't realize their same-sex attraction until adulthood. Once the orientation is honestly confronted, a conscious choice can be made as to how to handle it.

About twenty percent of gay men marry.[4] Whether they are unaware of their homosexuality, deny it, or consciously hide it, they want to have children and the security that marriage affords in a society that values the family. While they may genuinely love the women they marry, a study of gay husbands by Michael Ross suggests that internalized homophobia and social pressure are significant factors in their decisions to seek marriage.[5] Bisexual men who marry—the exact percentage is not known—are of course also sexually attracted to their wives. In contrast to gay men, most women who are sure of their lesbian orientation rarely consider marriage.

The majority of homosexual or bisexual men who marry say they sensed being different from other men or were aware of their orientation at the time. Rather than tell their fiancees, most decide to live a straight lifestyle, remaining gay or bisexual only in self-identity, feelings or fantasies. Many believe their love is strong enough to make them forget, if not overcome, their sexual attraction. This is an assumption supported until recently by many psychiatrists who counseled that homosexuality was just a phase that could be overcome by finding a good wife.

Once married, whether uncertain about their orientation or consciously hiding it, many husbands gradually heed latent or repressed feelings and begin to make secret gay contacts. Clandestine gay sex can be quick and anonymous without the possible consequences of affairs with women, yet with the constant risk of arrest if sought in public places. Laud Humphreys' study of anonymous sex in men's restrooms found that the married men who comprised fifty-four percent of his sample compartmentalize and isolate this "tearoom trade" from married life.[6] Men who then find lovers and begin secret liaisons suffer increasing guilt.

Most homosexuals and bisexuals who are not yet comfortable with their sexual orientation hide their secret lives. After stressful soul-searching a number come out to their spouses. The truth is usually revealed through one of the following ways: (1) disclosure— when telling the truth becomes more important than hiding or the pain of repression and guilt becomes unbearable; (2) confrontation— when the wife suspects; (3) mediation—when the couple seeks counseling; or (4) outside evidence—such as the husband's arrest for homosexual acts or an AIDS diagnosis. Many men remain closeted, some keeping their unsuspecting wives satisfied and fulfilling parental responsibilities, others neglecting and criticizing their confused spouses. The need to conceal sexual identity can be so overpowering that some keep silent even after being diagnosed with AIDS.

Lesbian wives typically don't seek anonymous isolated sex but develop a close relationship to one woman at a time. Once they discover and admit their homosexuality, most seem to come out to their husbands quickly.

Liberation

The increased incidence of husbands and wives coming out over the past thirty years reflects major changes in our society. Following the gay-baiting tactics of the repressive McCarthy Senate hearings in the fifties that aroused fear of homosexual men, the sixties brought a sweeping reversal of social attitudes that affected homosexuals along with other minorities.

The civil rights movement of African-Americans and the sexual revolution liberalized views held by the majority of society about minority groups and sexual behavior. By the late sixties African-Americans were participating in many levels of society from which they had previously been excluded. Human sexuality became a respectable subject for academic study, trade publications and individual therapy.

These liberalizing changes boosted the confidence of the homosexual minority in cities across the nation to lead more openly gay lives. The 1969 successful stand of gay men against the police raid of Stonewall Inn in Greenwich Village established a model of gay power strong enough to fight for and win their civil rights as an oppressed minority group. Within a short time gay baths, bars, tearooms and a variety of designated meeting spots mushroomed from coast to coast.

Meanwhile lesbians, having developed group identity during and after World War II, formed a separate strand of the growing feminist movement sparked by Betty Friedan's *The Feminine Mystique*. Soon they were a powerful minority with lesbian publications, public meeting places and bars across the country.

The seventies saw gay liberation stabilize and expand. In 1974, the American Psychiatric Association voted to remove homosexuality from the list of pathological diseases, lessening the stigma attached to gay persons and activities. The American Psychological Association followed suit. By the decade's end, bisexual persons, erroneously labeled gay by society and classified as such in many studies and the media, had formed their own network to celebrate their unique orientation. Expanding the sexual revolution, books and media publicized non-traditional relationships such as open marriage, menages a trois, communes and group sex.

In the eighties openly gay and lesbian individuals entered mainstream activities from business to politics. Gay and lesbian organizations were creating public identity and gaining political clout for homosexual persons nationwide. Gay therapists and support groups were available to counsel men on how to come out. More gay and bisexual husbands, gaining self-esteem, told their wives. More lesbian wives, having easier access to other lesbian and bisexual women, acknowledged their orientation and came out to their husbands.

In the midst of this ground swell of gay, lesbian and bisexual pride, three events rekindled negative social attitudes against homosexuality. First, the rising death toll from AIDS made many people fear gay men as potential carriers of death, even though the disease is not limited solely to the high-risk male homosexual population. Second, the 1986 Supreme Court decision to uphold Georgia's law criminalizing sodomy set the precedent for the potential application of such laws in some thirty other states. Third, the Vatican reaffirmed that same year that active homosexuality is a sin in the eyes of the Catholic Church. The resulting resurgence of anti-gay sentiment prompted homosexual and bisexual groups to escalate political action toward securing rights long denied to them.

The growing momentum of gay liberation, the feminist movement and the sexual revolution over three decades disrupted the lives of many mixed-orientation couples. As more gay and bisexual husbands acted on their homosexuality in secret, their wives, empowered by feminist pride and new sexual expertise, were trying to exert more power in the couple's sex life. The husbands' resulting feelings of being further trapped in marriage added fuel to their drive to come out.

The impact was more abrupt in lesbian-straight marriages, since both feminism and gay liberation encouraged lesbian wives to lessen the power husbands exerted over their lives. As they pursued women's rights and independence and recognized their homosexuality for the first time, a large number left their husbands.

No one foresaw the negative effects that the long overdue recognition of gay and lesbian rights would have on straight spouses and the family as a whole. The liberation cry of gay, lesbian and bisexual marriage partners became a sword that sundered the world of their spouses.

The Other Side of the Closet

The devastating impact of gay and women's liberation on the lives of straight spouses whose partners come out cannot be minimized. Most spouses have endured the struggle in silence on their side of the closet while their partners have benefited from the growing public awareness of and support for gay and lesbian liberation.

The coming out of homosexual partners, a cause of celebration for them, unintentionally creates profound trauma for their spouses. To them the disclosure seems like a denial of the relationship. Shocked spouses typically feel rejected sexually and bereft of the mates that they thought they had.

Whether twenty-three years old with toddlers or fifty-six years old with adult children, straight spouses are generally too traumatized at first to understand how the coming out will affect them. Only as shock subsides can they begin to grasp the implications of their partner's disclosures. Although relieved to know the reason behind changes in their partner's behavior or problems in marital sex, most feel hurt, angry and helpless. As they gradually begin to understand homosexuality and homophobia and how those realities affect them, the partner's closet can become as much a prison for them as it was for the partner. Emerging conflicts of interests may then appear unresolvable.

What seems to many like rock bottom at that point can serve as a stepping stone to new possibilities. Just as mythical heroes and heroines undergo seemingly impossible trials to reach their goal and in the process discover their true worth, so spouses can direct their lives toward positive change as they work through the painful consequences of the coming out.

The Other Side of the Closet outlines six major issues that the coming out raises for the straight spouse including: damage to the spouse's sexuality; destruction of the traditional marriage form; conflict of parental and spousal roles; crisis of self-identity; breakdown of trust and integrity; disintegration of belief systems. The spouse's reactions to the coming-out crisis, although individual and distinctive, appear to progress through these common stages from initial trauma to eventual transformation.

There is no single correct resolution of these issues although some coping strategies seem to be more constructive than others. While depression, illness and breakdown may occur, the struggle need not go that way. There are many alternate routes leading to acceptance, understanding and positive transformation within the marriage or after divorce. By seeking therapy, Hanna took such a route, gradually becoming a more capable and confident woman than she had been before her crisis.

The process of recovery and transformation is long and arduous, requiring patience, courage and persistence. Because of the profound shock of the coming out, it typically takes spouses at least a year to resolve the pragmatic issues of damaged sexuality, altered relationship and conflicting parent-spouse roles. Two or more years are necessary in order to resolve the psychological issues of shattered identity, integrity and belief system. All told, it generally takes at least three years to reconstruct a new life and far longer to look dispassionately at the coming-out crisis.

The length of recovery varies for each individual depending on competing demands of family and work, number of years married, number and age of children, length of time the partner's sexual orientation was hidden, quality of the relationship, extent of outside support, community attitudes, physical and emotional health, age, job skills, outside interests, and emotional maturity. Recovery tends to be faster for straight husbands than for straight wives.

The stories and analyses that follow present a collective portrait of how spouses come to terms with their partners' coming out. The stories are told in the voices of straight wives and husbands and a gay and a lesbian partner from across the country. Representative of common perceptions, feelings and coping strategies, each anonymous tale could have been told by many other spouses who have struggled with the coming-out crisis.

The stories are grouped into six sections, based on the most pressing issue the straight wife or husband faced. The sections are presented in order of the most common sequence of emotional stages through which spouses progress. Each section concludes with a discussion of the major implications of the highlighted issue and with constructive strategies for recovery. These analyses are based on five years of extensive research including discussions with professionals in the field, personal experience as a straight spouse and support group leader as well as interviews with hundreds of straight spouses and gay, lesbian and bisexual partners representing a cross section of age, education, occupation, community, and race.

Together the stories and analyses expose the closeted struggle of straight spouses, the unintended victims of victims of a homophobic society. However inadvertent the partner's actions, the painful consequences of the coming out on their spouses and children cannot be ignored. At the same time the coming out is in many cases the beginning of healing for all concerned.

Author's Note

The real life stories in this book, selected to illustrate common issues rather than private lives, are told in the spouse's own voices, with some alterations made for literacy and privacy purposes. Every effort has been made, to the best of the author's ability, to keep the spouse's privacy interest intact (except for the stories by Jane and Jim, who choose to come out publicly from their side of the closet). The conscious effort to protect individuals' privacy may inadvertently result in a description of a real person unknown to the author. Any such resemblance is purely coincidental.

Publisher's Note

The anguish suffered by both spouses in a marriage that includes major differences cannot be measured on a human scale.

It is our hope that *The Other Side of the Closet* will open doors of understanding for all spouses of mixed-orientation marriages and lead them from devastation and despair to hope and healing.

No condemnation nor justification is intended for partners who live either traditional or alternative lifestyles.

This book in no way attempts to take the place of professional counseling and readers are urged to seek help from licensed professionals as needed.

The Other Side Of The Closet

one

SEXUAL MISMATCH

DAMAGED SEXUALITY
OF THE STRAIGHT SPOUSE

When the initial shock subsides, straight spouses are typically devastated by what seems like a rejection of their sexuality. How to adapt to their partners' sexual attraction to someone of the same sex is the major concern for most spouses. They have suddenly become the non-preferred sex partners and often feel rejected as women or men. As partners celebrate their true sexual orientation and their courageous honesty in disclosing it, spouses feel bereft of their marital mates—causing confusion and anger.

Even though the partner may not have known, accepted or dared to reveal his or her homosexuality or bisexuality, the fact that the different sexual orientation existed at all makes the spouse typically suspect some dysfunctioning in the couple's lovemaking and some damage to his or her own sexuality.

For many spouses, the partner's revealed homosexuality or bisexuality alone prompts immediate divorce. Others try to work through it to preserve the marriage, as the stories in part two show. Whether they stay or leave, most spouses gradually realize that the hidden sexual disparity has already harmed their sexual functioning and self-image. This is particularly true for spouses of gay or lesbian partners who have little or no erotic attraction to them. The rage many feel can persist for years.

The following stories told by two wives and a husband of homosexual partners illustrate how unknown sexual incompatibility can profoundly affect the marriage and the straight spouse's sexual identity. The concluding section highlights major problems related to the sexuality issue and outlines several effective strategies for healing sexual damage.

Personal Stories

Brainwashed
Moira

I'm no longer that freckle-faced redhead who won the Good Samaritan prize and got engaged to Tim Conally shortly after high school in Brooklyn. That was someone else, who never made a decision and wanted to be cared for the rest of her life.

One memory stands out from that period, when Tim was on a construction crew and I was a clerk in an office near his job site. One evening, we were to meet after work. After an hour's wait, I called him from a pay phone.

"Why are you so stupid, Moira?" Tim shouted. "Use your head. Don't stand around waiting, for God's sake! Get a bus and go home, if I don't show."

A few weeks later, we were to rendezvous again. When he didn't come within twenty minutes, I caught the bus home. Just as I opened my door, the phone rang. It was Tim, asking, "Are you dumb or what? When I say I'll pick you up, you be there."

"Tim, a couple of weeks ago you said...."

The wedding took place as planned because I cared and would do anything to keep that handsome, black-haired man loving me.

For the next twenty years until the early eighties, I tried to comply with his confusing demands. "If only you were thin like our neighbor," he'd say or "Why aren't you a better cook like my sister?" Then, once I'd lose weight or try new recipes, he wouldn't like my figure or my food. In our sex life it was, "If only you did this, Moira...or felt like that."

After six months of not having sex very often, I asked him why, figuring I could do something to meet his wishes better.

"I like women to be aggressors once in a while."

That night, I took the initiative, and he turned over to sleep.

"Hmm, I'm doing something wrong," I thought.

The following night, I tried again, laughing a little and showing enthusiasm. The same negative response. "What I'm doing really must be wrong," I told myself. "Maybe my intentions should be clearer."

A few nights later, announcing my desire for sex, I acted highly seductive.

"No, not tonight," he said and rolled over.

Humiliated, I vowed never to try again.

Shortly thereafter, Tim asked me one morning, "Why aren't you pregnant yet, Moira? Go see a doctor."

Though I was furious, my sense of humor came to the rescue. "I'm not the Virgin Mary, Tim. You've got to have sex with me if I'm going to get pregnant."

I got pregnant by the end of the year, when Tim was working two jobs to make ends meet. Six months later, looking through one of the magazines he often brought home, I came upon several photos of naked men. Puzzled, I asked about them at dinner.

"God, you're dumb! It's normal for us men to be curious about other nude men."

Having led a sheltered life in a parochial school system and a Catholic family, I bought his answer. Being ignorant about homosexuality, I was scared not to accept what he said.

In bed that night, Tim asked, "Do you think I'm gay?"

"Of course not." What did I know? A wife doesn't think that about the husband she loves. Besides, he'd made me pregnant.

Three months later Beth arrived. Tim was crushed it wasn't a son. Two years later when Vicky was born, he was disappointed again. His letdown was so intense that the hospital staff talked about it. When Vicky and I got home, he ignored her. Never touched her. Within six weeks he started drinking heavily and blamed it on being trapped with the first daughter and super-trapped with the second.

By then I was trapped too, a twenty-four-year-old woman taking care of a two year old, a baby, and an alcoholic husband.

Tim drank for fourteen years, mostly in bars. He got through the day on a quart of vodka, staying drunk most of the time even at work, where they covered for him.

At home I wondered how much longer living with an alcoholic was possible. I decided that when the girls went off to school I would look for a job and get out of the house.

During the next six years we moved twice. Because sex with a drunk is not good, I avoided it except for one night after Vicky was finally old enough to go to school full time. A month later my doctor discovered that I was pregnant, sending me into total depression. A new baby would keep me home another five years.

When I told the doctor how Tim's drinking frustrated me, he said, "You're wrong, Moira. Count how many drinks he has. That'll prove that he isn't alcoholic."

In my low state, there wasn't much to fall back on. Then a friend said he'd seen Tim go into a gay bar one night when Tim had said he'd been someplace else.

That evening, when I brought it up, Tim said, "Oh, yeah. When I found out it was a gay bar I left." Then he added, "If you threaten to throw me out for this, Moira, you'll go first, bag and baggage."

By then I was totally out of control. Subconsciously I felt that if I found out that Tim was homosexual it would break me completely. "Let it go, Moira," I told myself.

Meanwhile I was losing my temper with the kids, screaming at them all the time—a real pain to live with—while Tim made it clear that was why he drank.

The few times we had sex during these months were more trouble than pleasure. Finally Tim asked, "What will we do about it?"

"I frankly don't know and frankly don't care," I sighed.

From then on Tim slept on the living room couch. Four months later Amanda was born. For the next five years until she went off to kindergarten, my depression and complaining tirades gradually became worse and I grieved for Tim as I watched him kill himself with alcohol. Day after day I asked myself, "What am I doing here?" I realized that I was really just an unemployed single parent of three kids.

Once Amanda started school a job became imperative. It would provide an outlet for my frustration, extra spending money and a way to support myself in the event of divorce. Yet seeing myself as lazy and stupid, incapable of performing—everything Tim said—I was frightened. Since I hadn't worked for so long, my talents were an unknown quantity. The part-time receptionist job that came up seemed like a good compromise.

A year later we moved to a four-bedroom house so everyone would have a bedroom. When the girls first saw it, Vicky asked, "Which bedroom is Daddy's?" "Of course," I thought, "all she's seen is Tim sleeping on the couch!"

The next year, seven years after Tim's retreat to the couch and no sex, his supervisor told him he'd be fired if he didn't quit drinking. In April 1980 he attempted sobriety for the first time.

A few weeks later, a friend I'd run into at the market said he'd seen Tim going into some gay hangout.

When I mentioned it after dinner, Tim said "Oh! That had nothing to do with me. It was just because I was drinking."

"O.K., forget it! It's behind us. You're sober now."

In this time of sobriety, Tim tried very hard to be nice to me, although he still blamed me as the cause of his drinking.

One night that summer, we were watching television with Amanda in the family room. Sitting on the hearth, she looked over at us on the lounge chair, where Tim had his arm around me and I was lying against him.

"Are you two going to get married?" she asked suddenly.

I looked at her, wide-eyed. "Amanda, we are married. We're your mom and dad,"

"No, you're not."

I laughed a little. "Why would you say that?"

"Because married people hug and kiss and hold each other and say nice things to each other. All you two do is fight and argue and scream." Then she smiled. "Are you going to get married?"

One night a few weeks later, after finishing the dishes, I popped into the living room where Tim was reading the paper. Feeling light-hearted, I said, "Hey! The kids are watching TV. Why don't we go up to the bedroom and fool around a little."

"They're watching TV."

"Tim, did you hear me? I'm not kidding."

"No, Moira. I just want to read."

And that was it.

So in my nineteenth year of marriage, I called up a man who had been pursuing me at work and started an affair, petrified he'd say, "My God! It's no wonder your husband doesn't want to have anything to do with you. You are horrible."

That was not the case. There was nothing wrong with me except for being totally inexperienced, fearful and very naive for a woman who'd been married for nineteen years. After eight months, though still frightened and unsure of sex, I realized that the relationship was only sexual and stopped seeing him.

With only Tim in my life again, my suspicions about him could no longer be ignored. Everything began to fall into place. Then one night when the kids and he were watching a TV show about gays, I heard him say, "Oh, those fags! Those queers! Ugh!"

In a rage, but waiting until the kids left the room, I accused him of being a gay.

"Yes," he screamed, spinning around to face me, "I occasionally get off on sex with a man."

Shocked, I began to look for evidence. Over the next few days, proof was everywhere—telephone numbers on scratch pads, reports from friends who'd seen him in gay places. Again I accused him. I needed him to confirm what I wanted to deny.

"Sure," he shouted, "a man's body turns me on."

I still couldn't believe it and we didn't discuss it further. By fall, all we did was argue.

Finally, Tim asked, "Just what do you want, Moira? Write it to me. I'm tired of talking."

My letter was very nice. It reflected the way I was raised. "If you're gay," I began,

> I want to know so you can get on with your life and I with mine. This isn't any good for the kids or us. We're miserable and the kids will be too. I want an answer soon because the holidays are coming."

When he hadn't answered by December, I asked him outright, "Are you gay, Tim? Are you?"

He started shouting. "Only you and your vicious, accusatory mind would suggest such a thing!" Starting out the door, he turned. "Try to kick me out and you'll see who's thrown out."

Come March, Tim still hadn't answered the letter. Mid-March, on my return from a weekend company retreat, he acted strange and the girls reported he'd been away most of the time.

At breakfast on Monday I asked, "So, are you planning on leaving?" "No," he said and went off to work.

That night I said, "Look, Tim, I wasn't kidding. Are you planning on moving out?"

Silence.

"What is going on? You haven't answered my letter. I can't live like this any more."

When he still gave no reply I yelled, "Don't tell me nothing!"

"Yeah, I'm gay," he said, matter-of-factly, "and I want a divorce."

No discussion. He was gay and the marriage was ending. I'd been married to him for twenty years and he'd never discussed it with me. As I found out later, he'd talked to gay men about it at a two-day gay conference that weekend.

When we told the kids about the divorce, they didn't understand. They blamed me for it, since I'd been such a grouse, yelling at them all those years. Within a few days we knew that they had to be told the real reason.

Tim drove them down to the park on Sunday afternoon to tell them alone. In ten minutes they were back.

"What!" I cried, as they walked in the door.

"I told 'em I was gay," Tim said, "and asked if they had any questions. They didn't, so we came home."

The girls' faces were ashen. "Mom?" Vicky said, her eyes asking all the questions that hadn't been voiced.

For the next two hours I talked to them about what it meant to be gay, the social and church pressures Tim had grown up under, the homosexual lifestyle—everything except the hurt and anger I felt. That was carefully concealed under the caring behavior I'd been taught to show no matter what.

"We're going to help him move and get set up in his new life," I told them. "We've got to make him comfortable."

Caring deeply for Tim's parents, I offered to help him tell them. Since he'd had a year of sobriety, none of them would understand our divorce unless he told them the truth. Reluctantly he agreed.

I called his mother to say we'd be coming down on Saturday. Halfway through dinner, Tim told them we were divorcing. In total shock, everyone let loose a barrage of questions. "Didn't you do this? Didn't you do that?"

Finally, Tim's mother turned to me and asked, "Didn't you love Timothy when you married him?"

"Yes, I did."

Then she turned to Tim, asking, "And you loved Moira?"

"No."

Time stopped. My face turned scarlet. My stomach twisted. Never had I sat through such humiliation. "I wish I hadn't come!" beat like a drum in my head.

Over the next tormented weeks, Tim told me how he'd fooled around before we married, and how the first year we were married, he'd started looking for gay men and going to gay baths, theatres and bookstores. He was so fearful somebody would find out he was gay that he wouldn't hug our male friends. He had sex with me just enough to legitimize the marriage, "and," I thought, "to have three kids."

Seeing my dismay, he said, "I really want to help you, Moira. You've got to remember when we married, the Catholic Church, family, schools, everybody said you weren't supposed to be gay. It was evil, vicious, dirty. So you had to try to be something you weren't—straight and married."

"Oh, I see," I thought. "You want to help me understand you. I've got news for you. I want to understand *me*."

The next night, I met Tim at the door, crying and screaming,

"You didn't love me! You married me just to look straight. You brainwashed me!"

"I refuse to deal with you, Moira," he called over his shoulder as he went to the kitchen, "since you can't act like an adult. When you decide to grow up and talk like an adult, we can discuss it." With that, he left for the evening.

A few weeks later we talked. "Consciously or unconsciously," he acknowledged, "I tried to make you kick me out of the marriage."

"And when I tried to kick you out, you threatened to throw me out! You had me either way, didn't you? If I had pushed you out or I'd left, you'd never have had to admit the truth to anybody. You'd have been the victim." My rage was mounting.

During this time Tim still went out cruising and had the support of gay organizations, activities and psychiatrists, while I stayed home with nothing to do and no one to talk to. Tim didn't want me to tell anyone.

"I'm dying," I thought, "and nobody knows why."

Then he moved out with our help. Once he was gone I never missed him. My crying came out of grief for the twenty years I had put into the marriage, not over the man who left. The fact that I no longer cared for the man I'd been married to for so long made me sadder.

One night shortly after he left, Tim gave me the book, *I'm O.K.—You're O.K..* Inside it he'd written, "You really are O.K."

He meant it nicely but I laughed to myself, thinking, "Now that I know you're gay, nothing's wrong with me. You jerk, now that you've gone, you think that you can eradicate all the pain you caused and get on with your life?"

Then I paused, appalled at what his legacy to me was. "How can I ever undo all the brainwashing that made me believe everything was my fault?" I asked myself. "You're not O.K., Tim, and I'm not either." Outraged, I closed the book, never to open it again.

Tim's brainwashing left me scared to get out on my own full time. Believing I was stupid, I went to see a counselor, someone to take care of me. "I don't know who I am," I began. "I kept changing myself to be so many things for Tim. It's what kept me in the marriage."

For five sessions I talked about the damage done to me and our marriage by Tim's behavior as a gay and an alcoholic. "I'm afraid of sex and question the motives of any man who wants to get close," I explained. "I don't believe in love or marriage. That makes me sad because I was raised to be married and have kids." Then feeling wistful, I added, "It would be great to get married again. But marriage has no value now."

With each outburst over what Tim had done to me, I said, "He did it because he was an alcoholic...because he was gay."

The sixth session the counselor asked, "Why can't you simply say, 'Tim did this to me.' Why do you have to excuse him because he's gay or alcoholic?"

"Because if I say, 'Tim did this to me and that to me,' without explaining his behavior, that makes him the most calculating and cruel human being I've ever known."

"So?"

That was the breakthrough. It finally dawned on me how terribly used I'd been. Tim needed the marriage and the kids for his respectability and then set out to make me divorce him. He'd used me the entire marriage—half of my life, my adult youth! My anger came pouring out.

"He didn't think twice about using me, a woman—the very type he didn't want around—as a shield," I screamed. "He has no right to take a woman as a wife and mother for his children just so he can look straight!"

My deep rage persists to this day, five years later. Anger is my only connection to Tim's gayness, though he's never felt it directly. He knows it's there when it comes out over concerns for the kids. Some day if the occasion arises, he'll receive my wrath. When he does, the issue won't be the Catholic Church's homophobia, which made him do what he did. The issue will be what he did to me— not asking me, not telling me before we married, not giving me a choice.

Because I'm A Man
Dan

We came from traditional backgrounds. We had a traditional marriage. We looked the traditional couple—I, tall, dark and fairly handsome, and Sally, just a little shorter and blonde. While I worked she took care of the house. Bringing in the money, I had the power. Sally felt powerless but learned how to get power by dispensing or withholding sex, almost like prostitution. If she wanted something we'd have sex. When she wanted to punish me we couldn't. Too naive to catch on, I thought we had a good sex life.

After we married in the early seventies, my salary as a pilot for a commercial airline put Sally through college. In the first ten years my job took us to three different cities. During our years in New York and St. Louis, Sally was always the first to try new things, always ahead of me, looking over her shoulder and saying, "Come on, Dan." Setting up activities, she brought me into them—natural childbirth, home delivery, breast feeding, child care. We delivered our two daughters, Ginnie and Sue, at home. Sally got involved in La Leche League and took parent effectiveness courses. She also hired as many women tradespeople as possible. Our gardener, our painter and even the car mechanic were women.

Our circle of friends was made up of her friends. Dear to her, they were her emotional support. That worked out well since I didn't have the skills then to express my feelings openly. When she lost those friendships each time we moved, depression set in. She became so close to one woman in St. Louis that when we left after two years to go to Denver, she was immobile for a long time. "I love her so," she told me, "but not in a sexual way," she added quickly.

Once we settled in Denver I became the one who tried new things while Sally stayed stuck in her depression. Through work I started some personal growth classes that were very helpful. Feeling I'd discovered a path of awareness, I kept telling Sally, "Hey! Here's a new way to think, to live."

The second year there I joined a men's support group, an off-shoot from one of my classes. Walking into my first meeting and seeing the nine men sitting there, I thought to myself, "Oh boy, a bunch of queers," just because it was a group of men. Like all the men I knew, my feeling was, "You don't touch men. You don't talk to men about anything but sports or finances." I soon found out that the other males in the group came from all walks of life and only one was gay. Gradually they became my emotional support.

About this time I took a weekend workshop on extrasensory perception. In one of the first ESP activities, a good-looking woman stood up to introduce herself to the group. "My name is Nanette," she began. "I'm bisexual. I've been bisexual for seventeen years."

Her words caught my attention. I was amazed that she had the courage to stand up before a room full of people and come right out about her sexuality. I listened hard to what she had to say.

Nanette had been married for sixteen years and had four kids. Throughout the marriage she'd brought home women to her husband and herself for threesomes—sometimes for a night, other times for months of living together.

The next workshop activity was to pick out the person we were most attracted to and go tell her or him. Right away I went over to Nanette. As we talked, her dynamic power attracted me. But it was a dark charisma.

Sunday night I told Sally all about the workshop and suggested, "Why not come to the next one in the series?" Since she'd finally shaken off her depression, I wanted her to share the high I was feeling from personal growth. Our marriage had never seemed better. We'd never been happier.

"O.K. Sounds interesting," she said and arranged for a sitter to take care of the girls.

When we arrived at the next workshop, there was Nanette. I introduced her to Sally. Immediately the two women connected. For the rest of the workshop, they were the only two people in the class who were in sync all of the time. Everyone expressed amazement at how they seemed to be in tune with each other—classic soul mates.

Ten days afterwards Sally ran off with Nanette.

I was completely floored, though not completely surprised. Sally had told me she was attracted to Nanette the night they met. "I'd like to experiment with someone of the same sex," she'd said.

Thinking "Gee, that's rather cool," I'd encouraged her to do it.

Once Sally announced she was leaving, feelings of guilt began to arise. "Did I subconsciously arrange for this to happen by introducing her to Nanette, figuring she'd be swept off her feet and run away?" The question agonized me for the next two years.

After Sally left, my first move was to try to win her back, to get her to come home and talk, to make love. Within a month I stopped trying. "I can't compete with this woman," I decided. "It's obviously some tricky technique in lovemaking she has that I can't duplicate because I'm a man." Again there was this sense of an evil force.

What a terrible blow to my ego it was! I'd rather Sally had run off with a man than a woman, a hundred times more. I'd have understood that and been able to combat it. "Sally," I would've said, "I can earn more money. I'm stronger. I'm faster." This way I felt I was not an adequate man. It completely destroyed my self-image.

It also destroyed my confidence in Sally as Ginnie and Sue's mother. "Their mother's a lesbian," I thought. "Therefore she's not a good mother so I'll keep the kids."

Sally's leaving came out of the blue to Ginnie and Sue. It wasn't as if it had been a bad marriage and everybody knew there'd be a divorce eventually. Their first reaction was, "Who's going to take care of us?"

The answer wasn't terribly clear for five months. My hurt wiped me out. At first I felt sorry for myself, moaning, "Oh I'll never find another woman to have such good sex with!" Then it was a rapid downhill course that lasted a year. I withdrew into myself, barely able to take care of myself, my children or my house. My neighbor kept sending me notes saying, "Your yard's a mess! Why don't you pull your weeds?" All I could do was eat until I was up over two hundred pounds.

Within weeks of Sally's running off, I had to go to a flight check course. It was bizarre. Every night I was on the phone calling my brothers and sisters to see who could watch my kids. Every day I was taking the course, which was taught by the only woman instructor the airline had. And, by God, it turned out to be the only time in my career that I flunked the final check flight—under the supervision of a woman. It seemed like there was a conspiracy of women against me.

So I operated as a flight engineer for the time being. In that capacity, there was nothing unsafe I could do. Had I been flying the controls, I would have grounded myself. As upset as I was, a crash could have been highly probable.

Soon my condition was so bad I arranged my flying schedule to have Wednesday nights free to meet with the men's support group. I needed people to tell my woes to. I didn't know how to unload to my male friends. Family counseling helped too. Each week Sally and I and the girls went alternately to a counseling center called the Center for the Family in Transition and to Family Services.

Ginnie and Sue, aged nine and five, didn't know what was going on. They had their mother coming in and out of the house to watch them while I flew, and me coming in and out of the house to and from flights. At other times they were farmed out to different aunts and uncles. Soon it was clear that a nanny was needed to watch them when I was flying.

A few months after the nanny came, I realized that a stranger watching them couldn't do as good a job as their mother. "Wait a minute!" I told myself. "There's no connection between Sally's sex life and whether she's a good mother." It had taken me a year to figure that out.

By then divorce proceedings had begun. Nanette filed for divorce too and left her husband, whereupon Sally and she moved into our house with two of her kids. Little Sue, by then six, immediately hooked onto Nanette and thought she was wonderful. I too still found her a special woman—a dark force, but special.

A month after Nanette and Sally moved in, our family counselor said in a session with just Sally and me, "The children want to know why their mother's in the bedroom all the time with Nanette. I suggest you tell them or they're going to hear it on the street corner from other kids."

Sally did the telling that night. "I'm lesbian," she said. "I'm in love with Nanette and we spend lots of time together doing lots of things."

The girls showed no negative reactions then, but it added to Sue's emotional upheaval from the divorce. She was so upset that one night she ran down the hall, through the dining room and out the window.

Five months later Sally and Nanette and all the kids moved into a house they rented together. When both divorces were final a few months after that, they each received enough money between them without having to work. So there were the two women and four kids in what was quite a nice household.

To come up with the money needed for alimony and child support, I rented out the girls' bedrooms. The first renter was a woman who told me she'd been a lesbian. The following week, there was trouble with the car. When I brought it to our woman car mechanic, I discovered that she was an active lesbian. "God!" I thought, "it seems like the world is filled with lesbians!"

After many months of feeling lonely I wanted to date. "But it's been years since I've pursued women," I realized with surprise.

My men's support group seemed like an obvious source of help. At the end of our next session, I announced looking around the circle, "I'd like to go out on a blind date. Could any of you give me a phone number?"

"No!" Eight guys faced me saying, "No, Dan, we won't give you any phone numbers. You're pathetic-acting and pathetic-looking."

I went out to my car and cried. The next day I joined the local gym and began exercising. It was the start of an uphill climb still in progress six years later.

The men were right. I was a pathetic jerk responsible for Sally's leaving. The next few days were spent mulling over the question, "Why else would a woman leave me other than that I was short-changing her?" That weekend I sat down and, with my logical mind, listed the areas where I fell short as far as women were concerned—touching, feelings, sensuality, sexuality, giving and receiving. "Building these up may not make your life work, Dan," I told myself, "but it's the way to satisfy a woman."

One by one I tackled those areas. I took workshops on massage and bought my own table. I took a course on sensuality and then began classes on human sexuality. Sexuality was a big issue for me because of Sally's rejection of me as a man on top of all the guilt about sex I'd grown up with.

Slowly healing began. In the process I was able to expand beyond the focus on my inner growth. I pulled out all the weeds in the garden and bought house plants which I tended with a real green thumb.

Four years after Sally left me, Nanette left her. Sue saw it as a second divorce. For weeks she wouldn't go to school, not wanting Sally out of her sight. Gradually, an hour at a time, she went back until she was there full time.

Soon my circle encompassed Sue and Ginnie. No longer heating up TV dinners, I began cooking for them. This spread to cooking classes and teaching them to cook. They got massaged on my table, we went together into our hot tub naked as a family and ran around without clothes on as a matter of course.

One day the family counselor told me, "You've got to cut down on the girls' sexual exposure, Dan. They're too agitated right now and too young to have an outlet. It's too much on top of Sally's lifestyle."

"That's a shame," I said. "It's important that my children see me nude. It's positive and healthy. I saw my parents nude."

About this time I took a course on "Surviving Divorce." In the third session the women and men separated to list characteristics of "the perfect person" of the opposite sex. When we compared our lists they were the same. "I didn't know we want the same thing," I said to the instructor, thinking, "Gosh! Many women enjoy sex!"

Inspired, I placed an ad in the local paper that weekend.

Forty-two-year-old male working on touching, feelings, sensuality, sexuality, giving and receiving. Looking for a woman to help me grow in these areas.

To my surprise six nice women answered the ad. One became a permanent friend. My dating had begun. Not wanting to be in another unequal relationship, I chose only working women.

That autumn a flyer for an Outward Bound program caught my eye—three weeks of winter mountaineering, the toughest of their challenges. "Aha!" I told myself, "this will be my test." I'd never hiked in winter. I'd never done ice climbing. I'd never been through any survival experiences but I needed to prove I was manly.

In January fifteen men—the other fourteen all twenty years younger than I—were ice-climbing, making igloos in blizzards and sleeping in the snow on pads with little canvas covers in twenty-below-zero weather. For three weeks I held my own.

Success made me feel proud. But the feeling of being okay didn't last. I needed to prove myself over and over. Getting strokes from others was great but my own were needed. Before long, I started training for triathalons and completed the "Iron Man" race in Hawaii—a two-and-a-half mile swim, 112 mile bike ride, and 26.6 mile marathon—making me very proud of myself.

From then on triathalon training was my primary hobby. Every day, I swam, bicycled and ran. It became a way to maintain my weight, my self-esteem and my emotions. Over the next two years I did three more "Iron Man" courses.

Now six years after Sally ran away, my health and life are all together. I'm a much better person than I ever was and feel better about myself. If we were still married I'd probably be soft, fat, and out of shape and never would have done any of these things.

My work towards personal growth was triggered by pain I wouldn't wish on anyone. Sally's running away was the most painful thing that ever happened to me. It was rejection of me as a person and as a man, the failure of our marriage and consequent divorce. Sally's being lesbian was only a minor part of it.

Sometimes I wonder that if I'd had strong self-esteem at the time, I could have said, "Well, it's her loss. She's giving up a good marriage." Then I laugh. "It is her loss. I am a special person."

Proof Of Womanhood*
Jane

This is the first time I've ever told my story publicly and I am afraid. I feel shaky and vulnerable and alone. Just as you felt alone and vulnerable and afraid when you found out your husband, wife, son or daughter was gay; or when you first risked telling someone you were gay and a look of horror flickered in his or her eyes; or when you first spoke publicly for gay rights. In facing the fear to speak openly, I experience a deep strength and power, a great sense of freedom out of doing and being what I must.

I met John in Taipei, Taiwan, in the early sixties. I was teaching and John was in the military. We were both twenty-three and we fell quickly and passionately in love. When our tours were up we returned to this country and decided to marry and settle in the San Francisco Bay Area where my family lived. Both families were thrilled. John's parents from Indiana called me the "pretty little wife from California." We had a family wedding, bought a Victorian house to renovate and pursued our careers. Our marriage was good. We loved each other and felt secure. We did the things our parents

*Adapted from a speech, first convention of Parents and Friends of Lesbians and Gays, Denver, May 5, 1982.

approved of and what we had grown up expecting to do. We were productive and we saved money. We had friends and had fun. Our sexual relationship was mutually satisfying. It was a safe, comfortable and well-programmed marriage. Life was the way it was supposed to be, just the way we'd always dreamed.

And then it changed.

Seven years after we married, Martin entered our lives. John met him through business and started spending a lot of time with him. He found Martin fascinating, a man with a wealth of experiences. As the weeks went by and the friendship grew, Martin told John he was gay.

John shared that information with me within two weeks, crying many tears about Martin's difficult life. "He's felt such prejudice! He had so much pain growing up gay," he told me. "He was alienated from his parents."

Five nights later John came home crying again, this time for himself. "I've fallen in love with Martin and I don't know what to do." Then he cried for us.

At that moment our lives turned upside down. The unimaginable had happened. Thirty years of dearly held assumptions blew apart. It was like trying to stand on water. Everything was in waves. There was no solid ground anywhere. "If this is real and all the former rules are untrue," I thought, "then everything might be false and then again, anything might be true."

It was terrifying and exhilarating! There was a sense of breathing free, of shattering old patterns, of opening up to limitless possibilities with no more boundaries to our lives.

Once John brought Martin home to meet me, the three of us began spending time together, trying to figure out what was happening. Martin didn't know what to do any more than John or I. John was the first straight man he'd fallen in love with and he didn't want to break up a marriage. So we spent hours and days and weeks talking and talking, discussing possibilities, exploring options.

I loved that period! New things were happening. A zest and liveliness entered our lives. John and I grew closer; Martin and I grew to love each other. Wonder surrounded us. I felt that on some very deep level nothing really had changed, that John and I were still a couple and we'd just opened up our marriage a little bit to include another person.

Then Martin left and I realized nothing would ever be the same. John began to face his own questions and his agony. "Was this just Martin or is it me? Am I really gay or not? What will this mean to our marriage? Who am I anyway?" As John went in search of his own identity, his exploration excluded me. I was left to face my own fears, my own pain and my own questions of identity.

The most painful part of this period was our isolation. We told no one about what was happening or the turmoil we felt. We had nowhere to go, no information, no support. Pulling away from our friends and families, we isolated ourselves in our questions and hurt.

My pain, isolation and confusion about my own worth led me to decide that all of our trouble must be my fault. I decided that I had caused John's homosexuality, that none of this would have happened if I'd somehow done something differently or been a better person. "Why wasn't I enough of a woman?" I wondered and began to view myself as incomplete, worthless, bad, wrong.

After years of not smoking I began smoking. I started drinking too much. Sometimes I'd leave the house, get halfway through San Francisco, panic, and have to go home. I was beginning to shatter and didn't know how to stop myself.

Then I discovered I was pregnant, making me sink deeper and deeper into despair. For several months questions hounded me. "Should I have this baby? Could I bring a baby into this marriage? Am I capable of facing an abortion?"

I decided to seek therapy. My first choice was a group in which the participants already knew each other. When I arrived, they asked me, "What's your issue?"

"I've just found out my husband is gay and I'm pregnant. I don't know what to do. I guess I need support."

The leader then turned to me and said, "I think you'll have to examine your part in creating this situation."

Then a woman in the group said, "Well, that's not much of a problem. I've got this problem and that problem..."

I felt attacked, invisible, unheard. I never went back.

Next I tried my family doctor who had told me I was pregnant.

When he heard the whole story, he wasn't unkind, but had no idea what to do other than recommend a therapist.

Happily the therapist was a woman but she was a Freudian analyst. I was in crisis and she wanted me to come three times a week to free associate. I was trying to make decisions about the life of my baby and she wanted me to talk about my relationship with my father! Six months pregnant, I slid further and further into despair.

The next month the baby was lost in natural miscarriage. While there was a great sense of relief on one level, on another the loss was the final blow. I was losing my husband, yet that baby was going to show me and everyone else in the world that I was a woman. Now I had lost the proof of my womanhood. Little of the following months remains in my memory. I was functioning but in deep, deep depression.

That spring I visited my gynecologist for a checkup after the miscarriage. Though I didn't know him well, I hysterically poured out my fears that I wasn't a complete woman, that I couldn't carry a baby, that there was something fundamentally wrong with me.

He sat listening until I stopped. Then looking directly at me, he said very slowly and clearly, "Jane, there is nothing wrong with you."

His words penetrated my darkness.

He repeated, "There is nothing wrong with you." Then he added, "Your head made the wrong decision to have this baby and your body made the right one. There's nothing wrong with you."

His words were my first glimmer of hope. Someone from the outside world heard me. Someone was validating me.

The next week, I wrote my sister about everything that had happened. Since we weren't close, telling her was a big risk. "I'm desperate," I concluded, "and have nowhere else to turn."

She wrote back immediately with love and support, telling me she'd get Mother to talk with me somehow. After years of closeness, my mother and I were now barely speaking. She had noticed my despair and withdrawal. Yet because of the need for secrecy I'd pushed away her questions, her concern, her love. Both of us felt sad and angry and guilty about it.

My sister put Mother on a plane to visit her in Denver. "I can't tell you everything that's going on," she told Mother when she arrived, "but it's Jane's issue and her life. There's nothing you can do but wait. No one's to blame."

When Mother came back to San Francisco, she called me right away. The tension between us eased.

Within weeks I called the office of my analyst. "Please inform Dr. Blum I'm not coming back." Five minutes later Dr. Blum called. "Don't you think you ought to come in and talk about it?"

"No," I told her, "I'm never stepping foot in your office again." What an incredible feeling of power and freedom! I was taking charge of my life for the first time in months.

Then I found myself a lover. This wonderful man let me know in no uncertain terms that I was a woman. Through his love and caring and passion, my shattered identity began to heal. I was going to live after all.

John and I stabilized emotionally at that point, although we didn't know what to do next. Knowing the old marriage was gone and our sexual relationship was over, we looked for a new direction. We'd gone through so much together we didn't want to part.

Our decision was to invite lovers to live with us communally. So he had his lovers in the house and I had mine. We had large family meals together. People drifted in and out.

John still hadn't come out to anyone else but me. Our family and friends didn't know what was happening or what we were doing. We avoided the issue when we couldn't avoid friends and lied outright when necessary. The secrecy became extremely distressing the summer we visited John's folks in Indiana.

On our return I said, "We've got to stop pretending everything's fine. We've got to begin telling people the truth."

But we didn't.

That fall, a year after Martin entered our lives, I realized I wanted a divorce. I told John one noon while we were eating in a restaurant in the city during his lunch hour.

Pain covered his face. Then he looked at me and said, "I'm afraid you're going to mess up your life if you leave."

That was the last response I expected, but his words released my rage and removed any doubts about my decision. "My God!" I shouted. "What do you think my life is now?"

Once the decision was made I wanted to move quickly. Knowing nothing about divorce, I called my sister. Her husband, a lawyer, gave me the information and advice I needed. Together they let me know that I had their love and support. "My family is beside me," kept going through my head. "I don't have to face this alone."

When divorce proceedings began, we had to tell people why. I told my mother first—the whole story. She was less concerned about John's homosexuality than about my "promiscuous behavior." Though upset, she was relieved that she and I were talking after a year of silent hostility.

John told his parents about the divorce but not that he was gay. Deciding that the failure of the marriage was my fault, they wanted nothing more to do with me and asked me to give back the family ring. The wrench of that final exchange has not gone away.

On January first we started living separate lives financially, but I couldn't separate emotionally. John didn't want me to go. Many friends wanted me to stay. The temptation was strong. The gay world seemed wonderfully nurturing. There was a place for me there. But John and I knew that for the sake of both of us I needed to leave.

Once I felt some hope of finding life outside my secure but hurtful path with John, I moved to Big Sur, a mountain retreat along the California coast. All summer I lived there by myself, camping, hiking, wandering the beaches, sleeping—very much alone. By fall I had decided to remain in that healing place. There was much to put to rest and to put together. I felt like a fawn—newly born, dependent, insecure, trembling— yet filled with the potential of growth.

That first autumn I enrolled in a women's workshop, "Liberation from Within." Remembering my negative experiences with therapy, I went to the first meeting with all my defenses up. Though I acted carefree and self-assured, I was trembling inside. The group was small, seven or eight women, with two leaders who were kind, gentle and intelligent. As they made me feel safe, I relaxed my guard.

One of our first exercises was, "Who Are You?" Separated into pairs, we were to ask our partner gently, over and over, "Who are you?" The idea was to uncover the richness and diversity of our identity. My partner began. "Who are you?"

"Jane."

"Who are you?" she asked again.

I had no answer.

"Who are you?" she prodded gently.

"I don't know," I whispered and began to cry.

This experience and the following workshop activities helped me understand it was all right not to know who I was, that when we let go of pretending to know who we are, true self-knowledge can begin. Saying honestly, "I don't know who I am," had begun the exciting journey of self-discovery which I have continued—with rests, backslides, and detours—ever since.

For the next three years I lived in Big Sur. John and I stayed in contact, dealing with our anger, guilt and grief individually and together. Sometimes months passed with no communication and then we'd come together to talk and cry, yell and laugh. As we shared times of need and joy, we each grew stronger. Gradually our friendship deepened, based on our independence, individuality and honesty.

While we lied to others, we never lied to each other. John's courage the night he told me he loved Martin was the single most important factor in my discovery of what truth is. His courage to speak his truth was his greatest gift to me.

Eighteen years earlier we had vowed to love each other until death do us part. Although the marriage is dissolved, we continue to hold the vows sacred.

❦   ❦   ❦   ❦   ❦

Seven years later, Jane is an ordained minister, counseling and teaching in Denver. She has remarried and become a mother to two stepchildren. John and she remain friends.

Healing Sexual Damage

Possibly the most devastating issue confronting a straight spouse is how their partner's newly revealed sexual orientation has affected marital sex and the spouse's own sexuality.

In the confusion of the coming out, straight spouses typically wonder, "What am I up against? What does homosexuality or bisexuality mean for me?" Whether their partners are homosexual or bisexual, the fact that there is any degree of same-sex orientation or behavior at all results in the spouses feeling rejected as sex partners. They must then contend with the ensuing pain and sexual difficulties.

Healing sexual damage entails five major steps:

- Identifying how the same-sex orientation affected marital sex
- Recognizing the damage to sexual identity
- Expressing pain from sexual damage
- Understanding homosexuality and bisexuality
- Restoring a healthy sexuality.

Identifying How the Same-Sex Orientation Affected Marital Sex

Determining how the partner's same-sex attraction has affected the couple's sex life is the first step toward healing sexual damage. It depends on how long the partner actually knew he or she was homosexual and concealed the information from the spouse.

Many of the couples studied for this book enjoyed satisfactory and for some passionate sex during the first years of marriage. Others always felt something was missing. Still others, as time went on, were falsely accused of being undersexed, frigid or oversexed. "Some gay husbands are terrified by their wives' sexual desire and interest in sexual exploration," says Jane Vennard, founder of the National Task Force on Spouses of Gays and Lesbians. "That's why they criticize the women's sexuality, making them feel 'wrong' to want sex."[2]

In many cases lovemaking decreases as the partner's criticism increases. Many straight wives, assuming that men have the greater sex drive, believe the criticism. The wives' false self-images are reinforced every time they desire sex with and then fail to seduce their husbands. Seeing themselves as sexually inadequate, they then repress sexual desire. Moira epitomizes women who, viewing themselves as sexless, give up wanting or trying to make love.

Straight men married to lesbians often develop a similar pattern, as their wives accuse them of not understanding women's needs and of not knowing how to give them sexual pleasure. One husband in New Orleans, for instance, blamed himself when his wife said she could reach orgasm only by herself. From such rebuffs, many straight husbands believe they lack the sexual prowess men are assumed to have and feel incompetent.

After the partner comes out, most spouses begin to realize that the partner's sexual orientation, not their own sexual deficiencies, is the real reason that sexual tension was missing or limited in lovemaking. Looking back, many begin to see how the sexual mismatch plagued the relationship from the start. Full sexual intimacy may never have been achieved. Without intimacy and sexual desire, all the emotional, physiological and spiritual responses that comprise human sexuality couldn't be fully experienced in the marriage.

While many partners who are aware of their different sexual orientations find others to satisfy their sexual needs, their spouses generally do not. In retrospect many spouses see their incomplete sexual experiences as a violation of their right to sexual pleasure. As one angry wife said, "I was just a way for my husband to masturbate!"

Outsiders often raise questions about the sexuality of people who marry homosexuals in the first place. Yet there don't appear to be any traits they share that distinguish them from their peers who marry heterosexuals.[2] Though a number of spouses of gays are sexually inexperienced, ignorant or insecure, so too are many spouses in heterosexual marriages.

The fundamental problem is that straight spouses are the wrong sex for their gay partners. Though learning better communication skills or sexual techniques may help, they can never totally bridge the gap. Without knowledge of the actual sexual incompatibility, straight spouses' efforts to attract their partners are futile and their images of themselves as sexually incompetent are constantly reinforced.

Recognizing the Damage to Sexual Identity

The discovery of the partner's same-sex orientation often seems to spouses like a confirmation of their own sexual inadequacy. More troubling, the coming out causes many spouses to doubt their manhood or womanhood. Such a devaluation of sexuality and sexual role deals a double blow to sexual identity. Unraveling the twofold damage, primarily the concern of spouses of homosexuals, is the second step of sexual recovery.

Rejection of spouses' core identities by the persons they are intimately involved with is one of the most painful aspects of the coming out. Since self-image is closely linked with sexual role, the rejected spouse may feel like less of a woman or man. This reasoning explains why Jane rejoiced after she got pregnant. Now she had proof of womanhood. And why Dan fretted that he was not enough of a man to win Sally back from her lover.

Some spouses begin to doubt their own orientation. According to sex therapist Sharon Nathan, Ph.D., wives who seek sex therapy often ask, "What does it say about me that I married a gay male? Am I *really* interested in sex (with men)? What was I getting out of it?"[3] One man wondered why he was attracted to his wife's female lover before she was and why he was drawn to two lesbians.

Similarly, Martha, a thirty-five-year-old actress who had always sensed something was missing from her marriage felt attracted to a woman artist who came on to her. Martha's husband's subsequent coming out increased her suspicion that she, too, must be homosexual until she took a Sexual Attitude Restructuring (S.A.R.) workshop to settle the issue. She found that she was not lesbian, simply attracted to the woman's body because of her sensual artistic nature at a period when she was starved for physical intimacy.

It would seem that the discovering of the hidden reason for sexual problems in the marriage would erase the spouse's doubts of sexual inadequacy. It doesn't. Guilt and self-doubt automatically resurface for many spouses. They typically wonder, "What did I do to cause the problem?" A more constructive response would be something like, "His (or her) homosexuality helps to explain our difficulties. Where do we go from here?"

The habit of self-blame is hard to break. Many wives relive every day of the marriage trying to see how they might have caused their husband's lack of response. By making themselves the culprit, they don't have to blame their husbands, an acknowledgement too painful for many at first. Supporting their husbands is top priority, even if it compromises the wife's sexuality.

Many gay husbands contribute to their wife's low self-esteem by blaming the wife's sexual inadequacies for driving them to men. Family and friends, too, sometimes compound the situation through lack of knowledge or denial of the partner's homosexuality.

As spouses gradually understand how the sexual incompatibility affected marital sex, they usually stop blaming themselves. Instead most begin to feel that their sexuality has been damaged as a result of the sexual mismatch itself and, in some cases, their partner's unjustified criticism. Many feel that these factors prevented full exercise of their sexuality. They fear, because of years of limited sexual activity, that they may no longer be able to function sexually.

The longer the sexual disparity has operated undetected in the marriage, the greater the damage to spouses and the greater their anger. This is more an issue for wives of gay and bisexual men than for husbands of lesbians, since lesbians tend not to conceal their orientation once discovered. Many straight wives feel cheated and robbed of their birthright. Those married for more than a few years often believe that their injured sexuality is as irreversible as their husband's gayness. They fear that the damage can't be repaired any faster than it took to be inflicted and never completely.

Wives whose husbands have hidden their active gay life for several years often come to believe that their sexuality was sacrificed for their husband's need for protective cover. Some feel exploited, used as a sex machine for childbearing until it no longer served that purpose. Moira called it being Tim's "shield" from society.

Even the most sympathetic wife may erupt in anger at being used as her husband's protection from social discrimination. As unintentional as his behavior may have been, the sexual harm she experienced seems unforgivable. Outrage may begin to outweigh compassion felt for his plight in an anti-gay society. Many then feel an urge to fight back. This is a natural reaction and a positive step towards recovery.

Expressing Pain from Sexual Damage

Anger and pain from damaged sexuality need to be released before such feelings grow out of proportion and provoke self-destructive or counterproductive actions. Sharing feelings is the third strategy for healing damaged sexuality and one that is crucial in every stage of recovery until the coming-out trauma has been resolved.

It is critical to find a friend or family member to share emotions with. The spouse needs to hear, "It's okay!" from people who care. A man, no less than a woman, needs a shoulder to cry upon without shame.

Yet many spouses don't tell anyone what is now "our secret" out of loyalty or embarrassment. Some are asked by their partners not to tell because of fear of anti-gay reactions in the community or loss of job. Others feel uneasy about broaching the sensitive subject, fearing "rejection, disapproval or ostracism, because of the stigma attached to homosexuality," report Dorothea Hays and Aurele Samuels in their 1986 study of twenty-one straight wives.[4] Locked into the husband's closet by the secret, wives feel the impact of homophobia without having an escape valve. This isolation increases their distress.

Friends or family sometimes suspect what's happened from their own observation, like Moira's friend who saw Tim at a gay bar. Or they guess there is some kind of a problem from the spouse's haggard appearance, weight change or hypersensitivity, or in a couple's constant bickering. While friends tend to keep quiet out of respect, denial or avoidance of the problem, their expression of concern can be a great relief to the spouse. By gently asking, "Is there something wrong that you'd like to talk about?" or "Do you think he's gay or might be leaning that way?" friends can let the spouse know that they are willing to listen and aren't repelled by gayness.

When the spouse finally shares the secret, it should be with someone who is a supportive listener. Friends often try to calm or discourage the spouse's anguish and anger. But what the spouse needs is someone to listen with empathy and respect for his or her feelings.

In many cases, spouses receive uninformed, stereotypical or moral judgments when sharing the secret. Many of the women in Hays and Samuels' study met disbelief or ignorance.[5] Some friends, feeling uncomfortable with the situation, may drop away. Anticipating such reactions, spouses need to choose carefully who they confide in and be ready to correct misinformation.

The most helpful support usually comes from those in the same situation—individuals or support groups. Other spouses understand the anger resulting from sexual rejection. They can suggest from their own experience effective ways of coping. A support group, run by a counselor or straight spouse, provides a common perspective by which spouses can handle trauma more realistically.

Other straight spouses can be found through the partner's contacts, counselors, churches, public health agencies, personal ads in the newspaper, gay and lesbian organizations, and resources for spouses listed in appendix B.

Anger and the feeling of being victimized may last for months until spouses understand more about homosexuality, the pain of hiding it and ways of tapping into their own resources to overcome the damage.

Understanding Homosexuality and Bisexuality

As spouses try to sort out angry, hurt and confused feelings, it becomes critical to find out what homosexuality really means on a practical level to them as straight spouses. Many wonder if the partner is lost forever or if their own sexuality is permanently damaged.

A factual understanding of homosexuality and bisexuality, the fourth task of restoring sexuality, helps spouses relieve anxiety and gain a more accurate perspective of their own sexuality. It is also necessary in accurately assessing the likelihood of continuing or reviving marital sex.

The partners of the spouses are a primary source of information about homosexuality. Ideally they can provide firsthand experience as well as intimate support that their spouses need during this difficult stage. In turn, the spouses' interest may help ease the partners' feelings of guilt and defensiveness, making the sharing of information easier.

Often support from the partner is not forthcoming. Preoccupied with their own problems, many don't understand the pain and confusion on the other side of the closet, which, in many ways, is similar to the agony they have experienced. Responding to their concerns would be tantamount to admitting that they have hurt their spouses. Yet this lack of support only increases the stress.

If the partner is not supportive, it may help to point out, "Look, I'm going through what you did before you could accept your gayness and come out. I need the same kind of support and information for my coming out as you needed then." Although being assertive is hard during a period of devastation, the urgency of the need for help may require it.

Ways for couples to bridge the gap of understanding are discussed in *When Husbands Come Out of the Closet*, by therapist Jean Schaar Gochros, Ph.D.[6] What spouses need most from their partners is loving support while they work through the coming out, an approach outlined in *Coming Out: An Act of Love*, by Rob Eichberg, Ph.D., co-founder of Coming Out Day.[7]

Up-to-date factual books on homosexuality and bisexuality are also key resources. Researching the topic is usually a more reliable way of getting information than through the partner or friends who may be ill-informed or biased. Through reading, spouses can gradually digest the facts and apply them to their individual situations, without the distortion of stereotypical notions about homosexual or mixed-orientation relationships.

It is often embarrassing for many spouses to enter libraries and bookstores on such a quest. They feel stigmatized along with their partners, guilty by association. To deflect possible raised eyebrows, statements like, "I'm doing a research paper," are effective.

Since much printed material about homosexual and bisexual orientations is inaccurate, it's advisable to check facts with a credible professional or support organization. Available by phone or letter to provide reliable information and counsel are many organizations devoted to gay, lesbian and bisexual issues such as the Institute for Advanced Study of Human Sexuality in San Francisco, the Bisexual Information and Counseling Services in New York City, the Gay Switchboard in most large cities, and the Federation of Parents and Friends of Lesbians and Gays (Parents FLAG) listed in appendix B. Such professional help is crucial for spouses in communities where little about homosexuality is known or accepted.

Getting to know other gay, lesbian or bisexual persons, such as the partner's friends, is another common and effective way to gain an understanding of homosexuality. Face-to-face encounters also help desensitize anti-gay feelings and correct misconceptions. Gay activities and meeting places abound in large cities, such as gay and lesbian bookstores, bars and public events like the Gay Men's Chorus. Though some women enjoy participating in such activities with their husbands, others find it too painful to see physical displays of affection between them and other men.

Through reading and direct experience, the spouse may be surprised by the diversity of homosexual and bisexual behaviors and lifestyles. At the same time, the distinction between the partner's sexual orientation and the spouse's heterosexuality becomes painfully clear. Dan, in looking back, finally recognized lesbian feelings in Sally's extreme devotion to women friends. Although each realization causes more pain, the spouse is one step closer to recovery.

When the spouse accepts the fact that homosexuality and bisexuality are irreversible, any hopes of "changing" the partner or restoring the old relationship fade. Now the spouse understands that the partner has no say about his or her orientation except how to handle it. There's no magic wand to change him or her into an exclusively heterosexual person.

The difference between the partner's and spouse's sexual orientations can seem like an uncrossable chasm. During the time it takes to accept the stark reality of this sexual disparity, it helps to remember that many other women and men have weathered its pain.

Restoring a Healthy Sexuality

Because of the emotional upheaval caused by the realization of the sexual mismatch, many months may pass before the spouse can ask, "What can I do about the damage?" Restoring a healthy sexuality, the fifth step of recovery, usually doesn't begin until the second year after the coming out, or when the couple's sexual disparity has been completely accepted. Typically it takes at least another year to achieve sexual confidence and even longer to feel fully restored.

The healing of sexual damage can be facilitated through study of human sexuality, therapy and dating. Courage, patience and faith in regenerative powers are also indispensable factors in recovery. Spouses who remain with their partners will need their cooperation too, to restore a healthy sexuality within the marriage, a relationship issue to be discussed in part two.

Since a healthy sexuality hinges on a sense of self-worth, it's critical to address self-esteem issues at this point. Many spouses find counseling, self-help books and introspection helpful in this process. Jane, for example, didn't come to terms with how John's gayness had affected her sexuality until she went to the mountains to sort out the truth about herself.

Once the spouse begins to regain self-esteem, a realistic view of his or her sexuality can be formed. There are many helpful books available on human sexuality, ranging from *Joy of Sex*, edited by Alex Comfort, M.B., Ph.D.,[8] to *Radical Love: An Approach to Sexual Spirituality*, by Dody H. Donnelly, Ph.D., Th.D.[9] Other books recommended by straight spouses are listed in appendix A.

Many spouses work through their sexual identity crisis with the help of counseling or therapy. Marriage and family counselors, social workers, psychotherapists, sex therapists, and doctors can be found through other straight spouses, the yellow pages of the telephone directory, the Department of Human Services, and gay, lesbian and bisexual organizations.

Because of the closeted nature of homosexuality, there is a dearth of knowledgeable counselors outside of metropolitan areas. For this reason, spouses should determine, before making an appointment, how much experience the professional has had with straight spouses or mixed-orientation couples and whether he or she addresses the unique sexual concerns of straight spouses in the actual sessions.

Once in counseling, spouses should be wary of advice that emphasizes marital, psychological or moral problems to the exclusion of sexual problems in a mixed-orientation marriage. If the sexuality issue is not addressed, spouses may need to supply factual information clarifying sexual problems that mixed-orientation couples encounter. If that doesn't prompt appropriate guidance, they may consider relying on supportive friends and family until other reputable professional help can be found.

Course work in human sexuality can provide fresh insight to spouses struggling with sexuality issues. Workshops on human sexuality, such as the Sexual Attitude Restructuring course sponsored by the National Sex Forum, are given in many metropolitan areas. More formal courses, like those Dan took to strengthen his understanding of human sexuality, are offered by many colleges, universities or learning institutions.

Alongside reading, counseling and classes, exploration of ways in which spouses can give themselves sexual pleasure, such as self-caressing, may help to revive moribund sexuality.

As the spouse gradually regains sexual confidence, he or she may feel ready to start dating. It's best not to begin too soon or wait too long. Dan felt so desperate that he asked his men's group for blind dates before he was ready, while many wives over thirty fear there is little time left to regenerate their sex life. Impediments women foresee in finding a lover or remarrying include age, few available single men and their own sexual insecurities. Those with school-age children often believe no one will want to marry a gay man's ex-wife with children. These apparent blocks to meeting eligible mates may seem more forbidding than the reality, as many wives discover once they take the plunge.

Whether dating begins during the marriage or after divorce, straight husbands generally find it easier to meet the opposite sex than straight wives largely because, until the current demographic shift, there have been more unattached women available.

For some spouses feelings of sexual inadequacy may persist even after they begin dating. "Why in the world would a man want to love me?" is a common question of former wives, reports a thirty-six-year-old administrative secretary who started a support group for former spouses after her husband of eighteen years came out.

Spouses' marital history may cast a shadow on their dating experiences, too. Many women learn not to mention that their husbands or ex-husbands are gay until dating becomes more serious because dates often jump to one of two conclusions—either, "She must have had a problem with sex," or, "She's starved for sex." Rejection or pressured sex may result, increasing the women's apprehension and insecurity about dating.

The threat of AIDS also poses a problem. As will be discussed in part two, HIV-antibody testing is imperative for everyone, including the spouses' and the partners' lovers, and should be done before engaging in sexual activities. When spouses are on the verge of entering a serious relationship, they have a moral obligation to inform their lovers that their partners or ex-partners are gay. Though the information may make dates pause, most will respect the honesty.

Because of the AIDS epidemic, it's crucial to find out about the date's sexual background before consummating the relationship, tempting as it might seem. Shared laughter and simple gestures of affection and caring—touching, kissing, hugging, or holding—can be immensely satisfying as a temporary replacement for sexual intercourse and can help the spouse prepare emotionally for the more complex sexual experience. For wives for whom infidelity may be out of the question, sheer affection and caring experiences alone are enormously helpful.

Gradually spouses begin to see themselves as normally functioning sexual beings. In time they may even be able to look back at the sexual mismatch with irony. As an ex-wife in Sacramento said with a half-smile, several years after her husband left her for a gay lover, "I had to seduce him every four months when I couldn't stand it any longer, enough so we had three children in five years."

Martha, the actress described earlier, blossomed with a heterosexual lover, "my sexual awakening at forty-five," she wrote. "It was an extraordinary spiritual experience. Incredible beauty was in everything around me, inspired by my renewed sexuality. I felt competent in everything. People saw me as a different person."

Despite seemingly overwhelming obstacles, a number of spouses, old and young, men and women, develop long-term heterosexual relationships including marriage. Five of the thirty straight spouses studied in depth for this book have remarried and one is engaged. While some spouses remarry soon after the coming out, it may be better to wait until all major emotional issues have been resolved and recovery is well under way.

For spouses who choose to stay with their partners, sexual damage may be healed within the marriage through various non-traditional arrangements, therapy and joint commitment to make the sexual relationship mutually satisfying. The stories in part two show how three women, along with their husbands, developed alternative ways to satisfy their sexual and other marital needs.

two

TRIAL
AND ERROR
ALTERNATIVE MARITAL STYLES
TO ACCOMMODATE GAYNESS

While some spouses are left by their partners after they come out and other spouses leave because of the sexual incompatibility, infidelity or existing marital problems, many spouses question whether the marriage needs to end just because the partner is gay or bisexual.

Usually it is straight wives, not straight husbands, who pose such a question, since often homosexual and bisexual men wish to stay married. Many gay or bisexual husbands don't want to leave because they still love their wives, give the marriage top priority or want its "cover," and desire continued contact with the children. Most lesbian wives on the other hand, seem to leave soon after accepting their sexual identity, as much because of a negative view of having sex with men as an attraction to women. Little is known about bisexual wives, although some stay married, as Nanette did in part one.

Many gay-straight couples have an unusually strong bond of friendship based on shared interests. The coming out threatens that bond as much as the marriage. Wives in such marriages often feel driven to try to preserve the bond and make the marriage work at whatever cost, despite disparate sexual needs. Typically they love their husbands too much to leave or fear the consequences of ending the marriage. Divorce would destroy both the bond and the family unit and in the case of spouses bound by financial or emotional dependence, severely affect the quality of their lives.

Few models of successful mixed-orientation marriages are available. As couples forge their own paths between the exigencies of their individual situations and conventional mores, the wife generally makes the most adjustments to accommodate the same-sex needs of the husband. Rarely does a husband decide not to pursue his gay interests in deference to his wife's needs.

Working out a viable alternative to the conventional arrangement is a process of trial and error that takes several years. Along the way, many couples discover that the marriage no longer serves their best interests. Yet working through the relationship crisis often results in a new and lasting bond.

The following stories illustrate alternative marital arrangements and ways of relating developed by three couples after the coming out. The concluding section highlights major problems mixed-orientation couples face and strategies for developing new relationship patterns that can endure whether or not they stay married.

Personal Stories

Nothing's Written In Stone
Rita

Though Hal was slightly younger, we'd been good friends since seventh grade. After dating in high school, we married two years later in Columbus. Our son was born two years after that.

Though we both tended to be heavy, we gave up smoking just before my second pregnancy. Hal ate along with me until his waist size was up to forty-eight at the time of our daughter's birth. Then we both dieted. In five months I lost eighty pounds and Hal dropped one hundred. With a waist of twenty-eight and a great build he looked terrific. Then suddenly he gained it all back and had a nervous breakdown.

Hal worked for a tool distribution company until the children were nine and eleven, when he left to work for himself. Then we began to spend time with a close friend Sue and her husband Eddie who worked in my repair shop. Although they were younger, in their mid-twenties, we had good times together.

Our relatives weren't so sure about Eddie. "Is he gay?" one or another would ask us.

"Oh, no," we'd say, "He's married."

One Saturday when Sue and Eddie were over, I said to Sue while fixing lunch, "Hal and I haven't had sex in three months."

"God!" she answered. "I've been married five years and have never had sex at all."

"What?" I thought, recalling Eddie telling me once when I was fussing about Hal, "I used to be impotent, but it's okay now."

Sue saw my disbelief. "Eddie's impotent, Rita."

A year or so after this, Hal's old boss wanted him back as manager. "Sure," he said, "but I'll need Tuesdays off."

His request made no sense for our schedule. Tuesday was my day off to go to my health spa.

Two weeks later Eddie had a nervous breakdown and started to say things at work like, "I'm going to break up your family."

After a couple of days Hal sat me down after dinner. "Rita, before Eddie blurts out anything more, I want you to hear it from me. He is gay, after all. The marriage was a show for his parents. And...we've been having an affair."

"A what?"

"An affair."

"You can't be that way, Hal. You don't act wimpy. You can't be!" I was shrieking by then.

"I am gay, Rita," he said and explained, "When I first had gay feelings as a boy, I was afraid to ask anyone about it but read all there was on the subject. The books said it's sometimes a natural feeling of young boys. So I repressed it as an adolescent feeling."

Stunned I listened to every word.

"Remember when I lost all that weight?" he went on. "Men started looking at my build which I liked better than when women did. Then, strong feelings came out toward Stan, my best friend! There was no way I could tell him how I felt, he's so straight. Scared of being gay with a wife and two kids, I had the breakdown. I repressed the feelings until Eddie."

I sat in total shock as he continued.

"When the shop was closed Tuesdays and you went to the health spa, Eddie and I had it to ourselves. When my old boss called me back, Eddie asked me to leave you. He'd leave Sue, he said, so we could buy a home and I'd take care of him.

"'I'm not leaving my wife,' I told him and went to a psychologist, who told me I'd better find out what my feelings really were."

After Hal finished I sat there paralyzed until way past bedtime.

The next day Sue called in a panic. "You won't believe it. Eddie's just said he's gay. He's known it since he was a boy."

"Yeah, I know," I said and told her my story, without giving her much sympathy.

For the next few weeks I walked around like a zombie. Yet as the shock wore off I began to feel hurt about being deceived.

One day, Hal said, "If Eddie hadn't gotten greedy, our affair could have gone on for years."

"Naw," I said, "something always comes up."

As Hal insisted he still wanted me, I became Joan of Arc. "We'll get through this together, hon. I still love you," I'd assure him.

The kids still loved their father, too. So Hal and I agreed to work on the marriage and stick with it, as long as it worked. We negotiated everything. First we decided he could be out Monday nights since I had Thursday nights for bowling.

On Monday nights after seeing his therapist Hal stayed in the city to hang out with the boys in bars until late. To get enough sleep for my job I went to bed early those nights, setting the alarm for one. He was never home by then, so I'd stare out the window and cry, wondering what he was doing. "There'll be a call," I thought, "saying he's dead somewhere without a head or arms."

Getting home at four didn't faze Hal. "Don't worry," he told me. "My therapist knows where I go. If anything happens, call him."

At first our relationship was like brother and sister. Then our sex got heavy and frequent for a month and then not very often again. Sex became "payment" in advance for a bomb he would later drop, like, "Rita, I am going to have sex with men and I'm not going to lie to you and say, 'I'm gay but you're the only one.'" After each bomb the sex became infrequent again.

One night Hal met a fellow at a bar who invited him to a married gay men's support group. He also told him that his wife was forming a support group for straight wives.

When Hal told me about the wives' group, I perked up. "Man, I'd like to talk to someone who doesn't have a totally heterosexual marriage and see how she handles it."

Going to the wives' session began a regular pattern. Soon I was open about Hal to my boss and everyone. I was on a TV show and did a radio interview from work with my co-worker's support.

Hal wasn't so open. He hesitated telling his best friend, Stan. When he did, Stan got angry, asking, "Why didn't you tell me sooner?" Yet he remained a compassionate and understanding friend.

Meanwhile after Hal had rebuffed Eddie, Eddie left my repair shop and I couldn't find a replacement. With only one other worker besides myself, it was hard to make a go of it. I was angry with Hal over the whole mess, but I didn't tell him about my struggling business. By the time he found out, the business had to close. We didn't go bankrupt or have to sell the house, but I ran up some bills and had to find another job.

Our bills were complicated by then since they covered additional expenses for Hal's mother and aunt who had moved in with us.

Within the year, Hal met Luke, who became his lover. Renegotiating, we agreed that Hal could be with Luke three nights a week. Since I liked Luke too we three did things together, including New Year's celebrations and family vacations. The kids liked him also.

Then Hal wanted to go away weekends with Luke.

"Well, we can work it out," I responded. "Why don't you take an extra week with him after our next vacation?"

If Hal was meticulous, Luke was super meticulous. Once Hal saw how Luke's single life allowed him to have things the way he wanted, Hal began trying to keep our house the way he wanted, too.

I laughed, "Hal, you can't have your kind of house here where there are six people, two cats and a dog. A house can't be dirt-free with that many people."

Before long Hal had taken over our bedroom, talking with Luke on the phone every night while I watched TV in the living room. I resented not being able to go to bed when I wanted and realized that Luke and I were competing for my room.

We were also competing for sex with Hal. Gradually Luke won out. Three years after Hal came out, he and I stopped having sex altogether.

By then we were going to the couples' group, an offshoot of his married men's group. Several of the women were from my support group. One evening the group was discussing what happens when gay husbands don't have sex with their wives.

"Sex isn't that important..." began the leader.

"Back up a minute!" I interrupted. "Do you have sex with your lover?"

"On occasion."

"Then it's important," I said.

"Well, it's not *that* important."

"If you've got to do it, it's important," I insisted. "Otherwise you wouldn't. So don't tell us wives that it's not important and that we should do without it. If you're not getting it at all, like us, every little bit is important."

He continued to argue the point.

"Come on!" I said, knowing how much his wife hurt from not having sex any more. "Don't patronize me because I'm not an idiot. If sex isn't important, then why are you in a gay relationship?"

For two more years Hal and I had no sex while he continued to see Luke.

Finally I told Hal one night, "This is unbearable!"

The next morning I told myself, "O.K., Rita, if you're not going to have sex with Hal, you've got to have somebody. You're a woman with needs and you're going to get them met. But if you're going to have sex, you're not going to get pregnant."

I made an appointment to have my tubes tied later that week. When the doctor examined me he found an extra heart beat. Though not serious, he had to monitor it for three months before operating. When the operation was over he gave me a prescription for heart pills, saying, "They're not essential."

"No way," I said. "As long as my heart keeps beating, I don't want medication."

Two months later I met Sam at the bowling alley where we'd both bowled for ten years without ever bumping into each other.

"Why didn't I meet you ten years ago!" Sam asked me on our third date.

"I wasn't ready before."

So Hal and I each had our own lovers. Within six months Hal was spending Tuesday, Thursday, Friday, and Sunday with Luke, while Sam and I were together after Monday bowling and on Thursday and Sunday nights. I still slept in the same bed with my husband and held him, but had sex with another man who desired me. Life was comfortable for awhile.

Thursdays and Sundays Hal and I went out at the same time but he came home at eleven while I walked in at three or four in the morning, thinking, "I don't care." That annoyed him.

One Saturday a year after meeting Sam, I had a funny feeling as I looked over at Hal while we sat talking in the kitchen, "I don't want any more physical contact with this man," I thought. "I give Luke a hello kiss faster than I do him. I wonder why. Am I afraid to lose control and want sex with him again?"

That evening I said to Hal, "I can't touch you any more. I don't know why because I still love you."

As Hal began to see how happy my relationship with Sam made me, his tune changed from "I'll stay with you, Rita" to "Our marriage isn't good. I want to get out."

"Hmm," I thought. "Hal's thinking, 'She's taken care of now. No more guilt over her not having sex with me.'"

That Saturday, about lunchtime, the phone rang. The man on the line asked, "Has your husband found his apartment yet?"

I choked. "What did you say?"

He repeated his question again and this time I understood. It was the first time Hal and I hadn't negotiated something that affected us both.

When Hal came home later I asked, my voice raised, "Why didn't you tell me you were moving out?"

"I never meant for you to find out that I was leaving that way."

"That makes no sense," I said. "If you didn't want me to know, why did you give out your home phone number? Since you're at work all day, and with Luke three nights and Sunday, how can I believe you didn't want me to find out?"

In preparation for the move five months away, Hal bought us each a car. The next day I found his address on the bills for both cars and I called him at work. "Why did you do that?"

"I was afraid you wouldn't pay the bills and would ruin my credit."

"Of course I'd pay them."

"Well, how would I know after what happened to the business?"

I screamed into the phone, "You rat! I can't afford to have my car taken away for not paying the bill. How on earth would I get to and from work without it? If I've got to support myself, I'll pay my bill. How dare you take it from me!"

I hung up in shock. "Our arguments have never been like this," I thought. "I've never called him names." Then I straightened up. "But I can't help it. He's treating me like a child. He assumes that what happened when the business went under will repeat itself. He distrusts me."

Just then the phone rang. It was Hal. "Sorry I upset you."

"Well, O.K. But did you really think you would have to pay my bills?"

"Well, no. Let's talk about it."

"Sure. Nothing's written in stone," I said. "We've thought that way all along. Why change now?"

When we finished negotiating, my car bills were mine to pay. Hal would write the house bills because I didn't want to be involved with him personally. The bank account was to be in both our names and everyone would contribute to it—the kids, my mother-in-law and both of our aunts who were living there by then.

"But," I added, "if anything has to be done around the house, it'll be deducted from your portion of the account and you'll have to take what you need for house bills from household funds."

When Hal left in May I thought I'd die from not being involved with him anymore except connected to the children. But it wasn't the time to sit and whine. Having a lousy attitude toward Hal wouldn't help the children keep their father.

The kids were hurt at first and discussed the situation with me for weeks until they accepted it. Hal's mother and aunt remained angry.

"He didn't do this to leave you," I reasoned with them until he was finally back in their good graces.

My relatives accepted Hal's leaving, taking a cue from me.

My friend Sue asked, "How come you're not upset like I was with Eddie?"

"Every separation's different. Mine was a long time coming with plenty of understanding. I did everything I could to make it work."

Once Hal was in his own place he became even closer to Luke. Within a few months he announced, "I'm going to find an apartment halfway between his house and ours, ten miles apart."

A week later he called to tell me he'd found a place. My son took the call. As he handed me the phone he whispered, "It's three miles from Luke's. How does Daddy figure that?"

Once on the line I asked, "Why did you pick a place so much closer to Luke's than here?"

"It was the only decent place."

"You shouldn't have been looking there," I said, furious, "if you were looking at places halfway between. You didn't want to be under our nose and now you're next to him. You just want to live with him."

"No, I'm making this apartment permanent."

"You mean we'll have to sell the house?"

"Of course," Hal replied. "Then we'll each do what we want."

"What about your mother and your aunt?"

"Oh," he said, "they can do what they want."

"Your aunt's sixty-eight and your mother's sixty-five. Why should they have to spend lots of money for separate apartments? Where is there a place with three bedrooms? We have six bedrooms here for five working people. Maybe I should buy you out."

After much discussion we decided I'd buy him out with my savings plus money we'd all put in over the next eighteen months.

A month or so later divorce came up. "I don't want a divorce," I said. "I won't be ready to commit myself to anyone for a long time. I'm too afraid."

So we worked out a legal document that stated what was mine and what was his, disclaiming any right to the other's assets.

I stayed on his insurance and the kids had theirs through their jobs. Hal kept me as his beneficiary since Luke, an only child, would get all his parents' funds.

Six months later I didn't miss Hal at all. Amazingly I felt happy and relieved not to have to compete with Luke in my own house and my own bedroom. Hal was just another friend, popping by after meetings and leaving with a care package I'd prepared for his microwave. When he asked to come by on Thanksgiving, I invited him for dessert along with other friends.

By Christmas, when he came for breakfast with the kids, Hal was down to a forty waist. But I had gained my ultimate weight to over two hundred pounds. I'd stopped smoking because of shortness of breath and back pain. So I started Weight Watchers in the New Year, inspiring myself to go. There was nobody else to do that for me any more.

Now another half year past, I'm on my way to recovery with Sam there to support me. Yet there are moments when I still feel strongly for Hal. One morning the radio played "our song." The tears that came made me angry. "I can't do that! It's that song!" I screamed silently.

It will just take time to get over him. Feelings, too, aren't written in stone.

Our Own Timetable
Carol

The day of reckoning for me came July 25, 1986. Dave and I, in our early twenties, had been married for three years. Our second daughter, Deidre, had arrived six days before and Mom was visiting to help me with her and two-year-old May. Dave got home from work late that night because of an appointment with his therapist, Roger.

"How did it go?" I asked. "Want to talk about it?"

"Yes, but later, Carol, in private."

Finally in bed, the light on and Deidre asleep in her bassinet beside us, Dave began, as my heart started beating faster and my palms became sweaty.

"Well, first, Roger isn't just a therapist. He counsels gay people." Dave paused and then he said, "I'm gay, Carol."

I waited for him to say it was a joke but he didn't. All he said, over and over was, "This is the worst day in my life."

I wanted to cry out, "Just what does being gay mean, anyway?" But Mom was there and the girls were sleeping so my cries were muffled.

When I saw the anguish in Dave's face, being the mothering type that I am, I tried to console him. We tried to console each other.

"I accept your being gay," I finally said, "but does it mean we have to divorce or we can't make love anymore?"

"I don't know," Dave said, "but I think it's best if you and the girls go back to Oregon when your mother goes next week."

All the next day I wondered, "How in the world can I organize a cross-country move with two small children in less than a week?" That night I told him, "I can't leave now. I need time for this to sink in before I move anywhere."

From then on I kept track of what happened in my journal as the meaning of Dave's words sunk in.

❦   ❦   ❦   ❦   ❦

August 11, 1986. Well, Mother is leaving Baltimore tomorrow and I'm packing a box of our things for her to take, going through all our possessions, trying to decide what to keep and what to toss. I even have to divide up the junk drawer!

I'm going to sell my wedding dress. It's just collecting dust. Besides it doesn't mean what it once did.

I'm resigned to the fact that life will never be the same again. It will be completely different from how I envisioned it, but that's not so terrible. I'm not naive. I'll be a single mother, support or not, and will have to work and put the kids in day care. That makes me sad, but there's no choice. Some people will think my life is forever ruined, but I don't. It's just changing, drastically maybe, but with these changes I'll grow.

August 30. I feel excited about my new relationship with Dave. Many people, especially women, can't believe how understanding and accepting I am of him. That says a lot about how they feel about their husbands! I seem to have a better relationship with my gay husband than they do with their straight husbands.

(Later) Maybe I have it together, but some days I feel as if I'm going to fall apart with sadness. When I move back home to Oregon, I'll be alone and so will Dave. I'll have two children to care for by myself, but he won't have the chance to care for them at all. When I feel sad like this, it shows and makes Dave sad too. Though he tries to console me, it doesn't help.

August 31. Sometimes I feel I'm the only person who has any compassion for Dave and what he's going through. Too many people think, no matter what I tell them, that he's found a new life and is sending me and the kids home so he can live unrestricted. But it's not like that!

His parents should know what a compassionate, thoughtful, generous, loving son they have. Instead they say that he's a "stranger" and, because he's planning to stay in Baltimore, that he's selfish. I know what they're going through, but they shouldn't lay that guilt on him. This is not easy to handle so why can't they think about what their son's going through?

September 5. Joy of joys, I'm not going back to Oregon after all! Dave's been a wreck all week. He finally realized what our splitting up would mean and it hurt too much. There wasn't a good reason to separate. We only thought we had to. We need each other. Who says we have to split up?

I've already sold the crib, so I guess I'll have to buy another.

September 10. Dave and our neighbor Curt went out to gay bars Friday night. Dave said it felt good to finally be a part of the gay life.

Saturday Curt and his wife Pat came over and as usual these days, the subject turned to sex. After a few beers it was obvious that Dave and Curt wanted each other sexually. Pat and I decided that if our husbands are going to sleep with men, it might as well be with people we know and like. So I went to bed alone and Dave went next door with Curt and Pat after I made it clear that I wanted to know if anything happened.

The reasons behind Dave sleeping with a man versus a woman are completely different. My reactions are, too. I cannot, try as I may, compete with another man. I can be gorgeous and intelligent, but if Dave wants a man, nothing I do can change that. I might as well be a frog. It's not easy, but I know he loves me as much as ever and I love him. We *will* be happy.

(Later) Dave did sleep with Curt, but didn't tell me until today, after we talked about the importance of openness and honesty.

September 17. It's so hard for me to face my insecurity. I never realized how emotionally dependent I am on Dave. I was basically insecure when I met him. Then I lost weight, became more confident and assertive. But now? I guess it was false security. Now I have to find real security within me.

September 26. I need to get a night job or something! Dave has this meeting on Tuesdays and that meeting on Thursdays and here I sit, telling myself I'm content.

October 3. Dave is coming out in more ways than one. He's having more aches and pains or actually finally acknowledging them. The real Dave gets headaches after all.

October 10. Well, he's not wearing his wedding band anymore. I guess he thinks that he can't be totally gay if he wears a symbol of heterosexual marriage. But it hurts!

It's ironic how I've been feeling so insecure just when Dave is feeling more secure about himself. For the most part, the changes in my life are good, but why does it have to be so different?

October 11. Dave had his hair cut and, boy, does he look gay! He's going through an adolescence of sorts, "boy crazy" and more than ever caring how he looks. I feel threatened, not as needed. I thought I could always satisfy him in every way, but it's clear that I can't.

October 29. Dave is depressed, mourning the "best little boy in the world" that he used to be. He always assumed that he'd be happy, not sad.

November 11. I resent the fact that if I want our marriage to work, I have to do all the accepting. Can I continue to accept all the changes I never bargained for? Or will I have to leave him—another change? I'm scared.

I don't give a damn if my situation isn't unique. As far as I'm concerned, no one knows how I feel. I'll never have all that I hoped for. Oh, I still hope, but not with the eternal optimism I once had. It's no one's fault, reality just slapped me in the face. Sometimes I want to slap it back. Is this why people become so cynical?

November 16. God, what was I going through on Sunday? It must have been the group therapy I went to Saturday. There are eight women including myself, the youngest. About half are trying to keep their marriages together and half are divorced or separated. I talked about fifteen minutes. Compared to the other women's problems, mine seemed trivial. Yet today I realized that if my problems make me cry and feel depressed, they aren't so trivial.

Sometimes I'm afraid I won't always be a strong person.

November 17. The Sunday paper had an article on gay husbands and a couple of them were on a talk show. They seemed to be doing a fine job of making their relationships work. Finally, role models!

December 12. Well, I just made a major decision on my own! The girls and I are going to move back to Oregon a year from now. Hopefully Dave will want to come with us.

December 15. Although Dave isn't wild about the idea, he said that he'd come with us. But he suggested that we move back sooner—this summer. If he has to leave his favorite city, he doesn't want to prolong the agony. I'm thrilled.

January 6, 1987. Dave now thinks it's inevitable we'll grow apart because we were brought up in totally different worlds. The "proletarian" Dave that he pretended to be isn't really him. It was a rebellion. He's actually more like his parents who are always doing this or that—busy all of the time. He thinks we're dull since we never do anything. He has cabin fever.

We may not be the socialites his parents are, but we're certainly not dull. So he's more frivolous and I'm more practical. Can't we complement each other?

Now I know there's no such thing as "forever." I always thought we were forever. That's why I left college after freshman year to marry Dave while he finished. What a fantasy! I guess no one's certain what their future will be. Nothing's guaranteed. Did I really think that once I got married I'd be immune? The sooner I can accept reality, the sooner I won't hurt so much. If there's any way I can prevent it, I'll never get hurt again.

January 7. We'll be O.K. Dave loves me, likes, appreciates and respects me. We've decided that if we ever show signs of growing apart, we'll do whatever it takes to keep our relationship alive, even if it means living apart.

January 14. I can't believe it's good or right to feel so much pain. After group therapy I came home and Dave did me a "favor" by trying to make me see reality. He said that there's a fine line between optimism and delusion and that I don't see the difference. But my optimism gives me strength. I know that Dave and I might live apart one day but why dwell on it?

January 21. Sometimes I think Dave wishes he had never married me or had kids, although he loves us all very much. Things would have been much less complicated. Sometimes I think it might almost have been easier, but not better, if Dave had died. Then there would be one grieving period, not something new each month.

January 28. For a while whenever Dave and I made love, I thought it was because he couldn't get it elsewhere. After finally talking to him about it, I now know that isn't true. We make love because he wants to and I want to. Meanwhile, when he goes out, he always practices safe sex.

January 29. I quit group therapy. My problems didn't seem bad enough to share and I felt stifled.

I know Dave may fall in love and move out one day. I'm not looking forward to that, but I'm determined not to be standing in the doorway wondering what to do next. I am going to be happy!

April 12. Now Dave is undecided about whether or not to move back to Oregon. Maybe he should stay here, not because I want him to, but because it's something he has to do. On the other hand, I think he should give Portland another chance.

April 16. Well, Dave has decided to stay here with the option to change his mind at any time. I'm relieved because the tension of wondering whether he will or won't go is gone. Now I can get on with the move.

April 22. Once again Dave has changed his mind! He will be coming with us after all! After he made the decision to stay, he never felt good about it. We're leaving at the end of May.

June 22. We're in Portland, renting a big house with a garden from my brother's sister-in-law. Sometimes I wonder if it was the right decision to come back. Would I have if Dave weren't gay? I don't think so.

Strange as it sounds, I'm happy he's gay. I've grown so much and become more open-minded. Our children are likely to be more open-minded also. One very important thing is that other people know I'm not ashamed. Maybe I'll write a book one day!

September 3. What a roller-coaster year it's been! Dave and I are in a sort of limbo as individuals as well as partners. He's trying to balance his gay life with his family life, but the two don't seem to be blending well. I never did think of him as a husband. The term doesn't fit. He's more like a "life partner."

January 24, 1988. I know I can handle Dave having an affair and am entitled to affairs of my own. But what will happen if he falls in love with someone? He assures me that he wouldn't drop me for another. Does that mean sharing him? What will that be like?

I really miss the romance in our life. When I met and fell in love with Dave in high school, I finally understood all the love songs. But now that I know he's gay, those same songs are hard to listen to. It doesn't seem fair. I feel a great loss.

Dave says his feelings for me haven't changed and he still feels romantic. When I feel the least bit romantic, I wonder if I'm a fool for caring and a fool for staying. But how foolish is it to love and care for someone who loves and cares for me? I want to be important to him. Is that so foolish?

January 26. It's been eighteen months and sometimes I feel I haven't gotten too far. Other times I'm amazed. When I reread my journal and realize the emotions that I've grappled with, it's clear that I've grown.

May 26. Despite our obvious contentedness, a lot of people have trouble understanding why I still live with Dave. Some think I should divorce him and move out just because he's gay. They don't think a gay-straight relationship can work. Others don't care to know about our lifestyle as long as we stay married and act like a couple.

Sometimes I wonder why I don't divorce him or at least move out? But we like living together, not to mention the financial benefits. For now this is what works for us. Without guidelines for a situation like ours, we have to create our own timetable.

One definition of marriage is "any close union, i.e., marriage of the minds." Our minds have been "married" for almost five years.

September 22. Dave read my journal today and said that it was too sugarcoated, that I wasn't being totally honest with myself. Maybe he's right. I always refer to his moving out as something that might happen in the future. Because it seems years away, I don't want to think about it until I have to.

But it will happen sooner than I think. We have an eventual plan to move into a flat his parents own in a nice neighborhood with good schools. Then, we'll save money so Dave can move out in a year. My logical side thinks it would be best for us both. My emotional side thinks Dave wants to leave because I stifle him. Maybe we're stifling each other.

It's exciting and scary all at once, but I'm grateful that there's time to truly prepare myself, not that it will be easy.

October 10. Two of our good women friends debated with Dave all afternoon and evening about our relationship. They were on the verge of outrage, telling him he couldn't be in love with me. Seeing him so upset, I reassured him.

January 22, 1989. Our friends were right. Dave can't be in love with me. I know he loves, cares for and respects me, but "in love" means deep devotion, passion and sole attraction, which isn't what he feels for me. And I'm feeling less of that for him. We haven't made love for two months and our kisses aren't much different from how I kiss my brother. Sometimes I hurt as much as I did when he told me two and a half years ago.

February 4. After rereading my last journal entry, I don't feel as bad. Dave and I have talked since then. It's clear that our relationship is still new to us. We're the only couple I know in this situation.

April 6. Having put on ten pounds and finding myself yelling at the children, I finally started seeing a therapist today.

July 2. There's never a perfect time, but now's the time to separate. The resentment between Dave and me has been building. Today in therapy I realized I had to get it over with. Dave's uncle, meanwhile, called us chicken for putting it off. We'll separate after our vacation, before the girls start school, so they won't have too much to cope with all at once.

November 10. It's working out as well as any separation. The vacation eased the hurt a bit. In a way I'm excited to be in total charge of the house and have more time to myself when Dave is with the kids. We have a joint checking account and pool our money. Since we can't afford to get Dave an apartment even with my waitressing, cleaning houses and baby-sitting, he's at his parents' house. Hopefully that will help them accept his being gay.

  With the kids' school, my jobs and home projects, I'm very busy. I need to be because the nights are lonely. I'm not ready for a new relationship and now with the risk of AIDS, flings are out of the question. It is so lonely, but not forever. It makes me feel better to remember that I still have my bond with Dave which we vowed was forever.

The Best Solution
Audrey

It was the mid-sixties when a friend wrenched me out of my family home to move in with her and another friend in Los Angeles. "What are you going to do, Audrey?" she teased. "Spend the rest of your life with your mother?"

Mama protested. Not particularly progressive, she frowned upon my leaving home without being married. She was anxious that I wasn't married or dating much at all.

My friends and I were twenty year olds playing at being adults. Soon after I moved in, someone fixed me up with a law student named Scott. When he walked in, attractive and dark haired, he smiled a beautiful smile. I liked him instantly, the first man I'd felt that way toward. "So friendly and open and sensitive!" I thought, thrilled by how comfortable I felt with him.

I'd always been concerned about my sexuality. From an early age, I'd felt different from other little girls, not knowing how to act with them as they talked about boys and flirted. Although I was fairly attractive with black hair and olive skin, thinking I wasn't like them put a stigma on me.

On my first date with Scott we went to the movies. As he guided me to my seat, his hand felt comfortable, big and warm and dry. That hand meant I'd be taken care of, unprepared as I was to get out into the world on my own. "This is the man I'm going to marry!" I exclaimed silently.

At home that night I thought, "It's perfect. Mama would die to have a Jewish lawyer for a son-in-law." Also some fears were dispelled. "Maybe I *am* okay!"

With Scott away at law school, our relationship was a long distance one. One weekend I went up to be with this prince, feeling insecure about the little sexual experience I'd had. Then when we slept together, everything that could go wrong did. But he continued to write and called me for a date when he returned to town.

"I don't understand," I thought to myself, "but I'll go for it."

We dated on and off for a year, during which time he got a job teaching like all the guys who wanted to beat the Vietnam draft.

He came over often and we began sleeping together each visit. It was much better now and I felt comfortable with sex for the first time.

Soon he was calling every day at noon. His predictability was a little confining, but I got used to it. Since he was a man I could be with, I wanted to safeguard this relationship.

We began to see each other every Saturday night and one evening sitting in my room one of us said, "Why don't we marry?" and we both agreed.

No rockets or fireworks, just the appropriate thing to do.

His family and mine were hoping for it. Both were Jewish, his from the old country and mine protective and conservative.

Since the next day was Mother's Day, we told Mama first before making the engagement official.

We didn't want rings or a big wedding. But Mama, who was dying of cancer, wanted a wedding. She won out. We were married in Palm Springs, California that winter.

We moved to a nice, neat community in Orange County where we set up a little apartment. We did everything expected of young married couples except join in the social activities of the apartment complex. We felt separate from all the other couples we saw going up and down the elevator. They seemed to be making friends with each other. Neither of us knew why we weren't. Though Scott was adaptable, I felt like an outsider, uncomfortable in my body and my identity which didn't seem to fit.

The first two years of our marriage were great. We laughed at the same things and shared lots of interests. We both worked, I at a part-time sales job and Scott as an intern in a law firm. He was wonderful around the house and taught me, who had never even had a fresh vegetable before, about everything. He didn't mind mothering me and we had wonderful times together.

Our sex life was easy. Scott wasn't demanding nor interested in a lot of sex. We made love once a week at the most, which was comfortable for me.

Scott masturbated a lot, but that wasn't a problem for me, having no reference point of how often married men do it. I was pleased he could relieve himself without making a lot of sexual demands on me.

Scott wanted children. Whenever he brought it up, I tried to put it off. Part of me didn't want to commit to children because I wasn't absolutely sure I'd be with this person all that long.

By the second year we'd made friends with two couples outside the complex. Weekends with them and working during the week was our life. Mama had died by then, as well as her expectations of me to be more like other women.

The wives of the couples were friends I'd known before I met Scott. Lil had been at camp with me and Mary was one of her friends.

The first time I'd met Mary was awkward. Lil had warned me that I wouldn't like her. When I picked them up to go for a drive that day, Mary acted strange. Looking at her in the back seat through the rear view mirror, we made eye contact and from that moment on, I felt off kilter. I couldn't handle it.

Mary couldn't either. We picked a fight and stopped speaking. A year or so later, I found out that she and Lil had been lovers. In a panic, I knew that it was absolutely necessary to stay away from them. I certainly didn't want to know a lesbian, much less be one.

Once Scott and I were safely married in our little nest, Mary made contact again. She was dating a lovely fellow named Don that Scott and I both liked. We began doing things with them and we four became close friends. Then they became engaged.

Tuesday before the wedding Mary and I went shopping. When she drove me home, we talked in the car and agreed to continue our conversation the following day at her place. She wanted help in lining her kitchen shelves. I called work to take the day off and told Scott where I'd be.

The next day changed my life totally and radically forever. When I got to Mary's apartment, there was no shelf paper. Instead she propositioned me.

I was scared to death. It wasn't because I was married and this would be cheating. It was, "Oh my God! Here it is. It's going to happen any second." Instantly I knew what had been suppressed all those years.

While Mary had had sex with other women, she was my first. It was unbelievable. It somehow seemed more reasonable that I was married than that she was about to be while coming on to me like this.

Watching Mary act the happy bride at her reception that Sunday, I was mesmerized. "How's she doing this?" I wondered.

Halfway through the party she came by our table and tapped me on the shoulder. I followed her into the ladies room. In a stall, in her bridal costume, she seduced me again. I couldn't believe it, thinking, "She's outrageous!"

After their honeymoon Mary and Don continued to get together with us on weekends. While Scott and Don watched old Twilight Zone shows on late night television in the bedroom, Mary and I messed around in the living room.

I had no thought about Scott or what he was doing or what he knew. All I felt was that it was great that he and Don were such buddies. It made life a little easier.

On July Fourth we two couples and Lil and her husband rented a house for a week. As the week progressed, something seemed changed in Mary's regard for me. Panicked I thought, "If she leaves, I have no other way of getting into the lesbian world."

Sunday morning Mary told me she'd met another woman and was leaving Don and me to be with her. She didn't tell Don why she was leaving him, but she told Scott, not mentioning her ten-month affair with his wife.

I was a wreck, not so much from heartbreak as from despair. "She's leaving Don in the marriage, but she's really leaving me and I have to go on living in this sham marriage," I thought.

All summer I didn't know what to do. I wondered whether I was sick or just thought I was. I was scared to death to tell anybody and get help. Then somewhere along the line a solution flashed in my mind: "Leave Scott and be on your own." It would be a first step toward telling the family my lifelong secret.

My gayness frightened me. Seeing women or men walking together holding hands or kissing, revolted me. Being so homophobic, I was afraid of Scott's judgment of me. "But I have to leave him and tell him why," I kept telling myself.

One night I finally got up enough courage. Scott was studying for the bar in bed as he'd done for weeks. Scared and feeling great pain, I entered the bedroom and sat down on the bed. "I've got something very serious to talk to you about, but I don't know how to begin." I was like a child, head hung low. I started stammering. "I-I-I have this problem...Mary's leaving Don has something to do with..."

"I know what your problem is," Scott interrupted.

"You couldn't possibly know what my problem is!" I said, feeling affronted. "How could you?"

Tears welled up in his eyes. "Because I have the same one."

"What do you mean?"

Tears were streaming down his face. "I have the same problem with men that you have with women."

"What!" I exclaimed, not very compassionately. I was flabbergasted and angry that he was stealing my thunder. "How could he be doing this?" I thought. Then I asked, "What are you talking about?"

Don poured out his heart. He'd known about and acted upon his homosexuality since his teens. "Having had experiences with men, I was frightened to marry. I knew what might have to be given up. Then I met you and liked you. Meeting you was my first chance to have a normal life. It helped me be willing to give up the other."

As he spoke I was thinking, "Here I was crawling in here mustering up enough guts to say this thing and he's now telling me his story. I've been blind to everything about this person!"

We stayed up all night talking. At first I couldn't believe he'd given up gay sex when he'd married me. As he shared more of his past, I no longer doubted him. He wanted so much for the marriage to work.

Then it was my turn to speak. First I told him about my decision to leave and then about my feelings and Mary.

"My God!" he said when I finished. "I sensed something going on but had no idea it'd gone that far. You were in love with our best friend!"

The next night I said, "I've got to leave you, Scott."

"Oh no, please don't," he cried. "Stay, Audrey, I beg of you. I don't know what form the marriage can take, but stay."

"No, I must go."

I told my father about my leaving the following day. This sent the family into shock. We had been married for three years and seemed like the perfect couple.

I found an apartment in the city but was so incapable of taking care of myself that I ended up at my father's place. I also kept checking in with Scott.

Each time I stopped by Scott fainted. Coming to, he implored me, "Please come back. I can't handle it."

The desperation in his voice made me realize how afraid he was of living the gay lifestyle openly. "If I leave," I thought," his cover will be blown, especially with his parents."

Our separation was too hard for me to handle also. One evening I went to see him. "O.K., I'll come back. It's the best solution, but let's get out of this suffocating community and move to the city. We'll have to have an open marriage with a twist. You go out with men and I'll go out with women."

"Absolutely fine." He smiled, the first in a long time.

Once we found an apartment we drew up a contract with one rule of the house: "Our house is not to be tainted in any way. We'll never do it here."

Living in Los Angeles, my life became more confused. Scott and I seemed the same to any outsider. But Scott, not interested in having a relationship, instead was having anonymous and bathroom sex, feeling a lot happier not knowing their names. And I was falling in love with a woman every other month, a kid let loose in a toy store.

Each time Scott came home I asked, "Where did you go? What did you do? How did you do it?" Hearing the drama of his activities excited me since my contacts were very different. His stories were fascinating. He told me of making eye contact and walking past the other man and then turning around to arrange to meet. "You know, the *Gay Yellow Pages* lists meeting places," he said one night.

"They're published?" I exclaimed.

"Sure," he said and brought out the book.

Reading it the next two hours, I burst out laughing. "I can't believe it! Pots and pans, fifth floor, of the department store in the mall and third floor stacks, west, of the main library. Where have I been?"

Experienced in gay affairs, Scott waited out each of my relationships until it had run its course. He never showed jealousy, although he acted irritable if I saw a woman for more than two months. I was the one who got upset, feeling pressured to be with Scott whenever I was distracted with my lover.

When I acted petulant like this Scott would say, "Now be a big girl with big girl responsibilities," putting us back into the child-parent roles we had established when we'd first married. Even though he supported everything I was doing to grow, he controlled my "allowance" and acted miserly about tuition money when I went back to college.

By then I had begun therapy to grow up emotionally as well as sexually, toward the ultimate goal of being on my own. After many of the sessions I would exclaim to Scott, "Oh, the world's so big! There's so much I don't know! And I want to know it all!"

Sometimes Scott would pat my head, saying, "Yes, dear, you'll find out," in the old-worldly way his parents had. Other times he made fun of my therapist.

"He thinks it's nice that I learn about myself," I thought, "but not too much."

For four and a half years I went in and out of relationships and Scott ran around with whatever men he could find. Gradually I got to know myself, building identity and confidence. Yet though part of me was alive another part was miserable.

All this time Scott and I had good times together, often traveling in the States and Europe. On one trip abroad we were laid up in New York. I was miserable but Scott went to a bar. When I finally joined him we made friends with another couple from California, Ben and Marge, also en route to Europe. Once on the Continent we four got together a few times.

Six months later Ben and Marge returned to Los Angeles and found an apartment near the new duplex we'd just bought. We saw them often, partying together until we passed out. Ben and I had a bantering relationship of one-liners. He seemed gay to me but Scott didn't know or care. As time went on it became clear that Ben wasn't in love with Marge and that she was absolutely mad for him.

One night when Ben and I were drinking, I told him about Scott's and my situation.

"Oh," he said. "I knew something was unusual about you two."

"Well," I thought, when nothing more was said, "I guess he's not going to admit to his homosexuality."

A month or so later when Marge was away on business, Ben hung out with us one night. Scott went up to bed at eleven, while Ben and I polished off whatever we were drinking. I began talking about gay bars, where he should go, what he should do and how he should do it.

By then Ben was drunk. "Maybe I'd be interested," he said.

"Scott's got a list of bars in the *Gay Yellow Pages*. It's up in the bedroom. Go on up and get it." With that, I passed out.

When I awakened several hours later, the lights were still on. "Where is everybody?" I mumbled, going upstairs to bed.

As I neared the bedroom I blinked from all the lights on there too. "That's odd," I thought. "Scott went to sleep way before Ben left."

When I looked in the doorway, they were both nude—Ben sitting at the edge of the bed looking the other way and Scott lying down, his head on the pillow.

"My God!" I gasped and stumbled downstairs, feeling betrayed and very angry.

A couple of minutes later Ben appeared dressed. We talked till dawn. "We had no idea how much we meant to each other," he said, "until we had sex tonight. We couldn't stop." Then he added, with a serious undertone, "You know who sent me up there."

Scott showed his head a few hours later. "Listen Audrey, we had no rule saying I couldn't have a relationship. I just didn't have one. But that wasn't how we set up this contract."

So our life changed again. As Ben and Scott continued to see each other over the next year and a half, I felt jealousy I'd never felt before and fury that I couldn't have my way any more.

It was a taste of my own medicine. Though Scott and Ben kept saying that I had pushed them together, I felt betrayed by them both. Before long being with Ben was no longer enjoyable. There was a cutting edge to our relationship.

Scott got Ben and Marge an apartment connected to ours by the roof, over which he and Ben ran back and forth to have their affair. Marge didn't know. They tried to stop for two months but it didn't work. When they resumed, Ben told Scott not to tell me. He did anyway.

Just as it got to be too much for me, a new woman friend captivated me. One night she called me on being married.

"It hasn't bothered anyone else."

"Well, it bothers me. Find someone it doesn't bother."

That was fuel enough to tell Scott that our arrangement was over. "You have your love affair that you can't give up and I've met someone who won't play this game. It's time we ended this."

Once again Scott fainted. When he revived he begged, "Don't leave me, Audrey," and began to cry.

Somehow I got myself together and moved to an apartment across town. It might as well have been another planet, I was so scared. It meant I had to take care of my entire life, including face up to who I really was—a thirty-one-year-old lesbian in her second year of graduate work in psychology.

For weeks Scott was a wreck. He lost weight. He took to his bed for several days until Ben came over and made him get up and go to work. He began to roam the city and bring people back to his house, living the single gay man's lifestyle. Ben stayed in his life but refused to leave Marge.

For two years, although we lived across town from each other, we double-dated and met each others' friends. The third year we went to New York together and I stayed on to visit a childhood friend.

On my return I announced, "I'm moving to New York."

It didn't happen, but it was a turning point. Scott went away with Ben that Thanksgiving, the first holiday we weren't together. From then on taking holidays without him wasn't a concern. Our social times together became less enjoyable and tapered off. Finally we separated legally.

It was another three years before divorce proceedings began, which didn't require much discussion. Only then, six years after I'd left, did we stop seeing each other socially and separate our friends and interests totally.

Over the next six years I had two lesbian partners and am still with the second. Ben and Scott developed a wide circle of friends and traveled together, a real gay lifestyle with lots of money between them.

Scott still calls every noon for a brief exchange, something about his mother, something about my work. He's my lawyer for whatever I need. I'm his psychologist. His call feels absolutely right.

My life would have been different if gays and lesbians were allowed to play the flirtation and mating games of adolescence. Part of me feels that would have been terrible because I wouldn't have met Scott, as dear to me as any of my close friends. I can't imagine marrying anyone but him. The feel of his hand nineteen years ago made him an immediate choice, absolutely normal.

On another level, where I am today and who I am is the right choice for me.

Redefining A Lasting Mixed Orientation Relationship

Although the traditional marriage form is shattered as a result of the partner's coming out, many spouses, particularly straight wives, still prefer the security of the broken pieces to an unknown future without partner, marital status or financial support. The need to keep the family together and to be a supportive wife is strong. Many have strong ties of love and friendship to their partners that they wish to preserve above all else. Also, wives who formerly felt estranged find hope in the intimacy of sharing their husbands' secret at last.

When these factors are enhanced by the husband's wish to stay married, a sizeable number of women will go to any length to make the marriage work. Out of blind hope or denial, many don't see the uphill battle ahead. They don't grasp the implications of no longer being their husband's preferred sexual partner even though they may still be their best friend, intellectual soul mate, or companion. They often deny the possibility that their husbands might be staying mainly for the security of the family or the facade of "married man."

Even spouses who accept the sexual incompatibility in the relationship often remain undaunted by the challenge. "Now that I know the facts," they reason, "I can make the marriage work." They become what support group leaders Sandra Auerback, M.S.W., and Charles Moser, Ph.D., term, "Superwoman."[1] They juggle marriage, job, home and children, as well as new gay-related tasks undertaken for the partner. In so doing, they may be required to make sacrifices for the marriage they haven't bargained for.

Although a number of couples succeed in preserving the marriage, the majority do not. Despite sincere efforts, the sexual disparity, competition for the partner's attention or unconventional and for some immoral arrangements eventually become intolerable for most spouses.

Coping with the marriage issue will be a more constructive process with greater promise of success if the couple, rather than trying to preserve the traditional marriage arrangement, is willing to develop a relationship appropriate to the new circumstances. This goal can be attained, whether or not the marriage itself lasts, through eight key strategies:

- Settling the AIDS issue
- Asserting the straight spouse's sexual needs
- Accommodating to the partner's sexual identity
- Reassessing the mixed-orientation marriage
- Putting the gay factor into perspective
- Rewriting marital rules
- Developing a non-dependent relationship
- Forming a lasting couple bond

Settling the AIDS Issue

Because of the far greater incidence of AIDS among homosexual and bisexual men than among lesbians, AIDS is primarily an issue for straight wives and gay or bisexual husbands. HIV-antibody testing, the first task to be accomplished in reestablishing the relationship, is essential for both husband and wife and, if they engage in extramarital affairs, their lovers. If for any reason the partner refuses testing, the spouse's fear of infection may never disappear and it will be much harder to resolve sexual and other marital problems constructively.

Being tested and waiting for results often cause embarrassment and anxiety. Apprehension so obsessed a pregnant woman in Los Angeles that, unable to wait for her partner's test results, she had an abortion one week before the test results came back negative. To lessen fears that might lead to rash actions, it helps to find a trusted friend who can offer support.

HIV-negative test results bring relief, yet anxiety can persist because of the long incubation period of the AIDS virus. An HIV-positive test result for the husband or wife calls for medical and psychological counseling and research into current facts. Wives who face their husband's AIDS diagnosis are likely to fear becoming infected themselves and often feel resentment at being put in a risk situation because of their husband's hidden activities.

Helpful advice for handling concerns about AIDS is offered in Jean Schaar Gochros' *When Husbands Come Out of the Closet*.[2] Actually there is reportedly a low incidence of wives who have been infected.[3]

Six of the twenty-six straight wives studied over a five-year period for this book have had to cope with their husband's HIV-positive test results or AIDS infection. For most of them, their emotional turmoil was eased by open, honest talk with the husband, counseling with a knowledgeable professional and participation in support groups with other couples in the same situation. The experience, though agonizing, can bring unexpected rewards of reconciliation and inner growth. Carol Lynn Pearson's *Good-bye I Love You* describes just such a moving story.[4]

Asserting the Straight Spouse's Sexual Needs

Even with an HIV-positive test result, the couple's sex life need not stop, although it will have to be altered to include safe-sex practices. Many husbands, particularly bisexual men, still feel attracted to their wives. Some men are more desirous than before, possibly because of the release from their repressed homosexuality or because of sexual arousal from gay contacts.

Given safe-sex protection, it is critical to try to continue or revive lovemaking. Making love is a primary way to affirm and express the union as long as it is a two-way experience. For it to be two-way, the wife needs her sexual needs to be fulfilled by her husband, the second step toward redefining the relationship.

Women who enjoyed marital sex before the coming out have less difficulty asserting their sexual needs. Wives habituated to thinking of themselves as inadequate, however, tend to acquiesce to their husband's disclosed needs without insisting that their own be met. Reminding themselves of the real reason underlying their sexual problems may help them to find the courage to be more assertive. Many find that the very act of specifying wishes reactivates dormant desires. If the husband is reluctant to try alternative ways to give pleasure, the wife will want to find out how committed he is to the relationship, uncomfortable as such probing might be.

Except in those rare cases in which the husband has not been and does not plan to be active with other men, there are but two options for continued lovemaking—safe sex or no sex. Because of the risk of exposing the spouse to AIDS, unprotected sex with a partner who is actively gay should not be considered. In addition, the spouse should insist that the partner limit gay sex to a single lover and only practiced safe sex, so that marital sex won't have to stop because of a deadly risk. Safe sex or no sex means that the wife, in particular, must give up the freely open sexual experience to which she has previously been accustomed because of her partner's lifestyle.

At the same time, the need to express his or her sexual orientation is extremely important to the partner. The 1987 study of twenty-five mixed-orientation couples by sex therapist George Deabill, M.S., Ph.D., suggests that husbands who engage in homosexual sex may feel more satisfaction in the marriage than those who don't.[5]

Maintaining a gay or bisexual identity in the marriage is so important to the husband that if the wife pressures him to limit or abstain from gay sex, he may ultimately feel less commitment to the marriage. The less committed he is, the less satisfied she will be, as in any marriage.[7] The wife's compromise then is to accept her partner's gay activities in exchange for a committed and affectionate relationship with limited or no sex. Not an easy bargain.

Many wives feel resentment about the limitations put on their sex life. Expressing such concerns in a calm manner can reduce tension and may motivate a husband to try other ways to increase his wife's pleasure.

Marriage or sex counseling with a therapist who is knowledgeable about homosexuality, bisexuality, and mixed-orientation couples can greatly increase the chances of salvaging the relationship. For bisexual-straight couples, it is crucial that they find a therapist who understands that bisexuality is a distinct orientation from homosexuality and not a transitional state. Without such a therapist, possibilities for the couple to revive sexuality may be bypassed. William Wedin, Ph.D., director of Bisexual Information and Counseling Service (BICS) in Manhattan, points out that some "bi" men think they're gay when in actuality they are only suffering from temporary impotence resulting from the stress of the coming out.[8] Some couples think that their problem is gay-related when it is just sexual boredom that can readily be remedied. In any case, a good therapist can assign exercises to enhance the couple's lovemaking. Spouses can learn to incorporate what their partners like in their same-sex activity into their lovemaking and partners can learn ways to give their spouses sexual pleasure.

Alternative ways to experience sexual pleasure can reduce the pain of limiting or giving up intercourse. There are some excellent books on expanding sexuality listed in appendix A. Using their own ingenuity, many couples devise other forms of physical contact that give the women sexual pleasure, such as cuddling, hugging, kissing, caressing, and massaging. Most of the wives in Deabill's study experienced sexual and marital satisfaction from such gestures of affection and physical contact from their husbands.[9]

For a majority of couples, however, marital sex doesn't last. Gradually the gay partner's sexual motivation and desire may shift as he or she follows the typical candy store syndrome, seeking varied experiences in gay bars, baths and meeting places. At home, sex often becomes infrequent and then stops, despite periodic increases after gay encounters.

Having to give up the sexual core of married life is agonizing for spouses, particularly if their sex lives improved after the coming out. Though love and friendship may compensate for the absence of sex, the feeling of loss is profound. Spouses may try to get along with shared interests and gestures of affection, but this may not be enough to alleviate the hurt.

Spouses who stay in a sexless marriage learn to sublimate, redirect or repress their desire. Many use alcohol, cigarettes, drugs or food as a substitute. More productive and healthy ways to utilize sexual energy include creative pursuits like art, music and dance or physical activities like gardening and sports. Masturbation is an effective way to release sexual energy, but even that doesn't wholly make up for the sexual deprivation.

Respect for the marital bond and strong commitment to husband and family are key reasons why many wives stay in sexless marriages. A Canadian couple married for forty-four years, put it like this, "We have a history, three children, and seven grandchildren keeping us together." Ray, a fundamentalist preacher, struggled with his homosexuality and Winnie agonized over his coming out until they eventually developed a devoted companionship. In the process she formed a close female friendship, a support group and a career. He became a counselor and took a lover, whom he sees weekly, just to hold and be held. They also use the support of several couple groups.

While many wives find the loss of marital sex so painful that they divorce, a number seem satisfied with perquisites like social position, financial security, emotional support or assured companionship. Some continue to live in substantial homes and lead active social lives twenty or more years after the coming out.

Accommodating to the Partner's Sexual Identity

Even if the wife gets her sexual needs met, nearly every aspect of her life becomes altered by the homosexual or bisexual needs of the husband. Compared to him, she has more drastic changes to make after the coming out. By the time the partner has revealed his orientation, he has already adjusted to it. For her the situation is new. Making necessary adaptations to the partner's revealed sexual identity is the third step toward developing a lasting relationship.

The husband's gay activities may first enter the wife's life as part of their everyday conversations. Some wives are eager to listen to what had been a secret. Curious about their husband's new world, they don't want to feel left out. Other wives don't want to know any details even if silence cuts them off from what their husbands value, because it's too painful or they feel uncomfortable or repelled by their husband's gay lifestyle or mannerisms.

Others may join in their husband's activities, such as Gay Fathers or similar groups, wanting to know what their friends are like and to support their partners openly. Fascinated by a hidden subculture or drawn to support an oppressed group, some like being a part of their husband's secret cause. Some even befriend their husband's lovers, seeing them as "special" because they share the love of the same man. While a few later join gay advocacy groups, many eventually feel isolated and stop all participation.

Most often, the wife is responsible for scheduling her husband's gay activities into the family calendar of child care, household tasks, careers, family excursions and couple activities, reflecting the traditional caretaker role of women. In addition some wives take on their husband's gay-related needs, such as baking a turkey for a Gay Fathers' party or handling the legal work for a husband's arrest for a sexual violation.

As the wife struggles to cope with all of the demands placed on her, she isn't aware at first of how much she is affected by her husband's double life. For example, she may not see the irony of scheduling quality time previously spent as a couple into the husband's gay agenda.

In the frenzy to keep the marriage going and be "the successful wife," she may think she has the situation in hand. In actuality she has little control. Almost all of her energy is directed toward accommodating her husband's new identity, with little heed paid to her own needs. As she focuses increasingly on supporting her husband's gay lifestyle, she gradually absorbs the gay perspective—becoming the "spouse of a gay (or bisexual)," defined by his identity.

At this point the couple risks developing a destructive co-dependency for the sake of sustaining the marriage.[10] The husband, needing his wife to shore up his self-esteem battered by homophobia, stays in a less-than-satisfying, restrictive relationship. The wife, in order to keep her husband, supports behavior that takes him away from her. In this instance, she may have to consider how much she is willing to sacrifice to make the marriage work.

Reassessing the Mixed-Orientation Marriage

Most spouses cannot sustain the merry-go-round pace required to maintain the semblance of the former marriage. As their energy wanes, it becomes necessary to step back and take an objective look at the marriage and how it is affecting them. This fourth strategy calls for slowing down and expecting to accomplish less than is normally done each day. Time needs to be set aside for introspection and freeing up emotions neglected in the struggle to make the marriage work.

Solitude is most conducive for getting in touch with buried emotions and gaining some insight on the marital situation. To release feelings, it helps to engage in activities that don't require thinking, such as exercise, meditation, music, art, dance, craft projects, day dreams, anything that allows emotions to surface. Tears relieve tension and reveal sources of pain. Laughter helps to create distance from the immediate plight. Each day presents something incongruous to rouse a smile, in the office, at the supermarket, on the bus, with one's children.

Alone and without distractions, spouses can gain the perspective needed to determine how to proceed forward. They may see for the first time how much the partner's "other life" has crept into theirs. Each change of schedule, each missed opportunity for affection, is recognized for what it is after being accepted unthinkingly for months. The relationship may no longer fit their expectations and may seem to be slipping away.

If couples have a contract or an agreed-upon arrangement, it may need to be revised to better serve their needs and to prevent further hurt. Walt and Sara, a young couple in Atlanta, were not able to negotiate a successful agreement. They drew up a contract after he moved out when their baby was three months old. He was to return and be demonstrative to Sara short of intercourse and to spend two nights a week and Saturday with his lover, while Sara was to lower her expectations of complete sexual pleasure. The following year, as Walt spent more than the allotted time with his lover and less time with Sara, she became clinically depressed until the separation she never wanted was the only tolerable option.

The unconventional arrangement itself often becomes the source of discomfort for spouses, arousing unwanted negativity against their partners. Gradually many wives feel jealous or resentful of the time their husbands spend with their lovers and the lovers may begin to appear to be a threat to the marriage. As the wife starts to feel that she has nothing while her partner has his other life, the marriage contract may no longer seem valid. At this point a single incident can seem like a blatant negation of the arrangement. When Scott started to go out with Ben, for example, Audrey, though empathetic with his situation that paralleled hers, felt betrayed. That marked the beginning of the end of their arrangement.

As the partner pursues a gay lifestyle, monogamy often becomes the paramount issue for the spouse whether or not lovemaking has continued. The partner's sexuality, in the totality of its physical, emotional and spiritual aspects, is no longer exclusive to the marriage. Spouses typically feel intense resentment toward this double life, but many are paralyzed and cannot take action because of fear of the future and guilt about failing. For others, their rage often forces the decision of whether to separate, divorce or reconstruct the relationship.

Before stress becomes self-destructive, it is critical to share concerns with a counselor or friend who can help the spouse look objectively at the relationship. A knowledgeable counselor can guide the spouse in resolving conflicting emotions and in sorting out priorities and responsibilities. This includes accepting negative feelings as normal and appropriate reactions to the situation, learning to take care of the spouse's needs first and discouraging wishful thinking or expectations about what "should" be done.

Since partners are going through their own stages of reactions to the coming out, counseling for them, as well as joint counseling, can help to clarify couple issues and raise their awareness of relationship responsibilities.

In such crisis periods when major decisions must be made, intensive couple counseling is very helpful since the partner and spouse often progress simultaneously through similar emotional stages.

William Wedin defines the stages as initial humiliation (the partner's guilt and the spouse's self-blame), a "honeymoon" of feeling mutually valued, rage (the partner feels misunderstood and the spouse duped) and final resolution.[11] Crisis counseling can help the couple get through apparent impasses as they progress through each stage. The goal of crisis counseling is to equip the couple with skills to resolve issues themselves in future crises.

Support groups for straight spouses and for mixed-orientation couples are key resources at this time also. In the growing sense of isolation that the spouse feels, finding just one other person who has been there can make a big difference. Through hearing others' reports of similar problems, such as dwindling commitment from the partner, less couple time and reneged agreements, spouses feel less alone and better able to handle their own crises. By talking with others in the same situation, Rita realized that a sexless marriage was a common problem. A support group can suggest practical options and provide firsthand advice otherwise not readily available.

Support groups can be located through the resources listed in appendix B. However, because there is a limited number of support groups outside of metropolitan areas, spouses in rural areas may have more success contacting a spouse network, such as the Task Force of Spouses of Gays and Lesbians (Parents FLAG) in appendix B. Some spouses form their own informal support groups which are often advertised in local newspapers.

Many spouses, in spite of outside emotional support, may be overwhelmed with anger and hurt at the destruction of their monogamous relationships. Often the partner is blamed for all couple problems, diminishing the chances of salvaging the relationship.

Putting the Gay Factor Into Perspective

As the spouse struggles with painful marital issues, the partner's gayness can assume disproportionate importance. Each time something goes wrong, it's tempting to say, "It's because he or she is gay (or bisexual)." But single-factor answers don't provide much insight into the larger relationship problems. It is therefore essential that spouses disentangle themselves from the polarized "gay-versus-straight" reasoning that they often fall into after the coming out. They can then put the partner's homosexuality into its proper perspective, the fifth strategy of establishing a lasting relationship.

The tendency to view marital problems solely in terms of the gay factor can blind the spouse to other possible causes: physical, psychological, educational, social, financial, work-related, religious, as well as sexual. Failed sexual encounters in any marriage, for example, can be accounted for in part by fatigue, stress, anxiety or alcohol consumption.

The partner's actions should not be judged exclusively on the basis of his or her sexual orientation. Like the straight spouse, the partner is motivated by multiple factors. Sometimes gayness operates; other times, non-gay motives exert a major influence. The newly-revealed sexual orientation doesn't turn the partner into a different person.

As in any marriage, personalities and personal philosophies play a large part in problems mixed-orientation couples face. This is not to diminish the issue of the mixed-orientation and the importance of how couples handle it. However, the spouse may need to reconsider each marriage problem—if the partner's gay behavior has contributed to it and if so, how significantly. In some cases, the unreliability, irresponsibility, inattention, or alcoholism of the partner plays a major part in the couple's problems.

Some estimates indicate that as many as one out of four gay men are alcoholic. Though the disease stems largely from hereditary factors, many men drink to alleviate the pain they suffer from the anti-gay social stigma or because of the large role alcohol plays in the gay lifestyle, from gay bars to private parties.[12]

Clinical psychologist Kathy McMahon, Psy.D., suggests asking the following questions to put the gay factor into perspective. "Does the gayness nullify any reason why we got married? Are positive aspects of the relationship still positive? Does the disclosure enable us to face the new, possibly fearful aspects and become more intimate?"[13]

To answer this, an understanding of the how the couple interacts is required. McMahon raises the important points, "Does his behavior hurt, deny, or affirm me? How much caring and sacrifice is there? How honest is he in admitting mistakes—rather than blaming me or society—and acknowledging any hurt his action may cause?"[14]

Spouses need to consider whether, if the gay factor weren't there, they would still continue to work on the marriage. To come to a satisfactory conclusion, they will need to discern what is needed not only for the partner's sake, but for their own sake and for the health of the relationship. Then they will be able to decide what to reject and what to accept in the marriage.

If the partner agrees to help solve marital problems, the next step is to determine how the couple's needs can be met within the marriage.

Rewriting Marital Rules

To satisfy the needs of both spouse and partner, alternative marriage rules need to be devised, the sixth strategy of this stage. The process is an ongoing one of adjustments and revisions throughout the marriage.

The breakdown of the traditional marriage form forces the couple to reevaluate its basic purpose and their own criteria for a quality relationship. As a wife of a bisexual man said, "We threw out everything we'd learned about the way you're *supposed* to be and figured out what we *were*."

Helpful examples of effective mixed-orientation relationships can be found in the few biographies that have been written, such as *Barry and Alice*[15] and in studies of gay-straight couples in general, notably *The New Couple*, by Rebecca Nahos and Myra Turley[16] and *Uncommon Lives*, by Catherine Whitney.[17]

The most effective straight-gay relationships appear to share non-sexual characteristics such as friendship, honesty and primary commitment to the marriage. The spouse accepts the partner's orientation. In turn the partner is sensitive to the spouse's needs. They each accept the other's need for autonomy. It's a special companionship not available to them in the gay or heterosexual community.[18] The healthiest relationships include physical contact, co-nurturing and commitment to marriage and family.

In working out an alternative marital arrangement, the straight wife usually has to make the greatest sacrifices. Each change from the conventional marriage form should take into consideration both the spouse's and the partner's personal, cultural and perhaps religious standards. If there are children, the arrangement must be appropriate for their needs for a stable home environment. Often the husband's gay affairs are considered by the wife to be beyond the purview of the traditional heterosexual marriage contract. Such a woman in Michigan contracted with her bisexual husband that he could continue dating men but not women. His dating women was too threatening to her.

Alternative marital arrangements are as diverse as couples. They range from a Philadelphia wife who invited her husband's lover to live with them; to a professor in San Diego who brings male graduate students home overnight; to a Chicago couple and the husband's lover who live together, by contract, as a menage a trois; to a socialite couple in Raleigh who each have lovers in another city.

The arrangement that seems to work for most couples entails that the partner have some gay activity and the spouse have limited or no marital sex and, for some, an outside affair. Taking a lover may be the only way the spouse can tolerate the lack of marital sex, as in Rita's case.

Most couples discover what works best for them through trial-and-error. Often spouses face negative pressure from friends, family or clergy, or begin to feel uncomfortable with the arrangement for personal reasons, forcing them to rethink their rationale and forge yet another concept of marriage.

Developing a Non-Dependent Relationship

Just as crucial as reaching an agreeable sexual arrangement is developing a healthy autonomy in the relationship. No alternative arrangement lasts very long without the couple's respect for each other's separate identity. In order to develop a non-dependent relationship, the seventh strategy of this stage, dependent behavior patterns, characteristic of many mixed-orientation couples, need to be replaced with reciprocal ways of interacting.

Three types of dependency patterns; clinging, pupil-teacher, and mother-child, are seen among many mixed-orientation couples. Polly and Mike, a childless couple in Buffalo, typify the clinging pattern. They shared a craft business in their home as well as lovers. In several years, a stifling symbiosis began to destroy their closeness.

Audrey and Scott illustrate the pupil-teacher relationship in which the better educated, skilled husband molded her into the perfect wife. This scenario of authority-submission enabled him to create a private world in which to hide.

In the mother-child pattern, as shown by Carol and Dave, typically the husband depends on the wife's nurturing while she ignores her own needs in deference to his.

Such dependency patterns resemble the behavior of couples in which the wife protects her alcoholic husband, denying that there is a problem, therefore enabling the destructive situation to persist. In this kind of co-dependent relationship, both the alcoholic husband and the co-alcoholic wife deny accountability for the harmful effects of their behavior. Similarly, the straight spouse who denies the hurtful effects of the coming out on the marriage is, in effect, helping perpetuate a painful situation.

Couples in dependent relationships need to learn how to relate in mutually constructive ways. Spouses who play the role of "symbiotic dependent," "pupil," or indulgent "parent" need to free themselves from the demands of the controlling counterpart. Realizing this, Polly, the wife in Buffalo, began teaching craft courses in the city, Audrey finished her undergraduate degree, and Carol found part-time work and entered therapy.

The spouse who develops autonomy is able to take equal responsibility for the direction the relationship takes. No longer dependent on the partner's needs, the spouse can freely decide if the relationship meets her or his priorities. Spouses who previously repressed their true feelings out of fear of jeopardizing the relationship can now express hurt from their partner's same-sex behavior while still showing empathy. "You have a right to be who you are," an Indiana wife often says to her husband, "but not to hurt others."

As spouses gain equality their partners may think that they've lost control. In response spouses can say to them, "You still have control, only it's equal now." Balance of power allows couples to make sounder decisions about what's best for the relationship in the long run.

Forming a Lasting Couple Bond

Developing a long-term bond is the final challenge for couples who want to stay together. To create an enduring relationship, both husband and wife need to commit themselves to work on it even under forbidding circumstances. The ideal goal is to try as hard as possible together to make it succeed and to keep communication lines open. Even if the marriage ultimately does not last, they will have the satisfaction of knowing that they made a sincere effort and will have gained a better understanding of themselves and the relationship. Many achieve a deeper bond than they had before.

In creating a lasting bond, the goal is not the romantic fantasy with which many couples begin marriage. It is a shared commitment to the concept of a community of two who care for each other's welfare enough to meet any challenge needed to resolve problems. This kind of dedication, psychiatrist M. Scott Peck explains, is necessary for the "security of knowing that the struggle over these issues will not itself destroy the relationship."[19]

Working toward mutual happiness, important in any relationship, is a formidable task for the mixed-orientation couple since the relationship needs are in direct conflict with the personal needs of the liberated partner. Having a shared commitment helps the couple to compromise some individual needs in the interest of the common good.

Deabill's research indicates that a husband's commitment greatly enhances his wife's sexual and marital satisfaction.[20] Miriam and Max, a couple in Denver who have been married for twenty-one years, illustrate this. Since sexual infidelity is unacceptable to Miriam, Max has relinquished gay sex to preserve the marriage and the family. In return he is allowed to engage in gay activities short of active sex.

"My thinking was black and white," Miriam explained. "Max helped me see the gray areas. Now when I get judgmental, I say to myself, 'Look Miriam, that's your husband. Think it through again.'"

Four qualities appear to enhance the development of a long-term relationship: openness, flexibility, candor, and humor. Many couples who survive the initial impact of the coming out displayed such traits before the disclosure. Others learn to develop them through deliberate effort such as counseling.

Both husband and wife need to be open about themselves, each other and the relationship in order to work through their differences. One way to foster openness is to replace judgmental behavior toward the other person's differences with acceptance.

Developing open, honest communication requires that the spouse and partner each take risks, such as rejection of their differing opinions or feelings. For those accustomed to hiding or denying their feelings, this can be extremely frightening or uncomfortable at first. But ultimately the couple will be rewarded with a deeper sense of intimacy or, as psychiatrists Patrick Thomas and Thomas Patrick Malone say, will "feel and know myself in the presence of another." [21]

Flexibility, the willingness to try alternative ways of interacting, is also essential. Being flexible includes the ability to be resilient in the face of failure or criticism. For example, Rita and Hal, despite upsets, adjusted and readjusted their relationship for five years, reminding themselves that, "Nothing's written in stone."

Honesty is the third key quality in preserving the couple bond. For example, marriages in which the partner comes out to the spouse early on tend to last longer than those in which the sexual orientation is concealed. Even after a delayed coming out, being honest is crucial in reducing hostility and restoring positive interaction. To express concerns candidly, it helps to concentrate on present feelings and proposed action rather than on past events which tend to arouse blame or excuses. If criticism upsets either person, he or she needs to be reminded that the purpose of the discussion is to solve the problem at hand.

A sense of humor is invaluable, although time may be required to get some distance on the painful events before they can be viewed with detachment. Eventually the couple may begin to appreciate the irony of their predicament. One young couple in Virginia, who forbid the word, "straight," in their house, have created a long glossary of synonyms they use with a secret wink.

Through cultivation of these four traits, most couple bonds are enriched and deepened. Reading self-help literature on relationships and talking with other couples, supportive friends and counselors will reinforce the process.

Many couples, especially those with children, desire to preserve their bond whether or not they stay married. As Dave and Carol vowed, "If a problem in the marriage ever threatens our friendship, we'll end the marriage."

Bond-building has been used successfully by separated and divorced couples too, although the physical separation and the hurt from divorce are formidable obstacles. A woman in Phoenix was married for twenty-eight years before her husband came out and two more years while he thought he was bisexual. When he realized he was gay and left, she chose to work through her rage to develop a platonic friendship with him. Though deeply satisfied when she succeeded, it had taken six stressful years to do so.

Maintaining the bond requires perseverance to work through issue after issue. Will and Betsy, a couple in Boston who have been together three years since the coming out, call the process "mending and tending." Facing their differences openly and honestly with guidance from a priest and support groups of gay professional men and mixed-orientation couples, they have grown in mutual understanding. Will, who stayed in the marriage at first because he loved their children, has developed unconditional love for Betsy.

A not insignificant number of couples stay married. While an estimate of fifteen percent is given in a number of studies, it is not known for how long they stay together. When research for this book began in 1986, eight of the twenty-six straight wives studied in depth, or thirty-one percent, were still married two to seven years after the coming out. Now after five years, only three, or eleven percent, are still with their husbands. Over half of the couples stayed together for at least three years after the coming out.

Couples who succeed in preserving their marriages share the following attitudes: the straight spouse accepts the partner's sexual orientation, the partner values the spouse as the primary relationship and they both hold a non-traditional view of marriage that they have defined together.

When children are involved, other issues come into play that can bring the couple closer together as a family or pit them against each other. Part three explores children's problems that parents, particularly the straight spouse, face in the coming-out crisis.

three

GROWING
PAINS

CONFLICTING ROLES AS
PARENT AND SPOUSE

While the children's needs may be overlooked in the initial trauma of the coming out, they soon demand attention. Of primary concern is how to preserve the bond between the children and the homosexual or bisexual parent. Positive identification with both parents is critical to the children's development of self-esteem, identity and sense of security. At the same time parents need to prepare their children for possible anti-gay attitudes in the community. How to protect them from the hurtful effects of homosexual prejudice without altering their relationship with the gay parent is the third dilemma facing the straight spouse.

Whether or not to tell the children about the partner's sexual orientation is the first concern of many parents. Most parents eventually decide to tell them. While it is important to gear the explanation to the children's age and level of understanding, the spouse's attitude toward the coming out is even more important in how well the children accept the gay or bisexual parent. It is imperative that the straight parent keep her or his personal pain from negatively influencing the children against the gay or bisexual parent.

A second major concern is how to help the children cope with negative effects of the coming out on their lives. Common problems they experience include embarrassment over the non-traditional orientation or lifestyle of the homosexual or bisexual parent; confusion about their own sexual orientation; stereotypical or prejudiced reactions of peers; conflicting loyalties to the two parents; and psychological turmoil resulting from separation or divorce.

Trying to maintain a positive relationship with the partner for the children's sake, as well as taking on responsibility for their needs, are among the many demands that prevent spouses from dealing with their own personal issues. Yet in working through the social, moral, sexual and sometimes legal concerns related to the children's well-being, many spouses gain insight into their own issues.

The three stories that follow, told by two straight mothers and a gay father, illustrate typical problems that children encounter after the coming out and the straight parent's conflicts in helping them cope. The final section of part three explores major family issues and ways in which both parents and children can cope constructively with them.

Personal Stories

Dad's Girl and Mom's Boy
Allison

Several years after Peter's mood swings began, when Nicolas was three and Courtney was six, he received a call at home one night. "I told you never to call me here," I heard him say as my heart froze. When Peter brought it up later, I couldn't talk about it.

We'd been married for eight years, after graduating from the University of Nebraska in the early sixties. Tall and dark-haired, Peter was the "boss" as my father had been, which fit right into my pattern of low self-esteem. I loved him dearly.

After the phone call, Peter's drinking became more of a problem. Whenever he was drunk, he accosted me with one of two accusations, "Allison, you're not very bright" or "You're a terrible parent."

"Of all the bad things I am," I thought, "it's not those. I'm a good parent and have above-average intelligence, thank you very much." I'd worked on being intelligent all my life, using books to hide my insecurity, especially with men. Outwardly I was a confident brunette, as tall as Peter.

After months of silence I confronted him one night. "Either you tell me what's going on or I'm leaving. I can't live with your excuses, hostility and verbal abuse when you drink."

"Okay, but later. It's something I need to talk to you about in private."

After the children were in bed I joined him in the living room, where he was sitting in front of the fire crying. Through his tears he told me that a psychologist had just confirmed that he was gay. He also told me that he'd been seeing men for four years. "I'm so frightened," he said. "I'd like to wake up one day and have it be untrue."

"It's as if he's said that he's dying," I thought. "Our marriage will end, but I can't walk away and leave him in such agony."

Before long I realized Peter had never been in love with me and could never love any woman the way I loved him. Though he cared about me as much as he could for a woman, I felt cheated. Feeling rejected as a woman, I resented the fact that he'd had my love but I'd never had his. All of my insecurity surfaced.

For the next four years I talked to no one about what was going on and how bad I felt. It was easier not to say it out loud. I plunged into community activities to distract my thoughts and to boost my self-esteem. Several sessions with a psychologist plus books on homosexuality helped me understand what was happening.

In Nebraska where I'd grown up, aberrations like homosexuality were ignored and homosexuals were carefully closeted, but my extensive reading convinced me that gays didn't choose to be gay. The hurt Peter was causing wasn't intentional. Because I loved him he could be excused. Yet the pain was no less profound and couldn't be ignored. To heal I had to learn to unlove him.

"You're on your own now, Allison," I told myself over and over, "without Peter." It took two years before I could tell myself, "I don't love him any more." But deep down I still did.

Peter meanwhile was on a roller coaster, acting like a straight family man for periods and then coming home at strange hours, drinking a lot and sinking into suicidal depressions that frightened me.

At home he spent most of the time with Courtney. She'd always been "Dad's girl," but more so when he started gay activities and stopped responding to me. Their closeness made me feel jealous. Our son Nicolas withdrew more. Since he was born just as Peter realized the straight family life wasn't meaningful for him any longer, Peter rejected Nicolas as symbolizing the truth he wanted to deny. So I had to be both Dad and Mom to Nicolas.

The fourth summer after he came out Peter bought me a car out of the blue and we began to remodel the house. Then he was stricken with a viral infection and confined to bed for three months. The constant noise of the workmen and the telephone irritated him. Since his income depended on commissions, this was also a very difficult time financially.

Each day after preparing his meals and leaving instructions with him for the workmen, I'd drive into Milwaukee to supervise preparations for a big fund-raising event. One night after coming home to find the workmen doing what I'd told Peter not to let them do, I blew up and Peter raised a fist at me. By then, I knew the end was near.

When Peter returned to work, Nicolas began first grade and seemed happy with it. Courtney, now in fifth grade, began to feel uncomfortable around boys and their teasing. I was named president of a prestigious community organization.

For the party honoring me and the new board, Peter promised to come but called halfway through the affair to say, "I'm downtown with the Wallaces. Join us when the party's over."

After bidding everyone good-bye with a frozen smile, I drove to the restaurant in a fury, not believing he was there. "You'll never betray me again," I muttered. "Never, ever."

He was there, but my outrage was so strong that I could barely speak until we were driving home. Then I burst out with increasing volume, "Peter, this is it. I can't take it anymore. I'll never let you do this again." I yelled all the way home and into the house.

When I finally calmed down Peter said, "I understand why you're angry. You've sensed something about Tom. You don't know him but he's been my lover for a year."

It also came out that Peter had bought him a car too, just before getting sick. "So that's why he bought me one," I thought, not pleased.

That night we decided that Peter would go live with Tom during the children's Christmas vacation, giving them time to absorb the news at their own pace. After talking with several counselors about how to tell the children, we agreed to state the facts and then explain what they didn't understand.

The night before we told them we rehearsed what Peter would say to allay any fears they might have. After breakfast the next morning we sat at the kitchen table while Peter told them. He ended with, "I'm moving out today to live with Tom."

"I just knew it!" Courtney said.

Nicolas, who was still distant from his father, accepted the news calmly.

"You'll still live here and go to your school," Peter went on. "I'll be in the city and will see you a lot. I want you to know that this has nothing to do with you and that I love you both very much. I'll talk about whatever you want and answer any questions you have."

Neither child had anything to say then or later that morning when Peter talked with them separately. That afternoon the children and I flew to New York to visit Peter's parents.

Peter called them there later that week. "I want to see you when you get home. There's a fair coming to town. Want to go?"

"Oh yes! We want to meet Tom."

After a successful day at the fair the children began spending weekends with Peter and Tom and went out to dinner with Peter during the week. The four of them also went on long vacations together with as little interference from me as possible.

Once I began talking to friends about Peter, feelings I had repressed for four years started bubbling up. I realized that his rejection of me, not his gayness, was the problem. "Being gay is the same as whether you have green or blue eyes," I explained to the children, friends and family. "There's no choice."

In September I went back to work to keep occupied while the children were in school. Soon my salary was needed to supplement Peter's fluctuating income. Divorce now seemed impossible since the house was collateral for many of his projects.

Every morning I left for the bus before six to be home early enough to drive the children to after-school sports where I cheered them on. They were both straightforward kids, tomboy Courtney and stalwart Nicolas, and they played every sport, every season.

The first year neither of the children wanted to talk about what was happening even when asked what they thought or felt. I told their teachers that we had separated but not why and asked them to call me if they noticed any behavior changes. Since both of them worked diligently at school, their teachers never called. Their grades went up.

When Courtney turned eleven she grew taller and more attractive and became aware of her sexuality. Although she was going through puberty, she remained even-tempered at home and she never fought with her many friends. She was a model child.

Unlike Courtney, Nicolas was angry, usually at me. Every problem was Mom's fault, like the broken shoe laces on his track shoes. "You should have known they might break! Why didn't you have an extra pair?"

Since this was much like Peter's way of relating to me, I had to concentrate on what Nicolas was doing in order not to react to the "Peter buttons" he pushed.

During the first summer after his father left he played with only a few friends. By fall he had withdrawn completely and was angry with all of his friends.

The second month of school his teacher called. "Allison, I don't think Nickie will complete second grade."

We located a psychiatrist and Nicolas went weekly, complaining all the way. He never said what went on but the psychiatrist reported to us every six weeks. Soon he appeared happier and resumed friendships and was promoted to third grade.

Meanwhile Peter was trying to mend his rift with him, but Nicolas no longer wanted to do things with his father no matter how great the activity. For the next two years he didn't even talk about Peter.

Courtney, by then in junior high, did talk about Peter and told a couple of good friends he was gay.

"So what?" they said.

Some months later the son of family friends, mad at Courtney for spurning him, went around telling their friends, "Courtney's father is a homosexual."

Again, the reaction was, "So what?"

By ninth grade Courtney had grown to nearly six feet, a stunning beauty whose slenderness was set off by the stylish clothes Peter bought. She was on the honor roll, all teams and the student council. Yet by February when we three visited Peter's parents, she was a teary-eyed, touchy teenager who snapped at everyone.

"Should I pay attention to this?" I asked myself, "Or quit worrying and let her be fourteen?"

Still anxious on our return, I told Courtney my observations.

"Oh, Mom, I feel so unhappy. But I don't know what about."

For the next few weeks, she would sleep every minute she could for several days and then would be up half the night crying for several days. "School isn't good. Sports aren't good," she said. "It's not Dad. I don't know what it is." She didn't want professional help and I didn't want to force it on her.

That spring she applied to a more demanding academic school in the city with my encouragement, hoping that a change of environment would help.

Two months later Courtney was working at a hot dog stand for a weekend track event. Suddenly her senses started to go, one by one. When her breathing stopped, a friend called 911.

On the way to the emergency room, the paramedics tried to read her vital signs. Courtney remembered floating near the ceiling, watching the scene below. "This girl's going!" one cried. "We're losing her. I can't get a heartbeat or blood pressure."

By the time the hospital called me Courtney had regained consciousness. A co-worker rushed me over to the hospital.

The examining doctor met me and said, "We insisted that Courtney must be on drugs, but she kept denying it. The blood test proved she wasn't lying. What she has is a circulatory problem linked with her menstrual cycle. Nothing can prevent a recurrence, although a high protein diet might help."

When our pediatrician confirmed the diagnosis the next day, he added, "This condition might be psychologically induced."

That Saturday Courtney came into my bedroom before going to sleep. "Mom, if my head's creating this problem, let's do something about it. I'd better see a counselor."

Starting in September she went by bus after school three times a week to a psychologist who specialized in counseling teenagers. Sandy was beautiful, intelligent and married with a young child, a good role model for a teenage girl.

For six months Courtney insisted that she wasn't angry. Then Sandy asked Nicolas and me to come to a session with Courtney. "I don't care that Dad's gay," Courtney explained. "His leaving me is what matters and his drinking. I was so close to him! I was Dad's girl and Nickie was Mom's boy. When Dad left I had nobody. That's why I did everything right at school because I was afraid I would lose Mom too if I screwed up. I kept thinking, 'What if he never calls me again and doesn't even take me to the movies on Sundays?'"

As she talked I thought, "This poor child must have feared offending me too, since our relationship was so tenuous. She lived in terror until she blew up!"

Describing the stereotypical gay mannerisms Peter put on when he was drunk, Courtney said, "I'm so embarrassed. He isn't the same person any more!"

Sandy, the psychologist, asked Peter to meet with her next. He went three times and each time denied his alcoholism.

As Courtney began to face her problem, Nicolas, eleven, developed a volatile personality. His main complaint was that his sister got her way all the time. "I'm always picked on and ignored," he said. "I never get new things."

By then Courtney was creating quite a stir. Even more beautiful, she still excelled in sports and her studies, a tough act to follow in the best of times. Though Nicolas was natively brighter, he rarely worked in school. So he picked on Courtney, being the peacemaker who didn't fight back.

Then Courtney began having trouble again. Sandy called to warn me, "Allison, watch Courtney carefully. There's a suicide possibility here."

A week later Courtney was riding with an unlicensed friend in her parents' BMW on a rain-slick street when they were hit. Just as the passenger side was demolished, Courtney was thrown into the back seat unhurt. She hadn't fastened her seat belt.

Her concentration level at school had dropped to zero. If she studied an hour before an exam, she remembered nothing an hour afterward.

After a few weeks, I said, "I'm going to call the dean of students to tell him what's going on."

"Thank you," she answered quietly.

After describing her suicidal behavior to the dean, I said, "I'd like her teachers to know but not to talk to her about it or do her any favors."

"Fine. I'll tell them and call if there's a problem."

After seven months with Sandy Courtney admitted that she was angry with Peter for deserting her. "I was so mad at him," she told me that night, "that I wouldn't let myself be satisfied with anything." After a pause, her brow furrowed, she said, "I can't believe I denied my anger all this time."

Courtney had another realization about her father her junior year. One Sunday she called me from Peter's house about some problem. That night at home she remarked, "I just noticed I didn't tell Dad my problem before calling you. Guess my best friend is my mother."

She also had a boyfriend, Robb, a tall, sensitive senior.

About this time, Nicolas started to give away favorite mementoes to his friends one by one. Concerned, I suggested he might like to talk to Sandy.

"Absolutely not."

"It looks like you're finishing business with your friends and I want to know what's going on."

"Okay, I'll go."

The afternoon of his appointment I came home early to drive him in. He was doing homework at his desk. Courtney also happened to be home.

"Time to go," I said.

"I'm not going," Nicolas announced, clinging to his desk chair.

Courtney, hearing this, came to his door. Together we picked up the desk chair with Nicolas attached and carried it to the car. When he realized that we intended to put him in the car no matter what, he got in himself.

All the way over to Sandy's he was screaming, "Why are you making me do this when you know I don't want to talk to Sandy? I won't get out of the car. You're a horrible person! You've always hated me!" His face was scarlet and he began to lose his voice.

Trying not to react and focusing on the rush hour traffic, I kept saying, "Nickie, I love you. I'm afraid. I love you."

Just as we came upon the first vista of the city skyline against the fall sunset, Nicolas suddenly stopped screaming and said, "Isn't that gorgeous?"

"Yes," I said weakly.

We drove the rest of the way in silence and he went into Sandy's office quietly.

After the session Sandy took me aside. "You were right to bring him in. Now just keep an eye on him."

Later that winter Nicolas was talking with friends on the playground after school one day when an older boy, Hal, shouted, "Hey! Did you know Nickie's dad is gay?"

The children standing next to him said, "What a jerk! Who cares?" His best chum didn't even respond. But Nicolas was upset. When one of his friends got home and told his mother what had happened, they returned to the playground, found Nicolas hysterical and brought him home. They stayed until he calmed down. His friend was still there when I came home.

Nicolas didn't want to go to school the next day so I offered to drive him.

"Mom, I'm so afraid. I don't want my friends to hate me."

"See if you can go to school knowing it's Hal's problem," I said. "He seems to think so little of himself that he makes others look bad in order to look better. Ignore him. Your classmates will. If you don't let on that it upsets you, nothing will happen."

"I'll try."

As we drove to school I said, "If the worst should happen, I'll pick you up after school so you don't have to be alone."

No one said a word about it to him that day or since. Nor did he ever mention the subject to any of his friends.

Five months later Sandy called me. "Nickie's very angry with his father over the desertion, but for now I think he can work some of it out by himself."

Courtney's senior year, Robb's family invited her to go with them to the Caribbean at Christmas. It sounded like a great idea and I decided to give her this trip as a combined Christmas and birthday present. Courtney asked Peter about it the next time he was at the house.

"I'd rather have you with me for Christmas," he said.

"Why do you say that?" I asked.

"Kids should be home at Christmas. My parents would like it."

"No, Peter, those kinds of arguments don't fly here."

He replied, "Kids have a duty to be home and we ought to insist."

"She lives here and I'm not insisting. So why should you?"

The following Friday night Courtney and I discussed the trip while Peter and Nicolas went out to dinner. When they returned Nicolas went off to study. Peter, pouring himself a drink, joined Courtney and me in the kitchen.

"Courtney can go," he announced, "the day after Christmas."

"It doesn't make sense," I said, "to fly alone a week later just so she can spend four hours of Christmas Eve with you. I've decided she's going when Robb's family goes and coming home when they come home. You're pressuring her unreasonably."

"I want her home because next year I might not be here."

"What did you say?"

"I may be dead."

"My goodness!" I cried. "What do you mean?"

"I was exposed two years ago to someone who has died of AIDS."

"Do you have it?"

"No," he answered, "I've tested negative and I'm well, but six or seven years after exposure it can appear."

Courtney ran out of the room.

I began screaming. "You don't have the disease! I could just as well say, 'Gee, I might get hit by a car crossing the street so I'm not going to work any more.' Peter, give me a break!"

He yelled back. "You're being flip about a serious thing."

"I'm sorry you've been exposed, but you will not use it to make your children's lives miserable. I won't stand for it. You're using what might happen as blackmail. How dare you!"

"But I haven't done anything!" he shouted.

"You've just said that you had sex with someone who had AIDS."

At that, Peter grabbed the garbage can and went out the door.

When he didn't return I went out to see what had happened. The front door was open, garbage strewn all over the walk and his car gone. Angrily picking up the garbage, I became frightened. "He's going to drive over a cliff or run into a tree on purpose."

Just then Courtney and Nicolas ran out, Nicolas crying, "He's probably going to kill himself. Let's follow him."

As we tore down the street in the car I thought, "This isn't rational." Aloud I was saying, "I'm so angry. I'm so angry."

The children were saying, "Relax, Mom. Calm down."

At the corner I turned back realizing it was a foolish exercise. Once home Nicolas and Courtney went to their rooms and I called Tom and asked him to let me know if Peter returned.

A half hour later Tom called. "Peter's coming up the steps and he's in one piece. So you can quit worrying about him."

As I hung up Robb appeared in the doorway. "Courtney called twenty minutes ago. She was upset and didn't make sense so I came over."

While Robb talked to Courtney I went into Nicolas' room and talked with him about AIDS until he fell asleep.

When I checked in on Courtney Robb had calmed her down. Robb asked me to tell him about homosexuality. Sitting on Courtney's bed I explained it to him for about an hour—that it's something some people are born with and which cannot be changed and that it has nothing to do with being a good or bad person.

What I didn't talk about was my apprehension about the effects of Peter's gayness on Courtney's attitude toward men, or my own terror of being rejected by another man. Nor did I speak of my anger over Peter's alcoholism, his unwillingness to deal with it and his irrational stance on AIDS. Nor my fear that Courtney and Nicolas might follow in their mother's footsteps and enter into a dysfunctional relationship out of low self-esteem. After all, Peter's gayness itself has never been the central issue.

Your Mother Cared
Grant

Coming out of an eleven-year marriage in the early eighties, I transferred to Manhattan to a good position which paid well. Most of the people in the office were single, divorced or separated, and without children. After work a group of us would go out for a drink but there was no further involvement. It was a great life for a single, attractive man in his late thirties.

That's how I got to know Karen. Ten years younger, pretty with auburn hair, she'd left her husband two years earlier. Mentioning being battered, she sounded gutsy. I felt sorry for her because she'd had to leave her two-year-old son, Cal, behind because she couldn't support him.

That spring I applied to law school, deciding that I didn't want to move up the ladder at work. Karen and I started dating and soon we were in love.

Karen moved into my place just when her parents were in town and they stayed with us. I hit it off with them, especially her mother, Shirley.

I started law school that fall and Karen filed for divorce. When she phoned her father to tell him, I could hear him yelling, "How could you, and give up your son?"

Again I was struck at how gutsy she was, standing up to him. Yet she loved her father and all of her family. One of five children, she talked often about their dinner table conversations and holiday get-togethers.

The eldest of three, I wasn't close to my brother and sister. At seventeen I'd left school to join the army because my folks had trouble supporting all of us. My parents were not high school graduates, but they came to my graduation to accept my diploma for me.

That Christmas Karen invited me to join her family gathering in Syracuse and I found out for the first time what fun it was to be part of a close family.

In February Karen enrolled in a financial planning course, so we both had to go to school after work. By the end of the year we were grating on each other. She was always saying, "Oh, Grant, I'm sorry. I'm sorry"—not so gutsy, after all. She did everything alone, unlike me who liked to do things with others. Complaining that I didn't communicate, she suggested that we go to counseling.

"Sure," I said, thinking, "Let's help Karen."

I stopped after a few sessions. Karen continued and began talking more about how much she valued family. By December when her mother was planning a family reunion for Christmas, she brought up the topic of marriage, something we hadn't wanted.

"Well," I said, "what about it? Will you marry me?"

"Oh, yes, Grant," she answered, hugging me.

At the Christmas reunion everyone toasted us around the tree. Back home we had a small wedding in Karen's community church.

For the next two years we both worked and went to school. Karen brought in less than I paid in taxes. When my courses ended I took leave to study for the bar which I passed just as Karen finished her course work. To celebrate we took off in a recreational vehicle to tour the States for several months.

While on our trip we decided to quit our jobs and fulfill our dreams, hers to be a caterer and mine to be a trust lawyer. "It won't be the same money," we agreed, "but we'll enjoy what we have more." There was also my savings, stocks and pension.

We rented a cottage in White Plains and Karen began work in a delicatessen Tuesday through Saturday at below minimum wage. That Thanksgiving two of her co-workers, Rose and Joline, joined us. Neither woman appealed to me, especially Rose, who dressed like a ragamuffin, smoked, used drugs and swore a lot. But I thought, "They're Karen's friends. It's up to her."

For a year we talked about having a baby. The next spring Karen said, "Grant, I've been reading the statistics on birth defects and the mother's age. It's now or never."

She was pregnant by summer. We each dreamed that it would be a girl and after much deliberation decided to call her "Heather." We both went to birthing classes and doctor visits where, thrilled, I heard the baby's heartbeat. Then Karen decided to use midwife assistants with a backup doctor if needed.

Three months into her pregnancy, Karen, along with Rose and Joline, filed an equal rights discrimination grievance with the deli and left. She found another job closer to the city working late hours to make breakfast and brunch specialties. As time went on her work hours were scheduled later and later at night.

"Well," I thought, wearily, "if she likes it, I'll put up with it." At this time my savings and stock sales paid the rent since free-lance legal work didn't bring in much more than Karen's salary, now barely above the minimum wage.

In late March after a false alarm, Karen went into labor and we went to the hospital's alternative birthing room with its two beds, cradle, couch, wallpaper, and stereo. I had my camera ready.

Suddenly Karen cried, "It's coming!" Since it was earlier than predicted, the assistants called in the emergency room doctor. Karen pushed once, twice, and out popped the baby into the doctor's arms. Snapping a picture, I yelled, "It's Heather!"

When Karen and Heather came home, aunts and Grandmother Shirley flew in to see the baby, who slept in a cradle beside our bed. Cal, Karen's son, came too, as a surprise. When Karen saw him peek in the door she started crying. Then they hugged and cried some more. Shirley stayed for the christening, performed by a woman minister in the church where we'd married four and a half years before.

When Heather was three months old Karen went back to her late night shift. Weekdays she went to bed at eight and I about eleven. She left at two in the morning for work and I arose at six to take the baby to the sitter's. Karen picked her up at two.

"With my weird hours," Karen said one Sunday while we were out driving with the baby, "I can't see any of my friends except Rose, since she has the same crazy schedule."

Rose worked and lived in the Bronx, not too far away. She and Karen jogged afternoons and talked on the phone after supper, while Heather nursed and I watched TV or worked at my desk. Soon, Karen was taking the phone into the bedroom to talk with Rose, who sometimes called after eight causing Karen to lose an hour's sleep and be irritable the next day.

When the phone bill arrived I confronted Karen. "Every day you call the Bronx for almost an hour. You've racked up twenty-five dollars worth! You see Rose every afternoon, so what's left to say? What are you whispering when I go by the door?"

Karen looked startled.

"I'm telling any caller after eight that you're in bed," I yelled. "I'm tired of taking the brunt of it the next day."

The calling slacked off a bit. Instead whenever Karen had to work late, she asked if she could spend the night at Rose's.

"Sure," I said. "This way I'll know you're getting an hour's extra sleep. You aren't getting enough."

Because of Karen's hours we didn't make love often. One night that fall when we did, I was surprised by how smooth it was. Always before after a lapse of several months, it was a bit awkward. This time it was as if we'd been having sex every two days. "Has she been with somebody else?" I wondered. Then I laughed, "How could she, with work and seeing Rose all the time?" But something in the back of my mind said, "Make note of this, Grant." I feared pursuing it further.

A week later we were invited to a Halloween party. Karen asked to go separately. "Rose will take me and Heather."

"Sure! What time?"

"About seven. Would it be okay if I stayed the night with her since I have an early order?"

"No problem, if she'll let you."

By the time I arrived at the party Karen was there with Rose and Joline. Since I was driving I didn't drink. About 9:30 P.M., well past Heather's bedtime, I gathered up her and the diaper bag and left. At home an hour later, opening the bag, I found Karen's keys. "Damn. Now she can't get home or go to work."

I called Rose's. No answer. "Strange," I thought. "She said they'd leave the party by ten o'clock."

Once Heather was in bed I called again. Still no answer. Then I called the deli where Karen worked. No answer. In case I'd missed them at Rose's, I called there once more. As the phone rang and rang, I recalled another time when Rose hadn't answered because she was mad at Joline. "Oh-h-h," I groaned. "I'll have to drive there."

It was midnight when Heather and I arrived. Karen's car was parked where she'd left it after work. I rang the doorbell with Heather in my arms. When no one came after a couple of minutes, I peered in the front window to see if Karen was asleep on the couch. She wasn't. "Odd," I thought. "Well, she's probably in the back room." Starting around the house, I noticed a couple of cops on the corner. "Oh, oh!" I whispered to Heather and hurried to the car.

I drove out to the deli. Since it was still locked up I used the pay phone to try Rose's once again. Still no answer. "She's got to be there!" I muttered and drove back over to Rose's.

Lugging the sleeping kid in my arms up to the door, I rang the bell over and over, getting more and more ticked.

Then that little voice in the back of my mind said, "Go look in the window." Fearing what might be there, I didn't. But the voice said, "Make note of it anyway," as I unlocked Karen's car, put the ignition key in the glove compartment, placed the door key in Rose's mailbox and drove home. It was now 1:30 A.M.

The next morning when I called Karen at work, she said that they thought it was Joline ringing the bell.

"What would have happened if I'd needed to get ahold of you because something had happened to Heather?"

"God! I didn't think of that."

"Well, look in Rose's mailbox. Next time come get the keys yourself." I was beginning to resent Karen's inconvenient schedule.

That Christmas Karen's church held its annual potluck and dance. Though I didn't want to go, we went anyway and brought Heather too. I didn't like to dance so Karen danced with Rose since there weren't enough men to go around. Then it was time to take Heather home.

Outside Karen said, "Oh, I've got to tell Rose something."

"You just saw her two seconds ago."

"Yes, but I forgot something."

As she went back to the church hall I strapped Heather in the car seat, hearing that funny voice inside say, "Go look." But I didn't want to leave Heather alone or carry her with me.

Over the next few weeks Rose drove out from the Bronx occasionally to go to a movie with Karen or a spa Karen had discovered with a group from church or a local tavern.

Then one night Karen said, "I'm thinking of going on the church retreat this weekend to think about things."

"Oh?" I said, scared. "She's thinking divorce," I thought, "I won't let it happen. I've seen too many broken families."

The next day I sent Karen a bouquet of roses with a note: "I know things haven't been going well. I'll do anything to change but don't know how to start. I need your help. Let's talk. I know we can work this out." Since we were both coming down with a flu bug, I figured this might tip the scales to make her stay home.

She called when she arrived home from work. "Thanks for the beautiful flowers! I'm leaving now for the retreat. See you."

As the weekend went on I decided between nausea bouts that we had to get counseling. "We have to hold the family together."

Since Karen didn't say much when she returned Sunday night I thought, "O.K., I'll bring it up next weekend."

The next Saturday Karen had dinner at Rose's to talk about what to do. At midnight Rose drove up with Karen in the front seat.

"I drank too much and fell asleep so Rose had to drive," Karen said, stumbling in the door. Her eyes were red and puffy.

"Well, have you decided what you're going to do?"

"Let's talk tomorrow," she said and shuffled to the bedroom.

On Sunday as we drove to the city to visit friends with Heather in the back seat, I asked, "Well, what have you decided?"

"I'm going to leave."

"Leave? Why?"

"We aren't getting along. You don't communicate." She rattled on about things that didn't warrant that drastic a move.

In between her reasons I kept saying, "Give me a chance."

"You've had a chance," she said finally.

"How could I have had a chance if I didn't know I was being given one? I'll make any deal if only you'll stay."

"No, I've decided."

"Where will you go?"

"I could go to Rose's."

When Rose came to help Karen move on Friday I said, "Gee, thanks for letting Karen stay with you while she's going through this."

Sunday I asked Karen to dinner on Monday. Taking off from work early, I bought Cornish game hens to stuff, vegetables for the kind of salad she liked, wine and candles. While Heather slept we had a nice dinner with lots of talk.

Then as Karen put on her coat to leave, I said, "Let's try to work things out. Come back. Give me another chance."

"No, Grant, I'm still leaving."

Once the door closed behind her I began to cry.

Every day that week when Karen came to take Heather to the sitter's and then to bring her back, I asked her to return.

When I asked on Friday she said, "No, I couldn't go to bed with you again."

"Who's talking about that? I'm talking about saving this family and making it work for Heather. I'll sleep on the couch."

That weekend I decided to write Heather a letter about her birth nine months earlier. It was important to put my positive feelings down right away as if Karen and I were still together so Heather would know her mother cared.

By then Karen had told her mother Shirley that she was leaving me. Shirley called Karen immediately. "I'll give you a year's salary to spend time with Grant and Heather so you can work things out."

Meanwhile one of Karen's church friends I'd asked for advice said, "She mentioned communication problems. Why not see a psychiatrist?"

Starting on Heather's first birthday in March, I saw a psychiatrist two or three times a week until October. "The faster you get to know me," I told her, "the faster you can help me get my wife back. Ask whatever you want. I'll hold nothing back."

I used up half her tissue box the first session. At the fourth session I said, "Maybe I drove her into being gay or something."

"Why do you say that?"

After describing our lovemaking incident the previous fall and the car keys incident after the Halloween party, I said, "I never followed up on these things until now."

In April Karen began to share Heather's care and Shirley came to visit. She stayed with me since my house had more room.

One night as we were having tea in the kitchen, Shirley said, "I told Karen that I'd watch Heather to give her more time with you. I also told her to get a decent day job to have a normal life with her family. But she said, 'No. No. No.'"

Shirley continued, "I told her there were only three reasons why she'd leave you: one, she has a terminal disease and wants to alienate everyone; two, she's had a nervous breakdown and doesn't know what's going on; or three, she's gay. She said, 'No,' to the first two and nothing to the third."

"Well, that's Karen!" I said, thinking she'd found the third reason too ridiculous to answer.

Over the next month my work went downhill but communication with Karen improved. "It took nine months for you to decide to leave," I told her one night. "I'm going to try at least that long to win you back."

Karen's son Cal came to visit that summer. I liked watching him and Heather play together with her toys.

Shirley visited again too, staying with me. One day Karen asked her to come to the Bronx to meet someone. Shirley took the train in and I agreed to pick her up. At dinner time she called to say that she'd take the train back and catch a taxi home.

When she arrived at midnight I'd just finished Heather's letter, describing her conception, the doctor, the delivery room, her birth and her baptism. My last words were, "We dearly love you and want only the best that we can provide for you."

"Shirley," I said. "I'll make you some tea and you can read Heather's letter to be sure there's nothing negative in it. I'm still hoping Karen will come back, you see."

Shirley read it in the kitchen with loud sobs as I watched TV in the living room. Then she came out, her eyes swollen.

"There's nothing negative, is there?" I asked.

"Oh no! It's very nice, Grant. Good night."

After Shirley left in tears the next day, I cried too. "Do I deserve this?" I asked myself. "I don't fight with Karen. I take care of her. I'm not a heavy drinker or drug addict or chauvinist pig. I was first to battle the company to get a woman in a top position. What's the real reason? If it's another man, I don't want to know it. But if I'm really nice to her, maybe he'll go away."

Six months after Karen left I told my psychiatrist, "Maybe she's homosexual. But it can't be. I know her."

Three months later Karen asked me to go see her counselor with her. "We'll drive separately," she added. "I don't want to be in the same car with you."

Once we were seated in front of the counselor Karen turned to me. "Grant, I've found myself. I'm gay."

"I thought so," I said, my eyes dry.

After we talked some, the counselor asked how I felt.

"Lousy. What do you think?"

For the next five days I sat in contemplation and cried. Unable to stop shaking, I didn't think I'd last the six days to my next counseling session. My dreams of a happy family were shattering and there wasn't anything I could do about it.

At some point Karen called to suggest that I do some reading about homosexuality. "I don't want to know any more than the little I know already," I thought.

Then I called Shirley, who said the evening she'd spent with Karen was a rap session with her gay group. Karen had told her that she thought she was gay and later told Cal. Shirley had urged her to tell me.

When I saw my psychiatrist, I told her with my eyes averted. She drew in her breath. "I never suspected."

After the session I decided to read everything available on homosexuality. The only way to fight Karen on her level was to know as much as her.

I felt like I was entering a dirty bookstore when I went to the library. The whole world seemed to be looking over my shoulder, thinking, "Oh, oh! Look at that guy." I snuck around the stacks and used the microfiche reader when no one was around. After finding four books I thought, "Oh! I've got to check them out." Putting the one with "homosexual" in the title on the bottom, I opened it to the date page so the title was hidden. The librarian turned it over anyway, giving me a look as she stamped it. Then I grabbed the books, ran outside, threw them into the trunk and sped away.

The first book I read that night, *Whose Child Cries*, described five gay situations from the child's viewpoint. Turning each page, thinking of Heather, I cried and cried. At one point I even contemplated suicide but knew I could never do that to Heather, sleeping in the next room.

For eight weeks I read these and other books, writing down my thoughts and feelings in a notebook. It seemed like a lifetime. At the end any hope I'd had was gone.

In late September Karen and I met with her counselor to discuss Heather. "Joint custody is fine," I said. "But I won't agree to anything more. When Heather's ready for school, I want you and Rose to move out here so she can come to your place or mine and still go to the same school."

Over the next nine months we worked out a sharing schedule for Heather. Even on Father's Day I had Karen pick her up as usual in order not to change our routine. Karen arrived with a Father's Day card for Heather to give me. As she went out the door she suddenly turned back. "I want to hug you, Grant."

"O.K.," I said, keeping my arms at my sides.

"You know," she smiled, "You're a wonderful father."

"Yeah," I thought, "but a lousy husband." If there were a way to keep Heather and not have to deal with Karen, I'd choose it. But I tried to get along with her so our daughter wouldn't see us fighting.

Yet I feared that a custody fight was inevitable. "If there is," I told myself, "I'll ask for a home investigation to determine what's best for Heather and find a house that is better than hers."

Although I was broke, I started house hunting. Shirley offered to help finance it if necessary. I also advertised for a single mother with toddler to share a three-bedroom place with us, so Heather would grow up with another child and see a man and woman together at the dinner table as a role model.

A woman with three children answered the ad. "Great!" I thought. Then, I caught myself. "Wait a minute! You're helping out women again."

Within three months I had made a down payment on a New England style bungalow with three bedrooms and a front yard in a complex that had a playground and pool. It was a quiet place with plenty of kids in the neighborhood.

Five years earlier I'd have said, "Kids? No way." Now I was elated.

Two years later it is still top priority that Heather have playmates as well as a home with a father who cares.

I Love You, Jeff And Peggy
Frank

We made a perfect family: two rosebud children, Jeff and Peggy, not yet in school, Patty at home cooking up a storm, and me at the university, supposedly making straight A's and preparing for my doctoral exams. We had a lot of friends and lived in a lovely apartment in Austin, after six years of temporary "homes" and separations while I was in the army. Making all this possible were the student loans we took out together so that Patty could stay home with the children.

Meanwhile I was being torn up inside, turning papers in late or not at all, running away from difficulty without telling anyone and inventing excuses to maintain my academic image.

Simultaneously, my homosexuality was growing more powerful. I felt confused, pressured and frightened. Any man or woman who's been there knows my pain—an incredible self-doubt, a contradictory yearning. I was too afraid to ask anyone what was going on and felt terribly isolated.

Our second year in Texas I met a man who pulled me across the line of my fear, from wondering to enjoying. Once across, I couldn't go back. Everything in my life became distorted, my judgment cloudy, my behavior erratic. I thought, "Here's this all-American, "Joe College" father having a secret romance with a young man and no one knows."

I learned how to lie, to cheat and be devious, not because I was a bad person but because I feared telling the truth and thereby suffering rejection and loss.

Patty and I could never deal with that truth. I recalled what Dad had said when we'd pushed up our wedding date. "Just as you're the product of your family and our values, Frank, and you can't change it, so Patty's the product of her parents' values and she can't change that. You two are so different in where you come from and how you see the world, marriage is premature."

Although I never opened up to Patty, she knew something was wrong. "I don't like you spending so much time with this friend of yours," she said one night. "It's quality time that you should be spending with us."

I stopped seeing him for the sake of our marriage. It took tremendous self-denial on my part to restore the sense of wholeness in my family life.

On that superficially happy note, our family set off for Germany for my doctoral research and dissertation. Kids in tow and spirits high, Patty and I thought only of my research and the experiences we'd share in Heidelberg.

Then one morning, in the university library I made eye contact with Emil and life for everyone was never the same.

Young and beautiful, Emil was connected with the world of intellectuals. He was my intellectual equal. He was also gay. In a matter of weeks I was swept away. And Patty was swept under the rug. I'd discovered something greater than my education and family put together: the deep satisfaction of having something I'd always wanted and of moving into a world where everything was right.

Though Emil and I were together every moment I was supposed to be studying, I still gave a lot of time to Peggy, Jeff and Patty, convincing myself that I could live two lives. The children blossomed! Patty was speaking German marvelously. Then we had to move to a remote village for my field research.

By then I couldn't even move without involving Emil, who went with me to prepare the house friends had lent us. The day Patty and the children arrived by train, he left to return to the city.

For the next four months the family grew closer and we explored a new part of the country. Jeff and Peggy were growing, learning German, attempting to swim and manifesting self-confidence. Patty was radiant, her skin glowing and her hair lustrous as she moved about in colorful Bavarian skirts. I missed Emil but knew I could manage for a while.

In September as my grant was running out, Patty returned to the States with the children so that they could start school. "I have to stay," I told her, "for additional research."

Back in the States Patty had to depend on parents and in-laws in New York and live in a state of waiting as she had during my army days. I returned to Heidelberg to live a gay lifestyle.

Even before Patty and the children left, I missed them deeply! Yet my heart pounded in anticipation of sharing every moment with Emil, of being free. Freedom didn't imply rejection. It meant the freedom to love someone.

My desire to love so overwhelmed me that I couldn't think through the consequences, not because I didn't care or wasn't frightened for Patty and the children and myself and Emil. I didn't know how to think and felt that no one could have helped me. If someone had said, "Get divorced," or, "Move home," I couldn't have done either. I couldn't see that my life needed simplification. Instead I wanted more and more of what I'd found, to wake up nestled against someone I loved without the fear of going home with a lie or an excuse.

Back in New York Patty and the children felt hurt. My mother knew something was terribly wrong with me because I wasn't with my children I loved so much. My brothers and sister, who had suspected my sexuality was confused, figured out why my life wasn't going normally. Out of caring for Patty and the children as well as for me, they talked with her one day about what I might be facing.

When they finished Patty became hysterical. "That's not true! You have no right to interfere in our lives!"

In late August Patty flew to Texas to find us a place to live near Austin and to start Jeff and Peggy in school. Without me, her main emotional support, she sought solace in a conservative church. The minister gave her the order in her life that she felt was missing, a structure that allowed her to make sense of things. Gradually she developed a reality system that included no ambiguity, no doubts, no unresolved matters. Things were to be the way she saw them because that way was right. Once the children were in school she organized a regular schedule for the three of them.

Meanwhile in Germany I was growing further away from who I had been before. I had a sense of wholeness as a man. I was gaining the confidence to express my true identity.

As summer ended my professor said my research time was up. In September I flew to Texas to resume teaching and begin the dissertation.

A very different family was waiting for me, just as a very different Frank was coming home. My hair was long and permed. I wore contact lenses. I was slender now, wearing tailored clothes and tighter pants, much different from the sloppy graduate students around me.

Peggy and Jeff were overjoyed to see me. Patty was shocked by my appearance and what she saw as effeminate behavior. She was angry that she'd carried all the burden of the children and that I'd been away so long.

The next four months were hell. I taught my classes but not well. I avoided responsibilities. I didn't know when I'd see Emil again and recapture the happiness we'd shared.

Because Patty insisted that we go to church I went, wanting to share something important to her on her terms. Her religious involvement over the years hadn't threatened my values in any serious way, although I felt more comfortable in churches in which instead of discussing Christian theology about sin and salvation, the congregation instead talked about the values of love and community with room for ambiguity.

Making a lot of moral compromises, I went to Sunday School and church and acted like a devout father and husband. It was the glue that held together the remaining framework of our crumbling family. In my dutiful role I was in fact, "crawling the walls." What was asked of me was too much for me to handle and I was ready to explode.

Being separated from Emil was part of the problem. Slowly several friends understood what had happened to me but they didn't offer support. Although I needed someone I could turn to, I was terrified to bring up the homosexuality issue with Patty. I feared losing the children because I thought she would be unable to deal with the situation. Then in my confusion, no longer able to deny my sexuality, I began to have casual sex.

In March, through my arrangements, Emil came to Austin for a symposium. Patty acted happy for me because she knew that he was the friend I'd lived with while finishing my research. Although Emil stayed with friends, I went out every night to see him. Every day while I was presumably at the university, I was with him. One by one, everybody close to us saw the reality except Patty.

Emil's part of the symposium was applauded by faculty members, students and intellectuals from the community. Patty, beautiful as always, helped me host the reception afterwards. It was an awkward occasion as I only paid attention to Emil.

The following day when Emil asked me for a commitment, I was like a jellyfish.

"O.K.," he said. "I'll return to Germany next month as planned and wait. If you choose to contact me, I'll come."

The next day I found out that I'd contracted a sexual disease from some casual sex experience during the preceding months.

All along Patty and I had continued to have sex. She was the only woman I'd ever had sex with. Now I'd exposed her to disease! I couldn't hide any longer. There was no escape, no denial left.

Sunday afternoon I took her for a drive to an outlying park. As we walked along the path that circled the gardens I began. "Patty,

I'm finally going to tell you why everything's been going wrong, why I couldn't answer your questions and why our relationship is so messed up." Then, I looked at her, and for the first time in my life said, "I am gay."

Everything Patty had feared exploded in her face. She fainted right there on the pathway.

As I held her I knew that our confusion and love were over. Years of anguish were lifted from my shoulders. "My door's open now," I thought, "but it's opened a terrible trap for her."

When Patty came to, she asked, "Emil...is he gay, too?"

"Yes."

"Could I have been exposed to a sexual disease?"

"Yes, Patty," I said, "there's a serious possibility."

We went home in shock. Patty was dazed. I was too except I knew that despite the pain I'd caused I could now live my life openly.

Once the children were in bed Patty went to see her dearest friends and I left to be with Emil. Everything then fell apart for the all-American family. Fortunately Patty wasn't infected by my disease, but we didn't know where to turn to get help in saving our marriage and the family.

Our friends became angry at me for my treatment of Patty and told her to get rid of me. Our pediatrician encouraged us to think of the children's best interests. "Lots of people work out arrangements to maintain family appearances, letting each partner dally on the side. You can be discreet in our town." But even if we had decided to do this, we would still have had to face our communication problems. This was something our pediatrician couldn't help us work out.

Next we went to Patty's minister. This time I needed his help to gain stability.

Once he heard our story he said, "Frank, homosexuality is a sinful abomination and a medical pathology. If you want to save your marriage, be forgiven by Christ and not go to hell, you'll have to renounce your homosexuality and cure this sickness. The only way to overcome something this powerful is by electroshock therapy."

I was horrified! The idea of someone burning my body to force me to give up everything that I wanted, that I was! "How terrifying,"

I thought, "to condemn someone in Jesus' name for wanting to be honest with himself and his family!"

That night Patty and I stopped sleeping together. The next morning Jeff and Peggy asked why I was asleep on the couch. We didn't know what to tell them since we hadn't made any decisions about the future. Patty wasn't interested in counseling and I clung to the fantasy that something might work out peacefully. Emil hadn't left yet and hovered on the side.

Patty gave me an ultimatum within the month. "Frank," she said, "totally renounce your homosexuality or move out."

The next day I went to see the university psychiatrist. He listened and finally said, "Do you want to be gay?"

"Yes, I do. I want to be gay."

And that was that. I'd acknowledged who I was and accepted the fact of beginning a new life. All the years of hiding from myself and Patty, all my fear, denial and suffering came to an end. Yet with the joy of liberation came pain and a sense of loss.

Within the week Patty said, "The only thing for you to do now is to move out as soon as possible."

So we had to tell Jeff and Peggy. Sitting at the table after dinner that night we said, "Mommy and Daddy are going to get divorced. We don't love each other the way we did, but we'll always love you."

The two ran from the table to their rooms and then back to us, saying, "No! No! No!" and holding onto us tightly. Then we were all crying.

It was the end of Patty's and my journey together over fifteen years. Yet I knew that as parents we shared a bond too deep to be broken by any legal institution.

Patty felt like a spurned woman who had been betrayed. She'd been doing right and I'd been doing wrong. That was her view and it was shared by many of our friends, some members of her family and the church. All of the insecurities, intolerance and fear that I'd noticed in her over the years surfaced to protect herself and the children. This isn't said to condemn Patty because I accept her for who she is.

When we separated Emil went back to Germany. He was to return once my life stabilized or I'd go there so that we could finally live together. Soon my going abroad as an unemployed graduate student was out of the question in the face of Patty's monetary needs for her and the children.

Trying to work out an amicable divorce settlement was difficult since there was a climate of intolerance toward homosexuality due to Anita Bryant's anti-gay crusade. The local court staff also included a known homophobic. I finally hired a young attorney and desperate to end the fighting signed away my life and chances for a reasonable scale of living.

Besides receiving a cash settlement Patty kept all of the valuables, furniture and car. In addition to her attorney fees, I was to pay hundreds of dollars a month in child support, the children's health and life insurance and payments toward the student loans that we had co-signed. Finally Patty received custody of the children, although I was awarded unrestricted visitation rights with certain holidays that we would share on an alternating basis.

Through the end of the academic year I saw Peggy and Jeff daily, driving them on errands, baby-sitting, taking them out, sharing dinners with Patty—anything to stay as close to them as possible and show how much I loved them.

Meanwhile Patty was impatient for me to get a job so that she'd have the support to finish college and gain more security than she had with my graduate school stipend. This meant finding a job in a city that offered higher salaries in my field than Austin. In August I moved to Chicago to work on a federally funded project, thereby relinquishing the hope of ever finishing my dissertation.

When I left Jeff was seven, an energetic, happy and loving child. Peggy was almost five, a red-headed jewel with a sweet temper. I felt they were forever my children and that I'd been with them long enough to instill the values of love and kindness, playfulness and sharing.

Although I only had three hundred dollars a month left after paying child support and loans, I scraped together enough cash to visit Texas and see the children, my friends and Patty that fall. Patty was dating a fellow named George, a pleasant, proper person who was defensive of her, fine with the children and noncommittal toward me.

Later that winter Emil joined me and we have been together the ten years since, outlasting my marriage to Patty.

A year after my move Jeff and Peggy began to say, "We don't want to come to Chicago." Sometimes they had legitimate reasons, like missing camp. Other times their excuses were flimsy, like fearing flying even though they'd taken long flights before.

When they came they always had a delightful time. We visited the Museum of Science and the Art Institute in the spring, walked along the lake in the winter cold and the balmy summer and saw the expanse of the city from the Sears Tower. When they got home, even as they were writing me effusive letters about the visits, Patty said that they spoke only of the plane trip.

When Jeff and Peggy were with me, Patty wrote them and they found gifts or notes or prayers hidden in their suitcases. She was there all the time, never completely releasing them to me.

The next thing I knew they started calling George "Daddy" and me "Frank." They stopped sending me Easter and Halloween cards or even birthday and Father's Day cards.

When I asked why they said, "We don't have money for a stamp."

I was sending several hundred dollars a month in child support and there wasn't enough money for a stamp! Gradually they stopped writing altogether.

Soon each time visitations came up, Peggy and Jeff said, "We don't want to go."

Patty said, "If you don't want to see your father, tell him."

When they expressed reluctance to come for their next Christmas visit Patty told me, "You can't make us do it, Frank. They don't want to and I'm not going to force them against their will."

Several things were contributing to their resistance. But primarily it was because Patty saw me as a threat to her fragile security. She'd pieced together what was left of her life to have the kind of lifestyle I'd never been able to give them. She and George bought new cars and a new house. He was devoted to going to church with her and the children.

I was no longer welcome in my children's lives. I was barred from seeing Peggy's and Jeff's counselors or teachers to find out how they were doing. My mother and Patty's mother were prevented from meeting. I wasn't allowed to contact any of her relatives. The children never saw the Baker side of the family. The lines were drawn tighter and tighter until I was effectively cut off from my children.

I was too far away and too poor to take legal action against Patty. Instead thousands of dollars went out for plane tickets whenever there was an opportunity for the kids to visit our meager but happy Chicago apartment. Then I was transferred to Philadelphia.

The move compounded all the problems of visitation. The first time I invited Jeff and Peggy they said that they didn't want to come. When I insisted, Patty told them to fight. They didn't come.

The next year the children's stepfather signed on with a company in Detroit much closer to me. This promised easier access, cheaper flights, more visits. I was exhilarated.

They were not. The message was, "We want less. Just bug off."

Since my business took me to Detroit regularly I saw them anyway. While Patty and the children fussed and fidgeted, I visited with the kids out of rental cars and ran them around like a baby-sitter. When I called their new school to see how they were doing, I was told that their records were in their stepfather's name as their legal father. This was against the court decree.

Visits became more regular the next year although each was like pulling teeth. When Jeff and Peggy went with me to my mom's in New York, they were well-behaved but wouldn't let me touch them. They never said, "I love you." They never called me "Daddy."

Several months later they came to Philadelphia, saw the Liberty Bell, ate our food, stuck their noses in the air and then flew home. Seeing my little babies act so rude and unappreciative hurt and confused me.

Emil criticized me for acting like the rich uncle who entertained them twice a year for a couple of days. Other friends said, "It isn't Patty's responsibility to remind the children that you exist. You've got a role in their lives to influence who they are." But I didn't know how to father except to send money every month.

Feeling discouraged and abused after two years of this, I began to go to a gay married men's support group. The group became close friends. They held me together, held me up and simply held me. They gave me belief in myself, helped me affirm the contributions I was making to my children and encouraged me to fight for my rights as their father.

Throwing down the gauntlet, I reduced my next child support check by twenty percent. By then I was working two jobs, but Emil and sometimes my mother often had to help me cover child support, loan repayments, insurance and plane tickets.

The following week the sheriff walked into my project office and came straight to my desk with a summons that stated I was in contempt of court for violating the divorce decree. I found an attorney in Detroit who set up an initial meeting with the judge. The judge said that Patty and I were to find a mutually acceptable psychologist for family counseling in which all of us would participate.

The selected psychologist held sessions with various combinations of us five. We all hadn't met together yet when he terminated the process. "The mother has resisted discussing her feelings," he told the judge, "particularly in sessions with her husband. Her disbelief in counseling and her manipulation of the process has undermined my role in this case."

The trial took place in the spring. George's testimony was key. Speaking of "Mr. Baker's lifestyle," he said, "I just wish he didn't exist. Life would be easier for us if he weren't alive."

When the psychologist came to the stand, the judge reminded him, "You're responsible to the court to share whatever you in your professional judgment believe is relevant to the case."

"I found a few answers," the psychologist said, "It was hard to get cooperation." After reporting on the children, George and me, he continued, "The mother seems to be deeply conflicted, over- protective of her children, quick to judge, slow to forgive and still at an unresolved stage, experiencing strong emotions toward her former husband. Because these emotions aren't resolved," he concluded, "no other family issue can be effectively resolved."

At those words Patty shrieked, "That's not true!"

The courtroom came apart. The trial was adjourned until the next day.

The rest of the trial went as expected. Patty's lawyer tried to discredit my lifestyle, while I described the rather mundane goings on around my house: "I go to my job, do the dishes, clean house, go shopping, do the laundry."

Several months later the court made its ruling. Monthly payments were reduced to the amount I wanted. Then the judge stated, "The father's rights have been violated. He is entitled to unrestricted visitation, provided he discusses visits in advance with the children and lets them participate in decisions about when and where visitations take place. They will alternate Christmas, Thanksgiving and Easter holidays between the mother and father and spend a substantial amount of time with the father in the summer."

The following summer I invited Peggy and Jeff to Philadelphia. Lo and behold, they didn't want to come. Patty said she wouldn't make them and would stand up against the courts to protect their right not to come if they didn't want to.

Once more I went to the Detroit courthouse, this time to take Patty to court for contempt. When the judge sat Patty, the children and me down in chambers with George sitting in the back, he first addressed Jeff and Peggy. "I do not accept your disregard for the laws and constitution of this state and the legal processes of the courts."

Turning to Patty he said, "It's your responsibility to ensure that the children comply fully to Frank's right to visitation."

Then he looked the children in the eye and said, "I never want to see you in this room again. You have responsibilities and rights and a father who loves you. The court has spoken."

Then, from the back of the room, came the stepfather's voice.

"Hey! What about AIDS?"

"Silence!" the judge roared. "You are totally out of order."

For the next year I didn't return to Detroit and rarely communicated with Patty. She never sent me copies of the children's school progress reports or samples of their work.

Jeff and Peggy came to visit me. It was the best period we ever had. They came for Easter, two weeks that summer, Christmas week, the following summer, and Thanksgiving. When it was my turn for Easter again they said, "No."

I let it go. Instead Emil and I decided to go to the Upper Peninsula of Michigan and stop in Detroit for a day on the way home. When I wrote Peggy and Jeff about the plan, they said they couldn't see me because they were leaving to see their aunts that day and couldn't delay their departure. That hurt. Yet it had been only four months since I'd seen them and Detroit was their turf so I didn't pursue it.

Emil and I camped and hiked for two weeks in March, full of vitality. It was the honeymoon we'd never had. We came back on March 25. On April 3 I was diagnosed with AIDS.

By mid-April I had regained my composure enough to tell my parents. By May I felt strong enough to tell my children. Through the principal of Peggy's middle school, I found out when her graduation was scheduled. Well in advance I wrote her to say that since I had business in Detroit then, I wanted to attend the graduation and visit with her and Jeff.

I wrote to Patty simultaneously about the children's expenses.

I'm as concerned about finances as you. Since I have to be in Michigan anyway, it would be a good chance for us to talk privately about money questions related to the children, such as paying for college.

Both letters were unthreatening. Peggy's reply was not. "I don't want you within the state of Michigan during graduation week. I'll be ashamed if you come to my school."

I wrote back calmly stating that I would attend the graduation and wanted to spend time with her and Jeff the following evening. I wrote Patty again also, reiterating the importance of meeting. "If we don't talk," I thought, "it will be her last opportunity."

Next I called Patty's former minister to come to Detroit that weekend to support her after I told her about having AIDS. A month later I was on the plane.

Graduation night I drove to the school and followed the pack of parents to the auditorium. Peggy was standing by the door talking with friends. When she saw me she turned away. I kept walking.

Then the ceremony began. Soon I was the proudest father there. Peggy had tied down every award there was—just like her father— and graduated at the top of her class. Her name was sprinkled all over the program though not once as "Peggy Baker."

The next evening I took her and Jeff to dinner. Jeff was nearly eighteen and so poised that he waved to a friend coming into the restaurant, unconcerned about how to introduce me if his friend came over to the table.

After dinner we drove to Grosse Pointe and walked along the lake. Jeff talked about his college plans. All Peggy wanted to do was skip. So we skipped together.

Then we sat down under a tree in the cool, quiet evening and I began. "I have the most important thing to say that I'm ever going to as your father. First I want you to know that I've always loved you. Do you understand that I've always loved you?"

"Yes, we understand."

And then I told them. "I have AIDS."

Jeff, his eyes full of tears, put his arms around me. Peggy sat paralyzed, not sure what to do, but understanding now why I had to come to her graduation. After a few minutes she held me too. We stayed a long time in the darkness holding onto each other.

Then we talked about AIDS. Both children seemed calm even when I told Jeff it would be harder financially now for his mom and him to cover college expenses.

"I've been reading a lot," he said, "knowing you're gay. I thought maybe you might get it."

I'd brought along a handbook from the AIDS Foundation, which explained ways families can help each other as well as the patient. Handing it to Jeff but speaking to both of them I said, "Don't be afraid of what it says or what you don't understand. I'll help you find answers if you're willing to ask the questions."

Then I asked, "Do you want to tell your mom or have me do it?"

"We'll tell her."

Then it was time to go. "I might not be here physically much longer," I said, holding them close, "but I'll always be here for you in my love and spirit. As long as my health lasts I'll do everything possible to see you. My home will be open to you as yours."

I drove them back to their house, told them I loved them one more time and watched them go inside. That was the last time I saw them.

Later that night Patty called and in a quiet, meek and secretive voice said, "I don't want anyone else to hear what I'm saying. I wish I could be there to hold you."

By noon the next day her minister described a different Patty. When he'd called to offer support she'd screamed, "How dare you get involved in my family affairs! I don't need or want anybody's support with this!"

"I guess she'd have preferred a letter, saying, 'I'm dying,'" I said. "She doesn't want to be exposed to pain so close at hand."

After that I wrote Patty three times trying to make her see that our reality as parents was changing. "I won't be here forever," I wrote. "My money will run out soon. We must discuss the children's education and insurance."

By the end of June my medical bills totaled several thousand dollars. I wrote Patty again. "To take care of my health, I've got to hoard every penny for when I can't work. So I can't realistically continue child support. Please understand."

She responded by phone. "Frank," she began, "you've gotten what you deserve. This is the consequence of the lifestyle you chose. It's God's punishment."

"This is the mother of my children?" I thought.

Patty was still talking. "This is just one more way to avoid taking care of the children."

I hung up on her. Then when I called back to apologize, she hung up on me. I called again and quickly said, "Before doing anything, take time to cool off, Patty. We share concerns about the children's future and have to plan for it. I've been thinking about a trust fund that could earn enough interest to replenish itself and pay for their college and beyond."

"That's not a good idea. I'll call when I'm ready to discuss it."

Instead of calling she went to court to garnishee my wages.

This time I knew how to find legal support. An attorney referred by the AIDS Foundation wrote me an ironclad will. My former lawyer in Detroit took my case at no cost. The Legal Aid office accepted my case in the "public interest." Many documents were prepared, specifying how many hours I'd been ill and what my medical bills were, doctor by doctor, month by month. Then I became too weak to work and it was a moot point.

"Let it go, Frank," my lawyer said. "There's nothing more she can do. You'll never owe her another penny."

"But what if AZT works for me?"

He smiled. "Frank, she tried to get you when you were dying. She'll probably sue you for surviving. We'll fight that battle when it comes. I'll be here for you."

It's been eight months now since I let the children off at their front door. Since then I've received one note from Peggy saying, "Thank you for my graduation present" and a Christmas card with no return address signed, "Sincerely, Peggy and Jeff." Not a call, not a card, not a message, not a peep.

Afraid to be hurt I've written them only twice. No more fights for me. I've run out of time and energy and purpose. There's no room left for any more tears. May my children realize some day that they are truly richer because I was their father, because I am their father, because I will always be their father!

I love you, Jeff and Peggy. My blessings on you always.

❧　　❧　　❧　　❧　　❧

Three months later Frank's parents, brothers, sister, lover, and friends gathered on Chesapeake Bay to celebrate Frank's life, which ended peacefully in a small AIDS hospice. A picture of Peggy, sent a month earlier, stood on his bedside table next to a letter he had just received from Jeff. It read, "I love you. You're always in my prayers."

Balancing Children's And Parent's Issues

L ittle information is available on how parents can help children understand homosexuality and cope with homophobia. The hope is that the children will continue to think of their gay, lesbian or bisexual parent as the same person who loves and cares for them. With this basic understanding, it will be easier for them to learn how to handle homophobic encounters constructively. The challenge is how to guide them so that gay-related stress becomes grist for growth rather than trauma. In bridging the gay and straight worlds for the children, the straight parent often assumes the major burden, particularly if the gay parent has left the family circle.

Recent media accounts like the documentary, *Not All Parents Are Straight*,[1] suggest that most children of gay and lesbian parents don't feel that having a homosexual parent is a negative factor in their lives. Yet the children and parents interviewed in such presentations are not representative of the whole spectrum. In many cases children experience serious problems ranging from negative psychological and physical reactions to a parent's coming out or separation from the family to the other extreme of resentment towards the straight parent for pressuring them to take sides against the gay parent.

The following concerns appear to be common among children whose parents come out: insecurity because of the parent's "difference" and resultant disruption of the family; confusion about their own sexuality because of the parent's sexual orientation; discomfort with stereotypical mannerisms or the non-conventional lifestyle of the parent; lowered self-esteem from the prejudiced reactions or ridicule of peers; and conflicting loyalty to the parents because of polarized gay-or-straight attitudes in the community.

While there is significant literature about children of gay, lesbian and bisexual parents such as the 1986 study of post-adolescent children's recollections of coming to terms with their parents' homosexuality or bisexuality by psychotherapist Jay P. Paul, Ph.D.,[2] as well as *Homosexuality and the Family* by professor Frederick W. Bozett, R.N., D.N.S.,[3] scant reference is made to the pivotal role of the straight parent in helping the children cope with the crisis.

Without clear guidelines, helping the children deal with gay-related problems may seem daunting, especially to the parent already emotionally overwhelmed. In the coming-out crisis, gay rights are no longer theoretical issues but tangible problems that real families face in an intolerant society.

Parental anxiety can be eased by remembering three axioms: a person's sexual orientation has no bearing on his or her capability as a parent; children's issues are separate from spousal issues and development of a child's healthy self-concept depends upon the love and support of both parents. Keeping these principles in mind can help the straight parent to act in the best interest of the children and to resist the temptation to sever the children's ties to the other parent should the couple relationship become strained or break up.

Five strategies help the straight spouse to be an effective parent and the family to survive the crisis:

• Maintaining the bond to the homosexual or bisexual parent
• Educating the children about homosexuality
• Helping the children cope with homophobia
• Practicing open parent-child communication
• Resolving fears about the effects of the coming out on children

Maintaining the Bond to the Homosexual or Bisexual Parent

The straight parent's attitude toward the partner is a key factor in how the children will accept the gay parent's orientation and in many cases, departure. Keeping the child-parent bond alive is essential for the children's development of self-concept and confidence. This first strategy calls for reaffirming the role of the gay or lesbian parent and the two-parent family unit.

Whether or not the partner is physically present, he or she needs to be seen as a continuing part of the family. Without the support of both parents children often don't feel valued, as illustrated in "Dad's Girl and Mom's Boy." Peter's departure made Courtney, who felt close only to her father, feel as though she had neither parent left. She then became a "model child," believing that perfect behavior was the only way to keep both parents from abandoning her. Finally she collapsed.

Separation or divorce usually compounds the sense of uncertainty from the non-straight parent. Courtney's brother Nicolas was never close to Peter and developed more severe psychological problems when Peter moved out. It therefore becomes even more crucial for gay parents to take an active role in their children's lives to compensate for their absence.

To minimize the separation crisis, communication lines between the gay or lesbian parent and the children need to be kept open. If a healthy parent-child rapport is not already established, the parents may consider family counseling to develop it.

It is crucial that the spouse avoid the temptation of using the children as pawns in conflicts with the partner. Hearing harmful comments about the other parent however factual they may be weakens the children's confidence in and link to the gay parent. To avoid such possibilities and to reassure Heather of her mother's love, Grant wrote her a "Birth Day" letter. Sorrow and pain can be expressed without faulting the gay parent in statements like, "I feel sad about what's happening."

This doesn't mean that the gay parent should be idealized or excused for wrongdoings by virtue of being a member of an oppressed group. It is helpful to remember that the coming out doesn't change his or her moral character.

Nor does the coming out change the gay parent's family responsibilities, often neglected in the stress of the transition. If any neglect, undue criticism, overindulgence, or denial of children's rights is noted, the spouse may need to point out the harmful effects on the children. Of course this applies to the straight parent's behavior as well.

If there is evidence of harm done by either parent, action has to be taken immediately even at the risk of severing child-parent ties. In such cases, it should be made clear that the purpose is solely to protect the child from the dangerous behavior and has nothing to do with the sexual orientation of the abusive parent.

Some spouses, believing that the partner's homosexuality is immoral, exclude the partner from the children's lives. While spouses have a right to their own moral and religious beliefs, keeping the children away from the other parent deprives them of the two-parent support needed to cope with the separation as well as the coming out. For example, when Patty used Frank's AIDS diagnosis as confirmation of his supposed immoral behavior, the children's communication with him stopped. Consequently their separation trauma was never completely healed.

Despite such obstacles children can maintain a connection to an outcast parent in memory and love. In the end Peggy and Jeff did contact Frank. How much richer their lives could have been if they had been allowed to enjoy continual face-to-face contact with their father. In contrast a nine year old in Atlanta was with his father as he died of AIDS, designed a square for the AIDS quilt and organized a memorial dinner for his father's closest friends, all because the mother, although angry about the coming out, kept the father-son contact alive.

Interaction with the partner's relatives helps validate the parent-child bond. It is crucial that children know their roots on both sides of the family. However awkward it may feel, the straight parent should try to stay in touch with in-laws for the children's sake. In turn relatives need to continue calling and visiting as always just as Karen's mother did.

Children may experience a division of loyalties between the parents as a result of outside social pressure. Children in conservative communities, out of a need to conform, may view the homosexual or bisexual parent as the bad guy and the straight parent as the good guy. In progressive communities, on the other hand, the non-straight parent might be seen as the underdog deserving sympathy and the straight parent become the oppressor.

Facing such conflicts, children may feel pressure to choose one parent over the other. Most youngsters do not want to take sides and many become so determined to stay neutral that they repress tension building up inside. Their conflict is heightened if the parents separate, especially if one begins to lead a gay lifestyle. Both parents can help alleviate their children's turmoil by reassuring them of their love and by explaining that the child's doing something special for one parent won't put down the other. No sides have to be drawn.

The task of preserving the parent-child bond and reassuring the children of joint-parent love is ongoing. Teaching them about homosexuality and helping them resolve concerns related to it is an essential part of this process.

Educating the Children About Homosexuality

Most professionals advise that children be told about the parent's coming out, especially if he or she leaves the family or begins an active gay lifestyle. However, if the gay parent lives at home, his or her gayness is well hidden from public view and it doesn't significantly alter the family relationship, the decision may be not to tell the children. This is risky since the children may be told by someone else in negative, stereotypical terms and suffer hurt from the parents' deception.

Children who aren't told may suspect but feel uncomfortable about bringing it up. "Adults can seek answers when they wonder about such things. Children need help," a mother in Denver commented. Many are afraid to seek the truth and remain in ignorance, feeling increasing stress. Some take desperate steps to end their pain. A nine year old in

Ohio, for example, confused over why his bisexual father lived else-where, asked for a gun at a family gathering to kill himself. Such pain can be avoided through open family communication.

It is crucial that three messages are communicated when telling children. First, homosexuality is a normal, though not common, sexual variation. It is neither a disorder, a sickness nor a perversion, as they may hear from others out of ignorance. Second, the partner's sexual orientation in no way affects his or her ties to the children. Mom or Dad is still the same parent. Third, the children aren't to blame for their parents' marital problems.

How the parents tell the children affects how well they accept the news. The most effective way is for parents to tell them jointly to demonstrate a shared concern for the children's well-being. For example, Allison sat by Peter when he told the children. This showed their united concern and reinforced the sense of family stability. The underlying message needs to be, "Our love for you hasn't changed. We're still your parents."

If the partner wants to tell the children alone, it is critical that the spouse know when and how it is done. If the children still have questions afterwards, the partner needs to be urged to talk again with them. If he or she doesn't cooperate, the task falls to the straight parent, a less desirable option because the information is secondhand.

If the partner tells only some of the children, arrangements need to be made to tell the others to avoid hurt feelings. It is critical that they be included in this pivotal event of their parents' lives so that they know they are a valued family member.

Once they are told, the partner may want the secret kept in the family. If the children ask, "If Daddy (or Mommy) is okay, why can't I tell anyone?" an effective reply is, "Yes, it isn't bad to be gay, but everyone doesn't understand that."

What the parents tell the children needs to be appropriate to their age-related stage of emotional, intellectual and social development. Since infants, for example, primarily understand loving attention and its opposite, anger, parents need to bury animosity when the baby is present. This is what Grant did.

Many parents with preschool children are ambivalent about telling them. On the one hand, they fear that the children might babble the secret to neighbors and playmates. On the other hand, they want to prepare the youngsters for possible taunting should the word get out. Fortunately at that age what the parent says is gospel, so children will discredit what friends or neighbors say that differs from what they've been told by their parents.

The most effective and reassuring explanation for preschoolers is a simple, brief statement that they can understand and remember. A young couple in New York, for instance, told their little girls, "Daddy likes men, but he and Mommy still love each other." Although preschoolers engage in genital exploration, they have no conception of sexuality, much less homosexuality. The implications of having a homosexual parent are beyond them. They can understand love however.

For children from five to twelve years old, more facts and explicit reassurance are needed. As Patty and Frank put it, "We don't love each other the way we did, but we'll always love you." If the partner has a lover, parents may want to add that he or she now loves someone else. Most important the children need to know that their daily lives will remain the same, especially if the parents are separating. Peter reassured the children after saying that he was leaving to be with Tom, "You'll remain in our house and go to your school." Preserving some semblance of structure helps compensate for the disruption of the family.

Innocent of prejudices, the five-to-eight year olds in this age group typically accept the gayness as a matter of fact. To them love between two people is normal regardless of age or sex. Yet their acceptance may be deceptive. Many later act out feelings not understood at the time, especially in the case of divorce.

A parent's departure is especially disruptive for the nine-to-ten year olds, who may experience reactions to divorce as intense as that of teenagers, according to the landmark study of children of divorce by Judith Wallerstein, Ph.D., director of the Center for the Family in Transition.[4]

Adolescents need special consideration in the coming out since they have the most complex needs. They require both information about the parent's homosexuality or bisexuality and guidance to assimilate it into their own growing awareness of sexuality. At the same time they sorely need reassurance of family security to cushion the insecurities of their growing independence.

Adolescents are the most likely of all age groups to have negative reactions about a parent's homosexuality even if it was revealed years earlier. In part discomfort comes from regarding either parent as a sexual being. As Jay Paul notes in his study, "It's less that they are bi/homosexual than that they are capable of having sex at all."[5] However, the teenager's adjustment to divorced parents' dating or remarrying is intensified by the gay parent's unconventional sexual behavior. This helps explain why Frank's daughter objected so strongly to his attending her graduation.

The negative reactions of peers, along with prevalent social stereotypes about homosexuals, compound teenagers' turmoil. When film maker Kevin White was in his teens, he felt isolated when his father came out, followed seven years later by his mother. Now married, he can't forget "the pressure of having other people question my sexuality."[6]

"How can my parent fit such a derogatory image? Could I be gay too?" are typical questions that plague many adolescents in the coming-out crisis. By learning about the variations of sexual orientation and behavior, some of their anguish and worry will be relieved. Parents can provide them with factual information about homosexuality and offer frequent opportunities for discussion. Paul's respondents whose parents discussed sexuality with them, compared to those whose parents didn't, seemed to be better able to "recognize cultural myths and prejudices about sexuality...and to be better equipped to handle them...with peers and others."[7]

Adult children, like preschoolers, tend to react to their parents' homosexuality matter-of-factly. Since most adult children have established their sexual independence and identity, they do not feel as threatened by the coming out.

However, they need sufficient information and support in order to reconcile feelings about their parents' homosexuality and to continue to accept them as adult role models. In particular they need to understand how important it is to clarify their own sexual orientation before contemplating marriage. They also should be prepared to explain their parents' homosexuality to prospective marriage partners who might be uneasy about joining a family with a gay, lesbian or bisexual member. It should be pointed out that children of gay parents have no more chance of being gay than children of straight parents.

As children grow older their needs become more complex. It is advised therefore that parents keep abreast of current facts about homosexuality and AIDS. It is useful to have factual literature available like the AIDS handbook Frank brought along in anticipation of Jeff's and Peggy's questions. Materials can be attained from bookstores, libraries, public health departments, universities, and gay and lesbian organizations.

Unlearning homosexual prejudice, a paramount factor in educating the children about homosexuality, isn't difficult if the family already values individual differences. If they do not, it is important that the family together learn to accept homosexuals and bisexuals as ordinary human beings with the same feelings and concerns as heterosexuals. They can educate themselves about homosexuality through factual information, the example of the straight parent and continued association with the gay parent. Eventually the children will know to ignore misleading labels and judge others based on individual character. It may help to reinforce the message that it's okay to be gay, although it's difficult to lead a gay life because of discriminatory attitudes in society.

Helping the Children Cope with Homophobia

No one can predict if, how or when a child will encounter homophobic reactions in the community. He or she may blurt out a problem during dinner or come home in tears because of a classmate's teasing. Often it's hard to determine whether the children's emotional problems are caused by the parent's sexual orientation or just ordinary growing pains. Since children will very likely experience traumatic incidents due to pervasive anti-gay attitudes in society, it is important for parents to be prepared to help them cope. This is the third strategy in handling children's issues.

Children's problems related to homophobia arise from three major sources: the homosexual parent's stereotypical mannerisms or non-conventional lifestyle; ridicule or rejection from peers; anti-gay attitudes in the community.

Some children are embarrassed by their parents' "gay" mannerisms or intimate behavior toward someone of the same sex. This is more likely for children whose parent lives a gay or lesbian lifestyle elsewhere. Courtney, for instance, was bothered by Peter's flamboyant gestures when he drank during her visits. Another young girl in New York recalled being upset when she glimpsed her mother and female lover nude together in the bedroom.

While it's important to maintain the children's contact with the homosexual parent, many straight parents feel that exposure to an unconventional lifestyle may be stressful for young persons, especially adolescents who are sexually sensitive and confused. Although adult fears are often worse than children's actual reactions, it may be best to minimize the possibility of children's discomfort until they become accustomed to the idea that the gay parent no longer fits the conventional image of a father, mother or adult in general. The parents can negotiate appropriate limits of exposure for the children and the gay parent may want to exercise discretion when interacting with the lover in front of them.

This doesn't mean forbidding the children from seeing spontaneous affection between the gay parent and lover. Difficult as it may be for the straight spouse to contemplate the partner and his or her lover acting openly in front of the children, it is healthier for children to witness a loving, supportive relationship between a same-sex couple than hostility between a heterosexual couple. Over time many spouses become more comfortable with the children's contact with the gay couple.

Ridicule for having a gay or lesbian parent, the second source of children's discomfort, usually occurs at school age when children are prey to classmates' name-calling. Taunting, however brief, is traumatic. When one boy blurted out that Nicolas' father was gay it caused him to fear abandonment by all of his friends.

Since children are vulnerable to assaults on their own and their parents' identities, they need reassurance about themselves and the gay parent. Parents can teach them not to take other people's teasing personally. It should be pointed out that others often don't understand what gay means and that the gay parent is still the same person as before. This knowledge will help them to not be ashamed of the gay parent's orientation and to not feel a conflict of loyalty between their peers and family.

Peer rejection can be used to the children's advantage as an opportunity for them to learn about the cowardice behind name-calling and to find out who their true friends are. Nicolas learned this when he returned to school and heard no more about the traumatic incident. It was the name-caller's problem as his mother had said. Dealing with teasing also helps many children learn to recognize valuable traits in friends such as trustworthiness and acceptance. [8]

A third source of discomfort for children comes from intolerance in the community. Children of gay parents who maintain a high public visibility are more likely to encounter anti-gay reactions from peers and others. It's one thing to attend a baseball game with a gay parent but quite another to have a mother appear in the newspaper as openly lesbian. This concern applies equally to straight parents who are openly involved in gay-related events, such as working a booth at a Gay Freedom Day event.

When contemplating "going public," parents need to decide if they are willing to allow their children to be stigmatized for something that isn't their issue. Many conclude that it isn't worth the risk of causing their children suffering, such as taunting from their friends. One such mother remarked, "A child's self-concept isn't an appropriate battleground for a parent's fight with society, however legitimate it is."

Children are more likely to be hurt by involvement in gay or lesbian events in conservative or rural areas where homosexuality and bisexuality are not widely accepted. In such communities gay parents often risk losing their jobs or arrest if their homosexuality is discovered. If such a threat becomes a reality, the children's welfare needs to be considered first when determining what to do. For instance, when a married peace officer in a farming town was accused of sodomy, the family moved quickly to a progressive city in the East to protect their children from the traumatic publicity that had already sent their reputation plummeting.

Decisions about children's involvement in gay events need to be based on the individual child as well as other factors such as community attitudes. Being seen as part of a minority group in a controversial social, moral or political realm can strengthen some children and unsettle more sensitive youngsters. Under some circumstances possible loss of self-esteem may be too high a risk for some children. In other instances reinforcing the child's acceptance and understanding of minority groups may be an overriding benefit.

Parents often disagree about their children's involvement in public gay events. On the one hand participation in such celebrations enables children to see people outside of their families accepting and respecting gays and lesbians. This is a very effective way for them to discover the range of homosexual persons and to break down their prejudices so that feelings about their own parents can be resolved. It is also a safe way for children to learn how to deal with homophobic reactions with parents and other children at their side.

On the other hand the straight parent may not want the children to march in a gay pride parade in the city, fearing possible harm if they are seen on the evening news by schoolmates or neighbors.

The gay parent may object, saying that the spouse is using the children as an excuse not to stand up for gay rights.

An effective reply is, "I support you in this but feel that it's more important right now that our children endorse you as a parent than the gay cause that might hurt them." Parents can compromise by finding low-risk ways to involve the children in the gay parent's life, such as Gay Fathers picnics.

The task of helping children cope with homophobia may seem overwhelming initially, but can be managed if one incident is handled at a time with trust in the children's resilience and creativity. Assistance is readily available from friends, family and community resources, such as the children's teachers, counselors, clergymen, parenting workshops and parent support groups.

Practicing Open Parent-Child Communication

How well the children cope with the coming out depends largely on the parents' receptivity to their feelings and concerns. Children who feel that they are listened to have higher self-worth. Those who aren't heard, feel inadequate and guilty and have trouble expressing their feelings. Communication with parents is especially important for sons who tend to have more difficulty accepting a parent's gayness than daughters.[9]

Parents need to make sure that they listen carefully not only to what their children say, but to what they don't say. This kind of listening requires what M. Scott Peck defines as "the work of attention."[10] This involves "bracketing" concerns about oneself in order to concentrate totally on what the child is saying and the feelings being communicated. Parents who don't feel open by nature can practice listening with a friend or family member. One helpful technique in effective listening is to rephrase what the other person has said to clarify meaning and to show understanding. Parents can also practice being open with each other to model the kind of openness they desire for the children.

It is critical that both parents set aside a "children's hour," time available for talking and listening. Even ten minutes a day will do. Since most children tend to confide more in their mothers than fathers, gay and straight fathers alike may need to make a greater effort to develop a rapport with them. This is particularly important for separated or divorced fathers of sons, who desperately need the reassurance of a father figure.

If children resist discussing feelings, it's helpful to talk about non-threatening topics such as their everyday activities and interests. They may need confirmation that their feelings and thoughts are valued before they dare to express sensitive concerns. Observing their parents discuss feelings openly may motivate them to do the same.

Signs of trouble like Nicolas giving away his mementoes need to be explored. If the child doesn't open up the parent can ask, "Is there something you want to talk about?" If done in a caring spirit, such questioning won't be construed as pressure or interference.

Parents may want to alert teachers to the changes taking place at home, even if the specific circumstances are withheld. Teachers can note behavior changes that may require professional counseling.

Expressing gentle concerns doesn't always guarantee that a child's pain won't remain repressed and become self-destructive. Each child has unique feelings and a different level of tolerance. Seven years after his father came out, an eleven year old in Texas tried to commit suicide. His psychiatrist explained that this happened partly because the family never expressed their hurt and confusion over the coming-out crisis. The most sensitive member, through his actions, did it for them. Children often take on the role of drawing attention to unresolved family conflicts.

Children may be more willing to talk with brothers and sisters than parents, especially when coping with peer prejudices. Other sources of support include a trusted relative, a knowledgeable therapist or other children of gay parents, singly or in support groups. Gay Fathers or similar groups of the Gay and Lesbian Parents Coalition often have children's groups.

If a child needs counseling it's important to screen therapists or support group leaders for sensitivity to both sides of the closet. Some mothers report that because of a leader's exclusive experience with the gay side of the issue, their children have blamed them for being homophobic or causing their father's stress.

Keeping the two-way communication going can help prevent children's problems from reaching a crisis point as well as encourage the development of their coping skills.

Resolving Fears About the Effects of the Coming Out on Children

As immediate children's problems are resolved, the spouse's fears about long-term implications of the coming out on the children can be resolved. This is the last strategy of this stage of recovery.

Many parents worry about how the coming out will affect the children, especially in the initial months. Factual information and counseling can disperse what otherwise might become a debilitating obsession. For example, mothers who become paranoid about their children kissing an HIV-positive father or using his water glass need only to review the facts on how the virus is transmitted to realize that their fears are unfounded.

Another common fear, even among spouses who appreciate the importance of coming out and know that sexual orientation isn't hereditary, is that one of the children will turn out to be gay. Sociologist Terry Arendell, Ph.D., points out a related misconception that children of single mothers may develop homosexuality.[11] There is of course no factual basis for these myths. Having a gay parent only widens children's awareness of the range of sexual orientations possible, according to Paul's study.[12]

In the rare case that a child is also gay and comes out, there is a repeated sequence of shattered expectations, shock and disbelief. The straight parent often feels as if yet another family member is now "lost" to a world separate from hers or his. But this time the major difference is that the child isn't a husband or wife. His or her sexual orientation isn't bound up in marital vows and the spouse's sexuality and therefore doesn't injure anyone else.

Yet the stigma of being homosexual is bound to hurt the child. The straight parent may feel resentment toward the gay parent for modeling the behavior. Or others may blame themselves for having accepted the partner's homosexuality so openly.

This crisis too can be overcome with the support of friends, appropriate counseling, development of healthy relationships with straight men and the inner work suggested in the last three parts of this book. A professional woman in Chicago whose son died of AIDS two years after the death of her husband from AIDS, eventually resumed a productive life and remarried.

Another concern is that the children may repeat the parent's pattern and gravitate toward a mixed-orientation marriage. As a bisexual man's daughter divorced from a bisexual man said, "Like children of alcoholics who marry alcoholics, a bisexual man was what I knew and understood best."[13]

While it can't be determined in advance how the children's lives will be affected by the coming out, parents can help them avoid much hurt by explaining the importance of being clear about their own sexual orientation in creating a healthy marital relationship. Children whose marriages are based on honesty will have greater promise of success than their parents. If a homosexual orientation is discovered in the child's marriage, parents can point out that they will have a better chance of working it out if the gay partner comes out immediately.

The effect that separation or divorce will have on the children is perhaps the biggest source of worry for parents. One of the strongest motives for keeping the family together is the children's need for security. This concern is valid since children in any divorce situation suffer insecurity and pain, according to Judith Wallerstein's ten-year follow-up study of divorced couples and their children, *Second Chances*.[14] Several children of spouses studied for this book still have physical ailments such as ulcers, resulting from their parents' departures more than ten years earlier.

Whether or not the effects of divorce are intensified by a parent's coming out has not yet been substantiated. Yet a sizeable minority of the children in Paul's study felt that learning about the parent's sexual orientation was more stressful than the divorce.[15]

Although parents can't insulate the children from the painful effects of divorce, they can give them the gift of how to cope constructively with such upsets of life. They can also minimize their children's distress by maintaining two-parent support.

Coping with parental concerns on top of spousal problems eventually takes its toll on the straight spouse. "Parenthood isn't easy under any circumstances," a mother in Phoenix remarked, "but with the gay issue, it's twice as hard."

Within the first year or two of the coming out, the triple burden of damaged sexuality, shattered marriage and parent-spouse conflicts becomes unbearable for most spouses. Exhausted from helping everyone else, many wonder, "What about me?" How two wives and a husband answered this question is portrayed in part four, which explores the crisis of lost identity and ways to regain a strong, authentic sense of self.

four

WHAT ABOUT ME?

IDENTITY CRISIS OF THE STRAIGHT SPOUSE

Many spouses are startled to discover that in the process of accommodating to their partner's coming out they have lost their sense of identity. Most have had little time or energy to notice how they have been personally affected because of the demands to adjust to their partner's new identity and changed behavior, make the marriage work or cope with separation and divorce and care for the children's needs. Typically by the second year after the coming out, exhaustion forces spouses to attend to what little is left of themselves. The identity crisis that they then experience is the fourth hurdle of their recovery process.

When spouses finally take a realistic look at themselves, they may not recognize what they see. Often body, mind and emotions are depleted or numbed with addictions to alcohol, caffeine, cigarettes or food. Many experience an overwhelming feeling of helplessness and feel abandoned by their partners. They feel devalued as people.

When the pain can no longer be tolerated, many spouses begin to ask, "Who am I?" The resulting quest for identity is the major turning point of the straight spouse's struggle. The journey is arduous but offers the promise of lasting renewal. Though support from others is needed, the spouse ultimately has to rely on her or himself alone. Even support groups for straight spouses which are invaluable at first may begin to seem counterproductive as the spouse's individual problems diverge from those common to spousal issues.

As the spouse searches for traces of her or his former self, buried passions and interests may be uncovered. Eventually, through self-exploration, the authentic "I" can be recaptured—an individual in her or his own right, no longer defined in relation to the partner.

The stories that follow portray different ways of coping with the identity crisis as experienced by two wives and a husband during or after their marriages. The concluding section examines the issue of shattered identity and outlines effective strategies to help the spouse reconstruct independent selfhood.

Personal Stories

On Trial
Catherine

The first sacrifice was to forego a marriage license. Larry, a radical liberal, opposed all institutions, particularly Christianity. A tall, gangly man, he was brilliant. I was tiny but full of energy.

We became friends in high school. He dropped out of college junior year to become a potter. While I majored in history and earned a teaching credential at the university, he made beautiful things out of clay. Although he'd said he was gay when we met, he took me out whenever I was home in Bloomington, Indiana. After graduation I taught school there. Eventually I left the job to live with him in the rustic bungalow his mother had bought for us near West Baden Springs to the south. The first year Emily was born and then William two years later.

Larry was so antisocial, he never had affairs with men. Yet his gayness colored how I approached our living together. "I'll work it out," I decided, "with whatever sacrifice is necessary."

Before long Larry's antisocial stance extended to his mother, who then terminated financial support. I was painting and making jewelry by then. Together we built up a solid reputation in the arts and crafts fair circuit.

Under Larry's strict direction, I did most of the leg work for these productions. He handled the creative aspects. With our proceeds we collected Oriental rugs and Indian crafts to add to the artifacts from my history studies. While I kept our accounts, Larry kept the house swept and tidy and cooked exotic meals. Sharing so many interests with him made me feel valued.

It was a busy, satisfying life most of the time except for Larry's streaks of violence. On one occasion he tied up our cat in a bag and threw it out of the house. The kids and I took it to the vet without letting on what had happened.

When William was five and Emily was seven, Larry told them he was gay and began to show them his pornographic gay literature. Sometimes when William was watching TV, he would run into Larry's workshop to say, "Come see the good parts of the movie." When I peeked in to see what was so good, it was men's bodies.

Then one day while Larry and I were working in the studio-living room, he suddenly said, "If only you were a man, Catherine, you'd be perfect." This was the first of many such remarks, each one further shattering my sense of self-worth.

Larry was unhappy about himself too because he hadn't had many gay relationships. Since he avoided social occasions, there were few chances to meet men at all. Whenever he did meet one he'd say, "Not for me. Nobody's good enough. I want someone who doesn't look gay and likes Indian culture like me."

His hopes went up when he met Stu, a handsome, intelligent, radical "straight," who agreed to sleep with him. Stu enjoyed sex with Larry—and with me. We three had a grand time together until one day Stu told Larry, "I'm not going to sleep with you any longer. What do I get out of it?"

Stu's departure put Larry over the edge. After that everyone was either pro-Larry or "the enemy." If you were Stu's friend, you were automatically in the latter group. Larry began creating straw men of all kinds.

Stu remained a close friend of mine. So did our neighbor, Louise, a practicing Christian. I therefore became the enemy and Larry moved out, suing for divorce.

Our common law marriage complicated the divorce process. I couldn't afford a lawyer since I was teaching without pay at a private school, so that the kids could attend tuition-free. So my mother, though preparing to go to Europe with my aunt, dipped into her reserve to lend me money.

At the first deposition for the divorce, the judge said we could sell the house even though it was in Larry's mother's name.

We decided to put it on the market once Larry's things were out. I suggested that he take the furniture, his rugs and the exotic spices he used for cooking. He took his clays, glazes and kiln equipment but left the other things behind.

"He must have forgotten," I thought, putting them in his workshop to pick up later.

He came by the following week while I was at work and put everything in the workshop back onto the porch. Discovering the pile there that night, I put it all back in his workshop. The next week he returned the stuff to the porch. This happened over and over until I finally gave up.

Louise said, "Stop taking care of Larry and take care of yourself."

I wondered how that was possible now that the house was on the market. The morning of my mother's departure for Europe, she called atwitter. "Auntie's ill and can't go. Pack your things and meet me at the airport at two-thirty."

A vacation sounded wonderful though I feared Larry would break in and take things in my absence. Louise, elated for me, offered to keep an eye on the house and take care of the kids.

When I called Larry about the trip, he said, "Give the keys to the realtor to show the house while you're gone."

"No. Not with my jewels here for my current project."

"Oh, I'll tell her to watch the people she shows it to."

"O.K.," I said and hung up, having to pack in a hurry. There were less than four hours to get to the airport, a two-hour drive away. In my rush I left the breakfast dishes in the sink.

Three weeks later when I returned, regenerated by my experiences in Paris, Florence and Madrid, I went straight to Louise's. "How did things go?"

"Not good. Not good. Have some coffee while I tell you."

In my absence Larry had borrowed the key from the realtor, telling her it was for a termite inspection. Instead he photographed the dirty dishes in the sink, the newspapers piled up for building fires, a dead mouse in the yard, cat excrement from somewhere and the piles of bric-a-brac in the living room that allowed us space for our craft work. No pictures were taken of eight-year-old Emily's room which was spotless.

Larry then took the photos to the divorce judge to ask for custody of the children because of the filthy house. Showing him the picture of cat excrement, Larry said, "This was in my daughter's room, but there's lots all over the house."

"If it's that bad," said the judge, "I give you temporary custody." The decision stated, "Catherine is an unfit mother."

The night of my return, Louise and I cleaned up the house in two hours. I photographed it the next day, then took the pictures to court and asked for another hearing.

At the preliminary hearing, two teachers, both gay men who had visited our house, spoke as witnesses. "The previous report is not true," each of them confirmed.

The following day a court-appointed probation officer inspected the house. At the hearing four days later, he stated, "The house was fine."

Larry spoke up. "Did you look into the cereal box? Emily discovered worms in it."

The judge ruled in my favor.

A week later we met with our divorce lawyers, who told us to divide our assets including the fifteen-year-old Indian collection worth about $30,000 and $35,000 earned from fairs.

"Well, the collection's mine," Larry said on the way home. "You can have an Oriental rug, a Hopi carving and some jewelry."

"And you'll have twenty-five rugs and thirteen carvings? What about my Indian things?"

Larry agreed to have a mediator help us divide our collection. When we entered the house with the man, Larry cried, "Open the window. I can't stand the stench."

Neither the mediator nor I smelled a thing.

The divorce trial took place several weeks later. Larry's theme was, "Catherine's a liar. She steps in and out of reality." As proof, he and his lawyer recounted false stories about what I'd done.

The judge believed both men. He was a narcoleptic with a heart problem. For most of the trial his eyes were closed.

When it was over, the judge delayed deciding the custody issue, while my lawyer tried to have him removed from the case. In July he made his decision. Larry was to have all of the money from the fairs, the craft tools, the Indian collection and all but two of the Oriental rugs.

By then I was seeing a psychologist. My mother and aunt lent me money to continue seeing him and to hire my lawyer to fight for joint custody.

When the psychologist heard that I wanted joint custody, he asked, "Are you willing to sacrifice your own happiness to keep the family together?"

"Oh, yes."

In August Larry called to say that he'd rented a house in South Carolina and wanted full custody. That required a court order, for which the four of us had to see a psychiatrist in separate interviews.

After the psychiatrist had met with all of us, he reported, "Emily talks as if she's thirty-five. Larry is manipulative and proscribes others." Nothing negative was said about me or William.

At the custody hearing the testimony sounded like a classic case from *Mothers on Trial*. When the psychiatrist took the stand, I held my breath. He repeated his judgments about Larry but made no recommendations.

After the trial Emily asked, "Who won?"

"It was fifty-fifty."

"Oh. I wanted Daddy because of the mean things you do."

I gasped, not having suspected brainwashing.

That night she wet her bed and came into my bedroom. "It's too cold in my room. Can I sleep with you?"

"Of course."

She crawled in, hugged me and fell asleep, her arms around me all night long. Over the following weeks this happened repeatedly, especially when she had nightmares.

A few months later after a weekend with Larry, Emily complained of bleeding in her crotch. I called Larry to find out what had happened.

"Oh," he said, "she fell on the jungle gym."

When our doctor examined her, Emily said she didn't remember what had happened. While she dressed, the doctor whispered to me, "I can't say anything about sexual abuse without her testimony."

Emily didn't remember the way it was before Larry left either. William recalled the violence. "Remember when Daddy threw out the cat?" he said one afternoon as we sat on the porch. He also reminded me of the time Larry wanted the dog killed. William seemed neutral about his father's behavior. He wasn't brainwashed one way or the other.

Emily saw it differently. To accept her father, she had to agree with his entire world view. An unspoken theme lay under every reference she made to him: "Daddy needs William and me to make it all right. If I don't do what he wants, he'll die."

One afternoon that spring, I came home from marketing to find the house empty. The kids weren't at Louise's or with friends. They didn't come home that night or the next day. The third day, having traced down Larry's post office box number in South Carolina, I drove there without stopping, straight to the post office parking lot and waited for him to come pick up his mail. In two hours, up came his van with Emily and William in the front seat.

I reported this to the police and the next day they cornered Larry when he arrived for the mail, charged him with kidnapping and brought the children back to me temporarily while the court decided what to do.

Again the narcoleptic judge delayed a decision. Larry's lawyer, his personal psychologist who was gay, and the court psychologist, a lesbian, kept stating that I didn't want Larry to have the kids because of his homosexuality. The psychologist recommended that Larry have either shared or full custody.

As legal proceedings dragged on, all but seven friends backed away from supporting me. Stu and Larry's brother stayed close by me, his brother at the risk of losing his inheritance since his mother was again supporting Larry. The five other close friends were women: Louise, Larry's brother's wife and three lesbian women from a women's rape organization who helped me work through the legal maze to prove my fitness as a mother.

Each time a crisis arose, I telephoned one or more of these friends to help me think it through and decide what forces to marshal. A minor problem meant one call. When the count went up to seven, I knew the problem was critical.

For months I had no energy even for housework. Toward the end of the year, Louise told me about a teacher's aid job in town paying $6.00 an hour.

"Well," I said, "that's better than lying in bed till noon."

At the interview it came out that I was qualified to teach adult education. On the spot they hired me to teach adults who had never finished high school. The job was low pressure but creative, perfect for my life at that time.

For the next two years, court negotiations over permanent custody continued. Twenty-three people wrote letters on my behalf. At home I learned little by little how to do the household tasks Larry had done except for his magnificent cooking. One night when Louise was over, I reflected, "You know, I'm happier living alone than the times I was happy with Larry! Now I'm an independent person and finally know what I like and who I am."

The third year I made my first foray into a singles bar and discovered that men found me attractive. Then several asked me out.

The first invitation startled me. "What? Someone cares what I think, where I want to go?" By the end of the year, I was dating one man exclusively. I wasn't the frigid woman Larry had made me out to be.

At work there were ever-changing problems that challenged my resourcefulness. "This adult can't read," I'd think with each illiterate student. "How can he or she get the information? What do I do?" Then I'd improvise and the student would always learn to read, no matter what the difficulty.

One day a filing cabinet had to be moved in the office. "You're strong," I told myself. "You can do it." So ninety-eight pound Catherine carried the heavy cabinet while men watched. What they thought didn't bother me because the strength I expected of myself was really there.

After three years of fighting for custody, I was afraid of what would happen to William and Emily if they had to live with Larry.

The more I read about brainwashing children through physical and psychological control, the more I feared. I knew from Larry's past behavior that he would control the children if he had custody.

Slowly it became clear to me what the trial was really about. Had I known in the beginning that joint custody keeps women who are in an abusive situation trapped in it forever, I would never have agreed.

❦   ❦   ❦   ❦   ❦

A year later, against the recommendations of the two gay psychologists, Catherine was awarded full physical and legal custody of the children with visitation rights for Larry. Recommendations from the court-appointed psychiatrist and the children's therapist, testimony from therapists who saw the family over the years, and interviews with Catherine and Larry verified the truth of her story.

That summer Catherine married the man she'd dated for two years. The following year Emily announced that she didn't want to visit her father any more because he had told her and William to hurt Catherine and her new husband and had given them knives and other implements to do so. When the sheriff came to hear Emily's testimony and collect the weapons, William claimed the tools were for gardening, fearing Larry's punishment if the court were to force visitations. The court ruled that there could be no further contact with the father.

Which Road?
Cliff

Problems surfaced after we adopted a three-month-old Salvadoran baby we named Curt. Married eleven years, I was a sales representative for a regional company and Priscilla was a middle manager in public health. We were a good-looking couple, Pris brunette and I sandy-haired. We had similar interests and a large circle of friends, many from our parish in Newton, Massachusetts, though I didn't go to Mass much. I was known for my sense of humor and easygoing nature.

Pris and I had serious talks driving back and forth to visit my mother in Worcester. Pris brought up what she felt was wrong with us, "Cliff, there are some things about women that men can never understand. You're so insensitive to my needs as a woman!"

"That's probably true," I kept saying, "but I can work on it if you'll tell me specifically what you need."

I didn't like how things were going either. Routine was sabotaging the relationship. There weren't the moments of total bliss I wanted. "To make the relationship work, Pris, we have to work on it," was my refrain. "We have an infinite array of options. We've just got to choose what we want and create it."

As the months passed, I began to wonder if Pris was looking elsewhere for the closeness we lacked. "Maybe she's searching among her friends," I thought, knowing she'd felt close to women ever since her friendship with a teacher in high school.

One evening as we drove back from Worcester, I asked, thinking of her work situation, "Have you and Flo ever slept together?"

"Yes," she said, half-wistful, half-bemused, "one rather bungled encounter a couple of years ago."

"Pris, there's no reason why you and I can't create that kind of intimacy. Our relationship could be more positive, but I can't do it by myself."

For two years our discussions went nowhere. My mother kept telling me that we were too involved in our careers to give enough time to each other. But we were both committed to spending as much time as possible with Curt, watching him grow into a little boy. We both adored him.

Just after his second birthday, we started joint counseling. As the sessions progressed over the next two years, Pris talked more and more about being attracted to women.

I told Pris, "We can make our relationship be anything we want. It's just a matter of making a choice."

"No, it isn't, Cliff. We're talking about something about which I really have no choice. I'm lesbian."

Momentarily shocked, I persisted. "I know it's hard to overcome things we're predisposed toward, but we do have a range of options."

On the way home Pris said, "Cliff, I've got to sort out my feelings about women and see where to go from here."

"I understand," I said. "And I've got to find a counselor to help me sort out my feelings."

Over the next few months, I met with a counselor who was gay and knowledgeable about gay-straight marriages and Pris joined a bisexual support group. On Friday and Sunday nights and often all day Sundays, she went to be with bisexual friends while I stayed home with Curt, who was then almost four.

After a month of this, I said to my counselor, "The odds of working it out are practically nonexistent now, but I'm not giving up hope."

A month later Pris announced, "I'm not going to the bisexual group any more."

"Oh?"

"It's for people who are just coming out."

The following month in May, she said, "It's clear, Cliff. I really am gay. We'll have to separate."

"Pris, let's stay under the same roof over the summer," I pleaded. "Things might change."

"Well, all right. It'll be better for Curt that we're together till he starts kindergarten. But things aren't going to change between us."

I continued to see my counselor over the summer. "If it weren't for her being lesbian," I told him, "we could work on the other problems in our relationship. As long as Pris thinks she's gay, she has no choice. My telling her she has one doesn't change how she feels."

By July Pris and I were further apart. I couldn't even rely on my humor any more to get me through. I told my counselor, "Even if she were to decide to stay in the marriage and give up her gayness, there would have to be a dramatic transformation for it to be the relationship I want." I sighed. "The odds for that are unlikely." Then after a long silence, I said what I'd never thought I would, "I give up."

For the rest of the summer, some days I felt depressed about the end of our marriage and what lay ahead. Other days I was "up," planning my future. My greatest worry was how Mother and Curt would react. I didn't want our son to be hurt.

During up times I took women friends out to lunch to determine if they were possible dates. Then very scientifically, I listed all the women whose company I thought I'd enjoy. If they turned out to be married, they could give me referrals. Then I started calling, one by one.

In September Curt started school and I moved into an apartment. Pris and I took turns picking him up at school and sometimes stayed for dinner at each other's place. As we went back and forth, Curt often burst out, "I want us to be together again like a family."

His schedule was floating, with Pris four nights a week and with me three nights including Fridays and Saturdays when she went out. The traumatic times were when I came to get him in the evening from Pris'. When we went out the door, Curt would burst out crying, "I want my Mommy!"

Back at the apartment, he would say, "I hate you. I want my Mommy. You're not my friend. It's not fair."

It was easier when I picked him up from school, especially when Pris came for dinner and then took him home. Those nights Curt would ask me, "Why don't you come over and stay with us?"

All this time Pris hadn't told her colleagues that she was lesbian and asked me not to tell anyone. One night I said to her after dinner while Curt played, "I'm not sure whether or not to tell Mother we've separated. She won't be able to handle the reason why."

"Why tell her? It's not critical."

"Well, she's got to know we're apart at least."

Mother wasn't surprised. "You were too devoted to your careers."

I wanted to say, "That's hogwash" and tell her the real reason. It was strange that someone so important in my life didn't know what I was going through.

Once separated, I set two goals for myself—personal growth and overcoming fear, things I'd always wanted to do. "It's a perfect time," I thought "the end of a stagnating situation."

First I rode the roller coaster at a local fair, the source of long-term fear. Then I decided to do something towards growth every day like exercise or finding a new client.

I also wanted to change how I looked and get back to my previous weight of 167 pounds. My public image worried me because of my job and dating.

From a book on calories, I figured out that I'd have to consume no more than one thousand calories a day to lose a pound every two days.

Each night I wrote out my next day's menu. For three weeks of my life I actually ate three meals a day! Combined with exercise, it was interesting and easy. In that time I lost fifteen pounds. I was three pounds from my goal.

The fourth week I stopped the evening meal and then breakfast. Back to one meal a day, I was eating what I pleased and keeping a constant weight of 174. Then I stopped exercising. I also stopped trying to overcome fear.

Meanwhile I answered personal ads and then placed one.

Forty years old, trim, six feet, zest for life, looking for attractive woman with zest for life."

The first response, "Mail artist, witch, and anarchist," so depressed me that I ripped it up.

The next response was an erotic letter from a psychotherapist. When I called her, she said, "I guess you placed the ad to get laid."

The following day, I went back to answering ads. The next few women I met had the attractiveness and zest for life that I sought. Some of them, hearing my circumstances, commented, "It's amazing you feel positive toward your wife after all she's put you through!"

"Look," I said, "I'm in a position to say my wife acted as honestly as she could. She's a good person and ought to be given credit for that." I felt obliged to stand up for Pris even though it often ended in a minor debate.

"You may feel that way now," several said, "but you've only been separated three months. There's got to be a lot going on inside that will come to the surface."

That ended any interest I had in them. "I don't want to be with someone who tells me I'm not dealing with emotions that aren't there," I thought.

Gradually I set criteria for the kind of woman I wanted. Yet even when I was face-to-face with someone who had none of the traits I wanted, but who found me attractive, I hesitated. I needed a woman so much!

Eventually I slept with one to prove to myself that I could do it. The next day I thought, "This is someone who'd be controlling if the relationship got serious. She isn't much fun either. I'd rather have sex with women I enjoy being with."

So I started dating a woman I had fun with, hoping it would go somewhere. After our third date, when I opened the newspaper to the Personals, there was her ad again. "Have we met?" I jotted on a business card, popped it in an envelope and sent it off with no return address.

After several months I thought, "I'm more likely to meet someone I'd enjoy while going up an elevator rather than from ads. Maybe I should take off an hour and ride elevators."

Midsummer, I felt the need to talk to other men who'd been married to lesbians to get a sense of what might lie ahead. My counselor referred me to the leader of a straight spouse support group, who arranged an evening get-together with two straight ex-husbands in a private home. It helped to know that someone cared about my situation and had been there. One man shared how he and his ex-wife divided up the care of their preschool daughter.

The other gave me tips for placing ads, my most urgent concern. "The more specific I was about myself and what I wanted," he said, "the fewer responses I would get, but the better quality of women I would meet."

A week or so later while talking about my dating search, a woman friend said, "I hope you don't get upset, Cliff, but I have to tell you that you're trying too hard."

So, trying to be more laid back, I reviewed my list of potential dates asking myself about each one, "Do you really want to pursue her or are you desperate?"

Counseling helped me cool down. I learned to say when a woman cancelled, "Give me a call when you want to get together."

One afternoon in Wellesley, I ran into an attractive woman I hadn't seen for two years. As we chatted, I asked, "Children?"

"Yes, fourteen and sixteen."

Noticing she wasn't wearing a wedding ring, I thought, "I'll risk calling her even though the bare finger may mean nothing."

Over lunch we discovered that we were both separated since fall, married seventeen years, and Catholic.

When I didn't hear from her later, I thought, "That's okay."

Soon it was fun just to flirt. One Saturday a younger woman and I went hiking. After an hour she said, "I really don't bite, Cliff."

I laughed. "I don't either, unless of course you ask me to."

By then I'd met three women I thought I'd like to get romantically involved with. One even said, "I'm attracted by your pixy charm"—me at six feet tall!

Dating reached its peak one Sunday when I went out with three different women. After the second I was weary. By Monday it was clear that refocusing was in order. Quantity wasn't what I needed or wanted.

"Well, what is a quality relationship?" I asked myself. "One in which we both agree enthusiastically that it's going in a positive direction!"

The next day I got back on my diet. Then I went to see my counselor. "I've got to start doing positive things for myself again like rope-climbing to overcome fear and drumming up business which I've neglected for three months."

A week later I was all over the Boston area contacting old clients. When I drove away from my last stop Friday night, there were two roads I could take to get home. I chose the less travelled one since it was safer at commute time. Fifteen minutes later someone hit me broadside. My car was totaled.

That was two weeks ago. Though I wasn't responsible, I felt somehow that I'd contributed to the accident by consciously creating the situation which brought me into contact with the other car.

Like my life. I still believe that I can control what happens to me even though I'm confused about which road I'm on and which one will lead to the love of my life. All I know is that the quality of the journey and the final destination will be a result of the choices I've made.

What The Buddha Said
Ling

Sometimes I look at Jack and think, "Why am I still here?" It's been eight years since he said he was gay. There's a lot of love between us—not passion but friendship from living together for twenty years."

It wasn't surprising that Jack married me, a Chinese student in graduate school at a midwestern university where he was a graduate student in religion. The Orient had fascinated him since he was a boy. College was his first chance to meet an Asian person. Most of his friends there were Asians.

He'd had two girlfriends at his rural high school and became engaged in college to a very American girl—blonde, blue-eyed, and beautiful. They didn't have premarital sex because it was sinful and they broke up before graduation. Then he met me.

When we met I thought, "Oh, he's American. That's a barrier between us." As I became acquainted with this tall, blond midwesterner, his interest in Asia and fondness for Asian people impressed me. I felt so comfortable with him that sometimes I completely forgot he was American and chatted away in Chinese.

He'd smile and say, "Ling-Ling, please speak in English."

After a year I felt so close to him on all levels that I said, "Yes," when he proposed.

His folks wanted him to marry the "girl next door." They still lived in the isolated area where he had grown up with only his brother for a playmate. He was the "perfect" son, raised without exposure to outside influences.

My parents too were against us. "You cannot marry an American," they wrote. Then because Jack's letter asking for approval, which I translated, was so sensitive, Father agreed.

Jack didn't want us to have premarital sex. "If you get pregnant and I'm killed in Vietnam," he said, "You'll have a hard time raising a child by yourself."

"This is true love," I thought. "He's the most perfect man I've ever met."

When we married, Jack decided to work for a design firm in Seattle. I couldn't work, lacking training or license for anything in this country.

Our first years I felt happy "until death us do part." We had sex. We went everywhere together. The only problem was Jack's strict morals because of his religious background. We couldn't dance since he felt it was a primitive pattern of intercourse.

"Oh my goodness!" I thought. "He's square!" Though my family had strict morals too, I went to dances as I was growing up. Dancing was considered a beautiful art form in China.

His family also objected to alcohol. Once when his parents were visiting, his mother saw my rice wine with a Chinese label in the refrigerator. Sniffing it, she asked, "What's this! Alcohol?"

Finally I told Jack, "I'm going to use wine in cooking whether or not your parents are opposed."

After that he gave up.

Four years after we married, Lionel was born and we moved to the suburbs. Janice arrived four years later. That same year Jack met a Japanese man and began inviting him to dinner and picnics. Fond of me, Michio became a member of the family. One weekend he and Jack went hiking in the mountains while I stayed with the children. All this time Jack was very loving to me.

Then there was a local fuss about homosexual teachers. Reading the news stories about it, I came across the word, "gay," for the first time although I'd heard of homosexual bars in Taiwan where I grew up. One morning, reading about a petition to dismiss gay teachers on moral charges, I said to Jack, "That's terrible!"

"Society is terrible for persecuting gay people," he replied. Over the next few weeks he talked increasingly about the issue. The more he talked, the more I detected a change in him.

One day a friend was discussing another friend of ours, Walton, with me. "His friendship with Jack seems strange. Maybe they have something going on."

Other things began to come together. One night I asked Jack, "Are you gay?" Though I understood by then why people are gay, I didn't want my husband to be.

His face turned pale and he got tense.

"I'm not against gay people, Jack," I went on. "I'm a very liberal, calm person."

"Then why did you ask?"

"I've got a feeling something is going on."

"Well, if you say so. I think I'm a bisexual."

"Have you had an experience?"

"Yes," he said.

"Then you had homosexual feelings before we married?"

"No, honestly not."

"Well, is it Walton?"

When he said, "No," relief flooded my being. Then after I guessed other men we knew, he said it was Michio.

"You've had a relationship with both him and me for the past four years?"

He nodded, tears rolling down his cheeks. "I couldn't satisfy my sexual needs with you, so I began to explore. It would've threatened you if I'd found a woman lover, so I turned to men. When I discovered my homosexual feelings, I was upset and couldn't believe it. But the more involved I became, the more wonderful it was."

As he told me about dating Michio and going to discos with him, I thought, "Jack—dancing?"

By then Jack was in shock. "Now I've broken up our relationship, Ling, and Michio said he'd stop seeing me if you found out, not wanting to hurt you. That's why I covered up."

The next day when Jack told him, Michio kept his word. "I must stop seeing you."

Then Michio called me. "This is the Asian way. You know that, Ling. Both of us are very Asian and our thinking is the same."

Jack said nothing more about it except that he was unhappy. "If only my gay feelings could be turned off with a switch, I'd go back to being straight."

I was devastated too, but my one thought was, "Poor Jack. I have to help him." I was nonexistent. So I did a funny thing. I went to Michio's apartment and begged him not to break up with Jack.

"No, Ling-Ling! I must stick to what I said."

In August Michio found another partner, but Jack hung onto Michio. When we went to concerts that fall, he hardly paid attention to me or the music. Watching him, I felt pain and anger. "I'm your wife. We came to see the symphony and you're thinking about Michio."

Our relationship deteriorated. Not knowing why, I didn't want sex with him any more. By November Jack became so depressed that he couldn't perform at work, which brought pressure from his boss.

Just after Thanksgiving we gave a party. After the guests left about eleven, Jack called Michio. It was the first time in four years he hadn't been invited to one of our parties. After the call, Jack joined me and my sister, visiting from the city for the weekend, for another glass of wine before going to bed. Twenty minutes after he left us, we heard a loud noise from the bedroom and rushed in there. Jack was on the floor. We shook him but he didn't wake up.

"It's probably the wine," I said.

Since he was too heavy to move, we put a blanket on him where he lay. Then he half rose and we half dragged him to bed.

The next morning, a Saturday, the kids came into the bedroom at five as they always did weekend mornings.

I shook Jack gently. "Let's get up."

"Go ahead without me," he mumbled.

As we started into the kitchen, there was another loud noise. I ran back to the bedroom. Jack was on the floor again, his head bleeding. My sister, now awake, called 911. When the paramedics came, Jack was still drowsy. Once they took his pulse, they called an ambulance.

I stayed next to him all the way to the emergency room. At the hospital the doctors washed out his stomach, assuming he'd over-dosed. By then he was unconscious.

I called Michio immediately. "Maybe he won't wake up. But, if he does, he'll want to see you."

Michio came at once and each of the next three days as Jack lay in a coma. Going home to check on the kids, who were being watched by my sister, I found an empty jar of sleeping pills in the bathroom.

The fourth day Jack came to. Over the next few days, he wrote a poem about wanting "to die for love not for the family."

Reading it when he finished, I thought, "His love for Michio is so strong that he wants to die because he lost him. I'm the wife, but he loves somebody else deeply! It's terrible knowing that it's a man he loves. If Jack wasn't gay and had a woman lover, maybe I'd have the energy and purpose to challenge her."

Once recovered, Jack didn't want to break up the marriage or family but wanted a private life. "If you really love me, Ling," he said, "you'll forgive me and accept the situation without questions."

That meant changing myself to accept his other lifestyle. At home he was still the same person who liked to be with family and close friends. But he never did things for the children's soccer and volley ball teams, never volunteered to help out at school.

In his other gay life, he acted macho. When he went out with a man, I got mad. When I objected, he got bitter.

For a year I talked to other women and counseling groups about how bad I felt about his other life, but it didn't help. After that Jack and I discussed separating but that ended in a fight. Then I just tolerated his double life.

For several years Jack hung onto Michio, even going to New York with him for two weeks. That didn't make me jealous because Michio was like a brother.

When Michio was with us, Jack was extremely good to me. He often said, "The threesome is nice."

The funny thing is that Michio never said he was gay. One day he told me, "I'm interested in a woman and want to get married."

"Please don't, Michio," I said, "for the woman's sake. Don't do that to her. She'd go through what I'm experiencing. Women are human beings, too."

"But that's our tradition. I have to have children."

When Michio found another lover, Jack wanted another gay relationship too, but was afraid of being hurt again. So he went out only on one-night stands.

Some months later with someone from his gay men's organization, Jack joined a support group for men who only wanted tricks. After two meetings they learned that it was a sex addiction not something related to being gay.

"O. K.," I said to Jack, "you're addicted to sex. So find one person. Reduce the chance of AIDS."

He responded with the same argument he always gave me. "You pushed me in this direction, Ling. You weren't interested in being a passionate lover. I wanted a two-way relationship. If you'd been..."

Finally I dropped the subject. After that I never knew where, how, or why he did anything and didn't ask. I survived by praying, "If this is your will, God, give me your strength to get through it. If not, show me a sign and then give me the strength to develop a new life."

My religious beliefs were based on both Christianity and Buddhism from my childhood. Buddhist nirvana is similar to the after-death of Christianity, but in nirvana you don't exist anymore, you just melt into nature. Not wanting to lose my soul to nothingness, I turned to Christianity when I became a teenager.

Though I was frightened by the Buddhist idea of seven bad natures of man which cause misery, it still made sense. Why struggle against suffering that is human nature when eventually there will be nothing anyway?

After four years of struggling with Jack's other life, I felt I couldn't handle the pain any longer. For three days I sat in the corner of the living room under my scrolls and next to a jade plant. I couldn't do housework or eat or take care of the children.

According to Asian tradition, when you're in turmoil, you have to take care of yourself and be strong. You may be mentally disturbed and need professional help, but you don't dare seek it because it's shameful. It shows you're weak. You must resolve your problems alone and not blame anyone else.

As I sat in the corner, I thought, "Why am I struggling like this? Eventually, I will be nothing." Then I meditated, repeating, "I'm struggling, struggling every day, staying in deep depression."

After three days when I couldn't stand the depression any more, I switched my feelings off, saying, "The hardship of the struggle gives me strength to accomplish whatever I need to do."

A month or so later I took a part-time job in a community center. Some time after that I began to think, "O.K., Jack has two lives. Why shouldn't I find a lover?"

When I told Jack this, he said, "I don't like the idea, but I can't tell you not to. I don't have that right." Looking hurt, he probably thought, "Ling's not going to take a chance on that." He was right. It was only a thought. I couldn't look for somebody else since I was married. From my mother, a school teacher, and my grandfather, a Buddhist priest, I had learned that women shouldn't be promiscuous but devoted to their husbands.

My grandfather had deep thoughts. "Have virtue, self-control and compassion," he often told me. "Don't stain morality." I respected his word, particularly after my grandmother showed me his beautiful will which was written by him in brush, the rice paper full of holes that moths had made.

Self-respect was important to me too. I had to be a good woman since Jack and I were married and living in the same house with children. I didn't want to look like a cheap woman in front of my children, going out with other men. It's hard to change an old-fashioned attitude instilled over many years.

Because we argued each time I said anything against Jack's gay activities, I thought about divorcing as many of our friends had done. One afternoon eight-year-old Janice and I were talking about a boy in her class whose parents had divorced.

All of a sudden she said, "Mom, if you and Dad divorce, I'm going to kill myself."

That scared me. I stopped thinking about divorce.

About the sixth year after Jack had told me about Michio, he no longer let me know when he'd be getting home from a night out. Once he returned at 3:00 A.M.

Hearing his steps in the hall, I came out of the bedroom, "I was so worried, Jack. I couldn't sleep."

"You pushed me to do this, Ling."

A few weeks later a friend told me about a woman who was dating a man who had married and divorced three times. He had told her, "Women are passionate only until they win the man. Then they become cold."

I told Jack the story that night. "See, I'm not the only one. I loved you sexually in my own way."

The following spring the center held an evening meeting and party to which I had to go. I didn't tell Jack how long it would last.

When I came in at 11:30 that night, he came out of the bedroom. "Are you alive or dead? Why didn't you call?"

"There was no telephone close by," I said, exactly the words he used whenever he didn't call to say he'd be late.

Nothing more was said.

Jack's nights continued in the same pattern, with different people every time. That made me think again about dating and perhaps separating from Jack, but I was too scared to act.

Then one of Jack's best friends, Greg, got AIDS. "All my life," I told myself, "I have controlled my own and my family's life very well. Now I have to face things I can't control. Today or tomorrow Jack may say, 'Ling-Ling, I'm sorry, I have AIDS.'"

I didn't know what to do. Insurance would cover medical treatment, but was my faith strong enough to watch Jack die?

Again I sunk into a deep depression.

When it was over, I brought up his promiscuity one more time. "You have a family and a social obligation not to spread AIDS. If you can't control yourself, you better talk to a counselor."

"You're overreacting, Ling. AIDS is mostly hysteria. It's very rare to catch it."

He saw a psychiatrist anyway. One night while the kids were doing homework, he reported, "Dr. Robinson says that as long as you're wrapped up in anger, Ling, our problems won't be solved."

"He blames everything on me because he hears only your side. I thought you went for help to stop one-night stands."

"You don't have any right to control what I do. Why don't you just accept me?" There was bitterness in his voice.

"What you're doing worries me, Jack."

A week later, noting he was nervous, I asked, "What's wrong?"

"Well, Greg's lover wants me to stay there tonight so he can get out of the house. He's exhausted and needs space."

"I don't mind since you're not planning to spend the night with a lover. It's wonderful that you're offering to help a friend."

"Well," Jack said, "I've got to change and start doing things for people. I've been selfish. After Greg goes, I want to work with the hospice."

After we talked a while about Greg's condition, I asked, "What causes the pain?"

"I don't know. He is dying so slowly."

When Jack left I thought, "Maybe this will make him realize how much burden he would be to me and the children if he got AIDS."

All this time I was thinking more and more, "If Jack stops acting gay, I can live with him. But, when we're in restaurants or on the street, he looks at men. When the waiter comes, he stares at him. I want my husband to look at me and be attracted to me. Jack says he cares about me, but without chemistry it's as if he were a friend or brother."

I saw the need to start taking care of myself so as not to get hurt any more. Separation seemed to be the only answer, but when I told Jack, it led to a clash. So I avoided the subject.

That summer we went to Taiwan to visit my family. Jack and the kids returned in August. I stayed on for a course on Chinese, thinking, "If I can live without Jack for two weeks, I really can separate."

On my return separation didn't seem so scary, but I still worried that Jack would get AIDS. For the third time I plunged into a depression.

Frightened, Jack called one of my friends to talk to me and to make sure that I wasn't about to commit suicide.

When I came out of it three days later, I took off my wedding ring. "Now I will be free of Jack," I told myself, "and available to meet someone else."

When he saw my bare finger, Jack said, "You're trying to punish me."

"No. I did it for myself. I love you, but I don't want my husband to be gay."

Jack, I'm sure, was thinking, "Dear Ling, she has said that for eight years. Eventually she'll accept my double life."

A month later I said, "You go your way and I'll go mine in the house. We'll eat with the children but have separate rooms."

That was a month ago. When I think of moving out altogether, the loneliness frightens me. When you're young, it's easy. In your forties and after twenty years of marriage, it's scary. Yet nothing stays the same. If eventually we are going to separate, why struggle to escape that suffering now? God will give me the strength to act.

❦   ❦   ❦   ❦   ❦

Two years after this story was told, Jack was diagnosed HIV positive. Though Ling was angry about his promiscuity, she didn't want to abandon the father of her children.

She began taking classes toward an advanced degree and continued her part-time job.

The following year, Jack became infected with AIDS. Ling stopped her courses to take a full-time job and to care for him. He prays that they each attain inner peace.

Discovering The Authentic Self

The spouse's identity crisis starts long before he or she is capable of doing anything about it. Most spouses are too disoriented or emotionally paralyzed right after the coming out to examine their pain. "I'd go to bed naked and hug myself to sleep," recalls a wife from Detroit. "Who else could I share that hurt with?"

Whether spouses divorce at once or try to make the marriage work, it may take months to realize the profound impact that the partner's coming out has had on them. Those who divorce are preoccupied with separation problems and those who stay married are adapting to their partner's homosexuality and gay activities. In either case, their own identities are slowly buried in the process of accommodating to the coming-out crisis.

For many spouses, keeping the marriage intact and meeting the needs of the children seem worth their self-sacrifice.

One such wife, Erin, married after high school, chose to help her husband accept his bisexuality as "good" rather than "evil," as a Pentecostal group had labeled him while attempting to pray the devil out of him. Later in their rural town where they were respected citizens raising four foster children, she stood by him when someone threatened to expose his gay activities.

Through each crisis her personal interests such as metaphysical reading as well as her own private love affairs, eased both her emotional pain and her physical symptoms including gastroenteritis and skin problems that had plagued her the last half of their fifteen-year marriage.

For most spouses the first clues of lost identity come sooner, sometime in the second year after the coming out. Married spouses, in particular, often find themselves drained of strength from the cumulative effect of the day-to-day struggles. Many have developed severe symptoms from physical ailments to depression. The desolation that all feel can be overwhelming.

Such despair overcame one young mother, Pamela, in Los Angeles. Empathizing with her husband's remorse over his gay affairs while taking care of three children under the age of eight, she could find no one who believed or understood her story. She finally cried, "I can't take it any more" and swallowed a bottle of sleeping pills.

Pamela survived and learned how to create her own happiness. So do most spouses, rising out of their nadir through self-nurturing, introspection, support from friends and family, therapy, peer support, outside activities, and spiritual nourishment. Straight husbands seem to recover faster than straight wives. Cliff, for instance, only a few months after Pris came out, began to feel more optimistic and plan his future.

Discovering one's true identity involves exploring inner emotional, mental and spiritual resources. Applying the coping skills used throughout the coming-out crisis, such as asserting needs and setting priorities, can help the spouse to succeed in this long and challenging process. The ultimate goal is to gain the inner strength to handle blows in life without losing self-worth and confidence.

Four steps lead to rebuilding a strong self-concept:

- Healing body, emotions and spirit
- Learning from the past
- Discovering an authentic identity
- Changing self-identity from "spouse" to "I"

Healing Body, Emotions and Spirit

The exhaustion and depression that signal the onset of the identity crisis can be used for healing inner wounds, the first strategy of this stage of recovery. Many spouses feel that their sense of identity has been damaged by day-to-day compromises, criticism by the partner or their own self-blame. As a working wife in Tucson said, "In the process, I lost self-esteem. The scars will never go away."

Fatigue often makes it impossible for spouses to continue all of their activities. In many cases they find that they need to stop being "the good girl" or "good citizen" and cancel or limit community, school, career, or gay-related commitments beyond the regular work schedule. Separated spouses often decide not to see their partners as much for awhile.

Domestic chores may also need to be decreased to derive the most benefit from this healing period. No longer can spouses drive themselves to be superwoman or superman. Rather, now is the time to seek help from others, a new experience for some spouses. This is when friends, family, and partner need to be ready to assist.

Self-nurturing is one of the best antidotes for the overpowering desolation that many spouses feel. Rest, balanced diet, physical activity, relaxation and recreation with children and friends are simple but powerful ways to restore physical and emotional strength.

It is best to minimize artificial supports such as alcohol, cigarettes and drugs in favor of psychological, physical or spiritual activities that help to relieve stress, release feelings and help each person discover his or her own inner resources. Letting the mind wander while allowing the emotions to have full play greatly enhance the spouse's recovery. It is a time simply to be, letting feelings previously held in check such as sorrow or anguish surface naturally.

Non-thinking experiences like listening to music can also enhance the healing process. Music often releases significant sorrowful emotions that the spouse has previously ignored out of concern for the pain of others. It is a time when tears, anger, despair and even daydreaming are to be welcomed, not resisted. Tears have healing chemical and emotional qualities.

Over a fourth of the spouses studied in depth for this book turned to some kind of spiritual realm to help them come to terms with their own disorientation. Meditation, for example, helped some spouses to get in touch with their own inner strength.

Theologian and author Dody Donnelly points out that "Meditating for fifteen minutes per day can let God into our lives, nourish us with Her love and heal us."[1]

Ling removed herself from the eye of the storm to recoup her emotional strength. Through meditation in the Buddhist way, she concentrated on her suffering until she could let go of it as an unnecessary burden. Reaching inner peace, Ling was then able to switch back to her daily life and withstand the tension of living with a husband who was leading two lives.

Other spouses gained enlightenment from spiritual readings found in every religion, from Sufi texts, to the Hindu *Bhagavad Gita*, to Navajo stories, to Old Testament psalms.[3] For example, the repetitive verse form of the psalms of lament, biblical scholar Walter Brueggemann explains, leads the reader "into the darkness to face it, then through and out of it."[4] Equally important, notes psychologist Jeanne Paradise, Ed.D, "Hope is interwoven with these laments."[5]

As their physical, emotional and spiritual stamina is revived, spouses gradually feel that day-to-day survival is no longer impossible. They realize that they can continue to cope with their problems and take care of themselves at the same time. Now a single manageable goal to benefit themselves alone can be met such as taking a walk or reading poetry or calling a friend. It is simply a time to be.

Learning from the Past

Even with physical and emotional strength recovered, the spouse's sense of self may remain fragmented. An effective way to discover individual identity is to examine memories of the past, the second step of this stage of recovery. Looking back one can find what remains, what has changed and what has been squashed or forgotten. Questions such as, "What used to make me happy or sad?" or, "What meant something to me then?" can help arouse memories that illuminate the true self. Discovering such clues to identity reestablishes continuity with the present.

Reviewing the past can help uncover self-identity. Childhood, school life and marriage come into view, forming a collage of favorite places, games, books, friends, hobbies, all once treasured. Gradually these positive recollections form a person with a distinct personality who was once responsive to life. Negative recollections that engender pain or sorrow also help clarify the spouse's self-identity. Reflecting on the marriage or the partner's coming out may be especially illuminating. Rather than turning away from such unhappy memories, the spouse may find it instructive to examine them by asking such questions as, "Why did I feel that way? What does this say about me?"

Many spouses, while reviewing the post coming-out period, experience an outburst of angry feelings hitherto repressed. Auerback and Moser, in their study of seven support groups, report that it took five three-hour monthly sessions before wives expressed delayed anger at their husbands. Some never returned after their outbursts, unable to deal with their negative feelings.[6]

The tumultuous rage of this stage is normal and necessary. This feeling is different from fury over damaged sexuality. Instead, there is a deep resentment at being devalued by the partner. There may also be bitterness, a feeling that the partner's problem has killed the joy in the spouse's life.

Reflecting too long upon unpleasant parts of the past, especially those concerning the partner's coming out, has its pitfalls. Since the spouse is looking back from a weakened self-concept and feeling tremendous anger, the tendency is to magnify problems and to forget positive, happy times that also occurred. Such selective remembering can sabotage the process of learning from the past.

Sometimes spouses may need to realize that the goal of their retrospection is to learn more about themselves instead of punishing themselves or anyone else because of what happened in the past. The point is to put the good and the bad aspects of past experiences into perspective. Since recollections of marriage may be the most difficult to view objectively, it helps to compare memories with partner, friends and family members.

Good times in the marriage need to be recalled and savored. Positive emotions felt then were valid under those circumstances. Imagining oneself in such situations can reveal many forgotten clues to self.

Discovering an Authentic Identity

Building on clues from the past will help the spouse to revive a sense of her or himself as a unique and valued person. This is the third and perhaps most difficult task of the coming-out crisis. The goal is to reactivate desires and interests which provide significant insight into who the spouse really is. Concentration on the self is crucial. Concerns related to the partner or marriage need to be set aside. To keep focused on self-exploration, it helps to use language that emphasizes the "I" nature of what is being done. This can be accomplished in a journal or by talking to oneself using self-dialogue such as, "*I* am going to work. *I* am crying. This is *me*."

Self-dialogue is a powerful technique for self-discovery. As clinical psychologist Pamela Butler, Ph.D., explains, it "determines the direction and quality of our lives...(and) can make the difference between happiness and despair, between self-confidence and self-doubt."[7]

Some spouses may need the help of a friend, therapist, support group or clergy person to turn their attention on themselves. For example, Catherine needed Louise's gentle push to stop putting Larry's needs first. When Catherine did, she rediscovered her love of teaching which had been set aside to live with Larry.

A first step for spouses is to resurrect interests long forgotten. One effective strategy is to engage in solitary pursuits and follow the natural impulses that arise. Any activity, whether serious or mundane, can stimulate the buried self. This can entail writing in a journal, singing in the shower, swinging on a park swing, walking in the city or country, anything as long as the activity is enjoyable. With no one else distracting the spouse, all kinds of elements can come freely into play.

In the pursuit of interests, the spouse needs to keep alert to the least flicker of something loved or yearned for. Once detected, such insights can lead to self-recognition. Cliff, for example, recalling how he used to look as a slim six-footer, methodically started a diet that succeeded in reinforcing his self-image.

Through reactivating dormant interests, the spouse will begin to gain a clearer sense of self. For example, Erin, the wife who stood by her bisexual husband in each of his crises, began making pillows after she recalled a forgotten yen to sew. Discovering the tactile pleasure of this hobby, she expanded to giving massages. Through these pursuits, Erin realized that the sensual side of her nature was a significant part of her identity.

Introspection and solitary pursuits need to be balanced by human contact to reinforce the development of a clear self-concept. Rather than participate in large social gatherings, it's usually better to be with close friends who can nurture the person hidden behind the "coping spouse" image. The spouse may need to seek out friends who have the patience to support the spouse in her or his inner work for as long as it takes.

Old friends are invaluable aids in ferreting out parts of the self that have been ignored or repressed to make the marriage work. Even brief contact such as a telephone call can bring powerful results. A professional in Los Angeles has lunch or an after-work drink with an old friend every week. Each encounter puts her back in touch with a meaningful part of herself.

New friends who share common interests with the spouse can be of tremendous help in reinforcing self-confidence. Though it requires self-motivation to meet new people, they can readily be found through a wide array of activities available in most communities such as those offered at the local gym, adult education school, community church, city museum, concert hall or sponsored outings to the mountains or seashore.

Individual therapy is extremely valuable at this stage since it focuses on personal development. With a knowledgeable therapist, the spouse can learn ways to correct her or his distorted self-concept created in the mixed-orientation marriage and to sustain the growing sense of self-worth. For example, a therapist showed a teacher in Ohio how to use creative visualization to affirm herself and not be torn apart by her husband's double life.

It is critical to find a therapist or counselor who understands the effects of the coming out on the straight spouse's identity. One young wife saw four different psychiatrists before finding one who, knowing that her gay husband couldn't change his behavior for her, helped her see that only she had control over her inner happiness.

Support groups for straight spouses may be less helpful at this stage than groups that focus on identity issues such as self-esteem and co-dependency. Many of these groups stress the Twelve-Step recovery process that affirms self-acceptance and self-love and is based on the premise that every person is responsible for his or her own life, not others.

A number of excellent books such as those listed in appendix A provide information and techniques for self-discovery. Literature can be useful if based on acknowledged theories of cognitive, behavioral or emotional development, and backed by research, clinical practice or personal experience. Particularly helpful is *How to Survive the Loss of a Love*, by Melba Colgrove, Ph.D., Harold H. Bloomfield, M.D., and Peter McWilliams.[8]

Gradually spouses get in touch with who they are. In many cases, they find that they have become far different from the person they were before the coming out and even before the marriage. Ling's experience is typical of spouses who feel uncomfortable about the strangers they have become, acting in uncharacteristic ways. Deep in her psyche, Ling wanted to be a loving companion to Jack yet hated his gayness and yearned for her own sexual life. While respecting her Asian upbringing that emphasized self-respect and virtue, she wondered if she was courageous enough to date and if she could support herself without Jack.

Once spouses discover the hallmarks of their authentic selves, they can use these characteristics as a basis for reviving their identities. Ling returned to her homeland to try living separately from Jack. Cliff set out to conquer his longtime fear of roller coasters and rock climbing.

It may take months or years to resolve contradictions between the valued self and the artificial person that the spouse has become. Recalling Reinhold Neibuhr's invaluable prayer adopted by AA may help spouses discover themselves: "Give me the serenity to accept what I cannot change, the courage to change what I can and the wisdom to know the difference." Through constant practice of valued behavior, undesirable characteristics will gradually disappear and be replaced by a stronger identity. After two years, Catherine, formerly under Larry's control, could decide for herself whether to move heavy furniture if not mountains. With her revived self-esteem came the confidence to be herself, married or not.

Changing Identity from "Spouse" to "I"

Once the spouse feels that he or she is a valued individual, the final step is to shed the image of spouse (or former spouse) of a gay, lesbian or bisexual partner and become an independent individual. This means no longer being defined in terms of the partner or ex-partner.

To redefine themselves according to their individual identities, spouses often begin to describe themselves in a different way. Some stop using any terms that signify the married relationship. Wives may refer to their husbands and themselves by name rather than by role, "Jack," for example, instead of "my husband." When meeting new people, spouses might say, "I'm Cliff," without adding, "Pris' husband." Former spouses speak of the ex-partner as "the children's father (or mother)." One former spouse changed her entire name.

If still married, doing things independently of the partner helps reinforce the sense of separate identity. Timothy Wolf, Ph.D., in his 1982 study of twenty-six couples, suggests that having outside interests, friends, job and sex life helps wives compensate for the "sense of incompleteness in the less than exclusive relationship."[9]

Going out alone with friends, plunging into a new project at work or buying clothes without consulting the partner can also create an inner and outer picture of an independent "I." A wife in Richmond who changed her hairdo and wardrobe, found a job and attended social events alone was seen as an independent woman. Many acquaintances didn't realize she was married.

Often the partner's criticism or blame may threaten the spouse's fledgling identity. Self-confidence can be reaffirmed by seeing such attacks as symptoms of the attacker's own pain, a method described by psychiatrist Gerald G. Jampolsky, M.D., in *Love is Letting Go of Fear*.[10] Viewing the partner's actions from this perspective may help the spouse realize that such criticism is unwarranted.

The identity crisis recurs each time self-concept is threatened by criticism or adverse events. Each threat provokes more soul-searching and struggle to regain peace of mind. In order not to be drawn back into the morass of lost identity, it helps to focus on solving the problem that has prompted the attack by expressing personal feelings about it as well as affirming oneself with such nurturing thoughts as, "I am a worthwhile, lovable person."

Each time the spouse withstands a challenge to his or her identity, feelings of self-confidence increase. On the other hand, if interaction with the partner continues to weaken the spouse's sense of self, leaving the relationship may be the only way to preserve identity.

As spouses begin to think and act as autonomous individuals, either within the marriage or after leaving, a surprising shift takes place. Spouses no longer act only in response to their partners, for example being sympathetic, defensive, or rebellious according to what their partners do. Instead, spouses now act according to their own needs and wants. Many begin to love and appreciate themselves for the first time.

As a stronger authentic self-concept is forged, many spouses gain a detached perspective on the coming-out crisis. Some even develop an ironic sense of humor about their situations. One such ex-wife calls her support group, "United Single Women in Search of Men Who Aren't Gay, Married, or Hung Up on Their Mothers."

Restoring self-confidence and autonomy are prerequisite for handling the most complex issue of the coming out, one that haunts many spouses for years. This is the partner's deception in hiding their sexual orientation. Part five examines how spouses work through their pain and confusion to rebuild integrity and regain control over their lives.

five

THE POWER OF THE LIE

THE SHATTERING OF INTEGRITY

Although not all mixed-orientation marriages involve deception, the vast majority of those between straight women and gay or bisexual men do entail deceit to some degree. Because of guilt, fear, or repression, only a small minority of gay or bisexual men come out before they marry or immediately after they realize their sexual orientation unlike lesbians who tend to leave the marriage once they discover it. Deception, therefore, is primarily an issue for straight wives.

The profound effect that the deception has on straight spouses isn't readily understood by others, especially their partners. However understandable or valid the partner's reasons are for keeping their sexual identity a secret, the severe stress that spouses suffer as a result cannot be denied. Betrayal by the person they love the most, in the most intimate of human relationships, shatters their trust not only in the partner but in others and themselves.

More devastating to spouses is the realization that they have been living a lie without knowing it. There is no certainty left about the past, present or future. Without confidence in their ability to discern fact from falsehood or right from wrong, spouses find it difficult to be true to themselves or act with moral integrity. While the partner's integrity is affirmed in the coming out, the spouse's integrity is shattered.

It usually takes a year or more before the spouse is ready to face the deception issue and another year to restore integrity. Only after the spouse has resolved pragmatic issues and gained some emotional distance from the coming out can she or he handle the more complex problem of deception. Even then the process of regaining control of the moral quality of his or her life is often prolonged by empathy for the partner's plight, anger at being duped or continuing spousal love. "If only I had an off button to stop loving him!" said one woman, four years after separating from her husband of twenty-eight years.

Since deception primarily affects straight wives, only women's stories have been included in this section to illustrate the issue. The two narratives that follow portray the most severe type of deceit—the partner being actively gay before coming out. The final section examines the problems spouses encounter as a result of being deceived and explores ways to restore integrity.

Personal Stories

I Hope You Never Find Out
Tracey

"Herb will be a better husband than Juan, mark my words," Mother said.

Juan was my boyfriend from high school until I was a twenty-one-year-old technical student in Pittsburgh. I was still cutting my blonde hair the way he liked and wearing the shade of green he liked. I broke up with Juan in March, met Herb in April, became engaged to him in May and married in October.

Heavily-built with brown hair, Herb joined the army after high school to get away from his mother. On his return he worked at a machine plant in Scranton, where he became engaged to some girl. Two weeks before the wedding, he claimed that he'd called it off. Then he started working in Pittsburgh. We met at the church where he assisted the director of the Catholic Young Men's Group.

During our engagement, a friend told me to break it off. "Tracey, you'll never be happy with Herb," he said.

I couldn't break it off. I was pregnant.

After we married I kept working as a medical lab assistant except for maternity leave with our first son. Two years later when I got pregnant again, Herb made me stop working. Two years after that son was born, I bore another making the total three sons, David, Edward and James, all under the age of six.

Those were the best times. Christmas shopping in toy stores, I'd grin watching Herb pick up the trucks and trains. "You're a bigger kid than they are!" I joked lovingly.

After James was born, it was a struggle to get Herb out to do anything. He'd come home from work, open a beer and then another until we ate. After dinner he slept on the couch until ten, when I went to bed tired from being with three babies all day. He stayed up with the television until two. The next morning twelve empty bottles awaited me on the kitchen table.

We had sex so often that I sometimes thought he was oversexed. That was all right. It was the weird things he wanted to do that made me uncomfortable. Whenever he suggested something like oral sex, I said, "That's stupid!" or "No! It's too perverse."

"You're just prudish," Herb said. "Your mother filled your head with garbage. Whatever a married couple does is fine."

"O.K.," I said, "as long as both parties agree to it."

Some things I did just to please him. Afterwards I hated myself, thinking, "Instead of enjoyment, I have turmoil."

When Herb got up to drinking five cases of beer a week and weighed 280 pounds, I sat him down in a sober moment and said, "You're passed out drunk all the time killing yourself. Worse than that, you're taking yourself away from your boys and missing so much important growth! It makes me angry."

"O.K.," he said. "What can I do to make you happy?"

"You know, what would be nice is if we went for a walk."

"That's crazy! Let's go out to dinner!"

So we went out to a nice restaurant, something grandiose that impresses people. We also went to Atlantic City three times with couples from the neighborhood though we couldn't afford it. "Everybody's going!" Herb reasoned. These times we spent with others were the happiest.

Home life was different. Each weeknight when Herb got home, I asked, "How was your day?" and listened to what he said about a job I didn't understand. Then I told him what happened at home including what went wrong with the kids and how I handled it.

Each time he jumped in, "That was the wrong thing to do!"

That hurt me and I eventually decided to see a marriage counselor. I told the counselor, "I expected someone who could give, like me. But his hugs have stopped—not even an encouraging word when I need it. I want to get out, but I don't want to leave my babies. What'll I do?"

"Go back to work."

All along I'd been working, though without pay. I organized food baskets and sold newspaper ads for the Lions Club, served on the PTA board and organized the Mothers' Sports Club for my older boys' teams. A paying job would be different.

Herb didn't like the idea. "If you go back to work," he said, "that's the end of the marriage."

"Listen," I said, "I need help. Go talk to this counselor. See if she can help you help me."

"No, it's your problem. I'm not going to sit in front of some woman. You women stick together."

So instead we agreed between us that I wouldn't work until James was in school all day.

The question then was which of us would take the responsibility of birth control. The pill was out because of my varicose veins. Dismissing vasectomy, we decided on rhythm.

During our ninth year of marriage, Herb went on afternoon shifts getting home after midnight and arising at noon. After an hour to shave and shower, he would eat and leave again at three.

At first I'd wait up for him to come home. While he watched television with his beer, I'd try to tell him what the kids had been doing that day.

"Can you wait for a commercial?"

"O.K.," I'd say and go upstairs. At commercial time he would come up, have quick sex with me and then go downstairs again. Once I called out as he left, "Just leave the money on the dresser!" Finally I didn't wait up and he didn't come up to wake me.

When James started kindergarten, I took some courses to get into social work. I also lost thirty-five pounds in three months for myself. The new life ahead excited me.

The next month I didn't get my period. I was pregnant again.

Eight months later, Paula was born. Still in postpartum depression, I telephoned a marriage counselor. "I can't take any more!" I cried. "I want to run away. Everything I do is wrong."

This man kept me talking for an hour and a half, getting me back on track. Then he had me make an appointment.

"It hurts so much," I said at my first visit, "that my husband puts himself first and can't give."

For five months the counselor gave me hints on how to get Herb to talk and how to show understanding rather than criticize him. "If you've got something serious to say," he said, "do it in public where he can't scream at you and you won't get off on a tangent."

These things helped for a time. Then the counselor said, "Without Herb working with you, you can't work on the marriage."

Herb refused. "You don't need your counselor. You need this," he said, handing me *The Total Woman*.

While continuing therapy for another month, I read the book from cover to cover, how the lady slipped suggestive notes in her husband's lunch box and how, wearing just a trench coat, she rang the doorbell and when he opened the door flashed him.

"O.K.," I thought, "We'll try it." I slipped notes into Herb's lunches. I called him at work to say I wanted his body, blushing later whenever I thought of it. I used perfumed oils, raspberries and cream, everything.

One night I lay on the living room couch in the buff while he watched television. "Hey, Herb!" I called, every few minutes. "Yoo hoo!"

"In a minute. In a minute!"

After half an hour I got up and threw the book into the fireplace. "This is it," I said, lighting a match to it. "I'm done trying, Herb. It's your turn."

Four years later the recession of the early eighties hit. Working only eight days a month, Herb drank more, smoked more and slept more. Worrying about unpaid bills made him irritable. I couldn't talk to him. The kids couldn't talk to him. We had no sexual contact for four months.

Come spring I said, "Herb, we're getting deeper and deeper into debt. I'm going to get a job."

"Where the hell do you think you'll get one?"

"I'll get one."

That afternoon the coordinator of social services at the local hospital hired me on the spot. Nervous about going back to work, I chose the midnight shift to be at home mornings to get the kids off to school and evenings to help with homework.

My high school had a reunion that September. Afterwards thirty classmates came back to my house including my old boyfriend, Juan.

His wife had gone home ill. Long after Herb went to bed, the group left, all except Juan, who suggested we take a walk to catch up on each other. Five months later he called.

"How about lunch sometime?"

"I'd love it."

We arranged to meet on the first day of May. In late April my mother was hospitalized with cancer that had spread to most of her organs. I was the one who had to tell Dad that she was dying.

Because of my part-time schedule, I was able to stay with Mother on nights off so that Dad could go home to sleep. Then I went home, got the kids off to school, did my washing and cleaning, dozed, got dinner, did the dishes and got back to the hospital.

Herb visited her only once. "As always, I put others first and he doesn't," I thought angrily.

Several times a week my brothers, Web and Mel, came to the hospital. One night Mel sat with me, talking about his wife.

"You really love her, don't you?" I asked.

"Oh, yeah. She's everything. She keeps me going. She picks me up when I'm down."

"God, it must be nice."

"Tracey, what's the matter? Aren't you happy?"

"I haven't been happy for so long, Mel, I can't tell you when I was," I sighed. "What love we had has been slowly chipped away. One day I'm going to divorce Herb."

"Well," he said, "when and if you do, let me know. I have something to tell you."

"Tell me now."

"No. When the time comes, I will but only if necessary."

The day Juan and I were supposed to have lunch, I left a message for him to call. When he heard about Mother, he came to sit with me for four hours.

He came the next two nights too. The first was Mother's seventieth birthday. The second night I told Dad to let her go. "You're just prolonging her agony," I said.

Four hours after Dad left, Mother died. There was nobody there for me except Juan.

He and I were beginning to feel an attraction between us though we didn't know whether it was just a midlife crisis or us trying to be fifteen again. When he hinted at an affair, I said, "No. I've got to give the marriage one more try."

In June Herb and I vacationed with some couples at a resort. The first night I came out of the shower wearing a lacy black thing bought for the occasion and stood between Herb and the basketball game on the television.

"Can't you wait?" he said. "It's a good game."

My heart sank. "That's it. I can't give any more."

Once the basketball game was over, we had sex. The nightgown wasn't mentioned.

We had sex in August too, the third and last time that year. After that when he went by me in the house, I flinched. In bed I prayed he wouldn't come up. If he did, I pretended to sleep or kept reading so he'd go to sleep first.

One night as he got into bed ready for sex, I said, "No, Herb, I don't want you near me. I don't know what's wrong."

"Get your hormones checked. Must be a change of life."

The next morning a doctor at the hospital took several hormone tests and reported, "Everything's fine."

When Herb heard that, he said, "Then see a psychiatrist."

"No," I thought, "all I can see is getting a divorce."

In September I found another counselor. "I don't have the guts to divorce," I said. "Teach me how to be strong enough."

But the counselor wanted me to work on the marriage so I stopped seeing him. I went back to my obstetrician who told me to see a psychiatrist. Instead I just tried to keep on with the kids' sports, school activities and daily needs. On vacations I took them along so that Paula and I could share a bed and Herb had to sleep with the boys.

Then I got depressed and began to lose weight. The kids often found me crying when they got home.

When I bought my oldest son, David, a four hundred and fifty dollar car for his job and school, Herb screamed, "What did you do that for, Tracey? It's just junk."

A few months later Herb's mother called me frantically to say his father was in the hospital. He'd been ill for years. "I need your help, Tracey," she implored.

For the next three weeks, I went every other day to see Herb's dad and check on his mother. Herb went three times. The twenty-first day as I sat with his dad, my son Edward called to say that my father was having a stroke and needed me to get him to the hospital.

I drove to my father's house, put him in the car, got him into the emergency room, and went back up to Herb's father's room. He had died. So I had to tell Herb's mother, all the brothers and sisters and my husband as they came to the hospital one by one.

Herb didn't cry when he heard.

"It's okay to cry," I said. "It's your father."

"As far as I'm concerned, he died when he first got sick."

The viewing of the body in the funeral home took place a few days later on a hot and humid Saturday. The whole family met at Herb's mother's house so that we could car pool.

When we got into our car, I said, "Follow David. His car isn't running right." Then as we pulled away, I cried out, "Wait! We're missing a kid. I didn't see Paula come out."

Herb kept on driving. "You're crazy. They're all here."

"Let's check your mom's house to be sure."

"She's in someone's car, Tracey. Don't worry."

Just then David's car stalled. As Herb made a U-turn to get behind him again, he started shouting at me, "I had to watch the damn kids when your old lady croaked. I was stuck baby-sitting the damn kids when my old man croaked and now I'm stuck baby-sitting again. All I asked for was some support during this time. You haven't given me anything."

Stunned by the violence I heard in his voice, I thought, "This isn't grief. This man hates me." With growing anger I recalled what I'd done for him and his family and what he hadn't done for me.

By the time we were at the funeral parlor, I was in tears. As I opened the door, I asked, "Does anybody here have Paula?"

When no one spoke up, I turned to Herb, "Look, you're the oldest son. Take your mother in. I'll go back and get Paula."

"No," he said, turning toward the door. "You no-good mother. You can't even keep track of your children. I'll get her." As he passed me, he gave me a shove.

"Herb," I whispered, my voice shaking, "if you walk out the door, the marriage is over. I've had it."

He walked out. I took off my wedding and engagement rings and threw them on the floor.

"Tracey!" his brother-in-law said. "I'll get Paula."

Everyone stood paralyzed. "There, there, we understand," one sister-in-law said. "It's only a year since your mom died."

Another whispered, "We know. Herb told us that you're seeing a counselor."

After Paula arrived and we viewed the body, I left with the grand-children and some girlfriends to prepare the post-viewing dinner at Herb's mother's house. It was ninety degrees, one hundred percent humidity by then. When the others arrived, David took me home. By the time Herb got home that night, I was on the couch with my pillow and blanket.

"What do you think you're doing?"

"Filing for divorce. I'll never get in the same bed with you again. It's over. I'm tired."

He stood at the end of the couch and laughed. "You know, you really are sick!" he said and walked upstairs.

I filed for divorce a week later and slept on the couch for a year until it was final.

Herb was served the papers on our eighteenth anniversary. "Why are you doing this?" he asked. "Letting you work was my mistake. Those divorced women you hang out with gave you this idea. I gave you everything a woman could want, a beautiful home, luxuries, travel. What more did you want me to give?"

"Yourself."

After this exchange I began wondering about the secret my brother Mel had mentioned. One day, talking with my other brother's wife, I couldn't contain my curiosity. "Mel has some secret he wants to tell me," I began. "Gosh, I wish he would. I should know."

She started crying. "Tracey, I hope you never find out."

"You know?"

"Yes," she said, "Web told me years ago."

"Years?"

She nodded. "I hope you never find out."

That night I thought, "This secret must be powerful." Then I remembered a scandal about the director of the Catholic Young Men's Group, something about pornographic photos and fondling some boys. "And Herb was his assistant," I thought. "It's the only thing explosive enough to be kept secret."

The next week I went to watch Edward play field hockey. As I sat on the bleachers with the other Sports Club mothers, one began telling me how she'd discovered that her "ex" had chased women during their marriage.

"Did you know about it, Tracey?"

"Uh huh. He chased me for a month until I stopped him."

"Why didn't you tell me? You were my friend," she said.

"Because you seemed happy." I squeezed her hand. "Don't worry. My brothers are keeping a secret about Herb from me."

"Do you have an idea of what it is?"

"Uh huh. I think it has to do with sexuality."

"You're right."

I sat up rigid. "What do you mean, 'I'm right.'"

"About his sexuality." She stopped for a minute and then took a deep breath. "Herb went around the Men's Sports Club asking friends and neighbors you know for sexual favors."

Shock, anger, and hurt shot through me all at once. My husband, my partner, the father of my children, doing this?

Regaining control, I crawled off the bleachers and went to the school pay phone. The only number I remembered was Web's. "Web," I said, "I want to know the secret now."

"Mel will tell you. He brought it up."

"I know. But I want to know how you know that Herb is bisexual."

Web was quiet. Then he asked, "Are you okay?"

"It's the truth, isn't it?" I persisted.

"Yes. Remember when I was hospitalized and Mel spent the night? Herb came to visit once and pounced on Mel. When he resisted, Herb said, 'There's nothing wrong with it. I did it in the Air Force.'"

"'Well,' Mel said, 'not with me. I'm getting out of here. You do this again and I'm telling Tracey.' The next day Mel talked to a counselor who told him to inform you."

As Web talked, I wondered if Herb had been drinking or was joking. Maybe these guys had misinterpreted what he said. "How did Herb say it?" I asked.

"Well," Web said, choking a little, "I can't say exactly."

Driving to work in agony, I wondered, "Why didn't Mel tell me? Maybe he thought that what I didn't know wouldn't hurt me." By the time I arrived at work, I couldn't function. The next day I called Mel. "Did Herb approach you?"

"Yes, three times. The third time was when you all came for dinner at our house. I came home late and took a shower. When Herb came in to use the bathroom, he made a grab for me."

"Well, that's that!" I said, hanging up. "I can't protect Herb from this as I have with the drinking and his other faults."

That night I called New York to talk with a male neighbor Herb had supposedly approached years before. Only his wife was home.

"Yes, it's true, but I assumed that you knew about it," she said, "and that you and Herb had an arrangement."

Since the holidays were coming up, I kept the secret inside me until Paula's birthday in January when we all went to eat at a restaurant in the mall, somewhere public enough to discuss it.

When the kids were off playing video games, Herb asked, "Tracey, why don't you stop the divorce!"

"I can't now."

"Why not ?"

"I have to ask you a question, first. Are you bisexual?"

"Yeah. So what?"

As I told him what Mel, Web, and the neighbor had said, he nodded, emotionless.

"Now what about the Young Men's Group? How could you work so closely with the director and not know?"

"I never was aware of it."

Then I asked, "Have you ever touched one of our sons?"

"No."

"That's all I want to know."

The subject came up once more, one night when he was drinking. "You never pleased me as a woman, Tracey," he said. "That's why I had to get it from men. No woman would want me this fat."

Over the next few weeks, I called friends who might know something more. They told me that he was involved in the Young Men's Group scandal and that it was his first fiancee who had cancelled their wedding at the rehearsal dinner. Some people thought I knew. Most believed my happy face and didn't want to rock the boat.

The more I found out, the more I suffered abdominal pain, vomiting, diarrhea, headaches. My best friend didn't want to talk about it. The girls at work were no help since they had no experience with it. I couldn't find any books on being married to a gay person. In February I went to a psychiatrist.

Then one afternoon in March, the left side of my face and left arm became numb. "My God, it's a stroke!" I said and drove myself to the hospital. Going up the steps to the emergency room, my left leg gave out so that I had to drag myself to the door.

They were about to admit me to the cardiac unit when they called my doctor who said I had a chronic blockage in my nervous system. "Give her tranquilizers and send her home," he said.

When I called my doctor the next day, he said he didn't tell me before because it was something one can live with.

Three months later my co-workers noticed my left cheek drooping and my eyelid half closed. When they took my blood pressure, it was 150/110. Once chest pains started, they got me to the emergency room at which point my heart rate was jumping all over the place and my blood pressure was going up and down. This time I was admitted to cardiac care and a cardiologist was called to see me.

All I was aware of was the kindness and caring in his eyes as he asked calmly, "O.K., what's the problem?"

He heard me out. Then, after asking if I wanted an AIDS test, he told me about his own bitter divorce and the emotional and physical symptoms that many people experience in such trauma. "We'll do some testing, but I think it's apprehension and anxiety. We'll get you through it."

After thirty-two hours I was sent home with orders not to do anything but sleep until testing on Monday. Not wanting to call on Herb for anything, I had my neighbor drive me home.

On Saturday Herb came home with a swollen arm. Taking one look, I sent him to the hospital clinic. It was a blood clot. He was admitted for five days.

The first day I was able to rest. The second day Herb called wanting clean underwear. The next day it was something else. The fifth day he asked for a ride home. When I arrived, his mother was there with her car.

Over the next five months, we just existed waiting for the divorce to be final. I went to work, exercised on the treadmill in the cardiologist's office, and helped the kids with school activities. Herb moved out when the divorce was final.

We put off telling his mother until the holidays were over. In February I took her to lunch to tell her gently.

"I knew something was wrong," she said, wiping her eyes. "Oh, Tracey, don't let me lose the grandchildren."

"You won't," I said, putting my hand over hers.

"I hope we can still be friends," she smiled. Then she asked, "Is there anything else I should know?"

Afraid that she'd find out from the other family members I'd told, I said, "Yes, one more thing. It's a big one."

When I told her, she said nothing for a moment. Then she asked, "Tell me, did a Francis Locke ever call Herb?"

"Yes."

She started crying again. Francis, I found out later, was a known homosexual Herb had hung around with after the army. The family knew about him and didn't like the relationship.

That was the last time I saw or heard from Herb's mother, though she spoke of me to others saying that I'd had affairs with men at work through the last years of the marriage.

For weeks after the divorce, anger and guilt plagued me. As I folded laundry, I wanted to rip up the clothes. I kept saying to my psychiatrist, "I busted up a marriage and family."

"Listen to yourself," he finally said. "What other choice was there? Did you want to stay miserable all your life?"

"Well, maybe I'm the type who likes being a martyr."

"No, Tracey, you're not!" he said.

I went to my priest with my guilt. "I was taught by the nuns that marriage is forever and not to be selfish. This is the first selfish thing I've done. It benefited nobody but me."

"In order to take care of others," he said, without a pause, "we must take care of ourselves first."

Then my fortieth birthday came. As I woke up that morning, lying in bed, I vowed, "This is the day I'm taking a step forward. I am not ever going to take a step back again!"

Siempre Manana
Caitlin

I had a traditional image of what life would bring me. I'd go to college, become a teacher, marry, have kids and stay home, working for the PTA and volunteering. Life would be wonderful for me.

In high school, I didn't date much. In college, I saw my male classmates just as intellectuals I could have wonderful discussions with. That's how I controlled relationships.

My heart was first touched doing community work in Washington. Miguel was bright, attractive, popular and had a tremendous amount of energy and skills. When he said that he planned to get a doctorate from Harvard, I thought, "I can't believe my luck! It's everything I wanted and more."

Miguel grew up poor, the son of Puerto Rican immigrants. He was the first of his family to graduate from high school, not to mention college. His parents were so proud! When he wanted to get a master's degree, they were impressed but could no longer identify with his goals. When he joined the Peace Corps and then wanted to get a Ph.D., they sat back and smiled.

Education was the way Miguel could leave his background. He dreamed of financial security, professional acclaim and a close family that he hadn't had because of his father's absence from home working long hours to make ends meet. Like me, he'd been raised as a good Catholic and shared my values to be loving, kind, get married and have kids.

So we became engaged. We were a handsome couple, Miguel with his brown hair and flashing eyes and I with auburn hair and the translucent skin of the Irish. We were two liberal kids of the sixties.

One weekend after our engagement, we went to lunch on the coast. Watching the fog circle outside the window, we felt close. All of a sudden Miguel stopped talking and his brow furrowed. Frightened, I wondered what I'd said wrong. After two days he came out of it. All was well again.

After we married, we found an apartment in Boston where he got a job and started graduate school. Then he quit his job to study full time, day and night.

"That's O.K.," I said to myself. "We can put off quality time until he finishes school."

Our sex life wasn't terribly exciting but it was regular. When Miguel's course work was finished, we decided to have a baby. We moved to Hartford, within driving distance of Harvard, and both found positions in the school system. Miguel planned to finish his dissertation later.

Gradually our sex life improved and I got pregnant. I stopped teaching just before our son, Felipe, was born. Fifteen months after his birth, we decided to have a second baby. Lo and behold, it was twins. Confined to bed toward the end, while Miguel travelled and started his dissertation, I kept thinking, "Of course, he has to do this for his career. So what if I have a toddler and a difficult pregnancy! I can handle it. My husband is going to have his Ph.D. A few years of struggle are necessary for life to get better afterwards."

Lucy and Maria were born in the fall. Once I regained my strength, I shared baby-sitting with friends so I could do consulting work in the schools again. My career took off.

When the twins were a year old, we decided to adopt. Good community-minded people of the sixties, we'd planned to adopt two underprivileged children after having two of our own. Since we now had three, we decided to adopt only one. A month after our decision, a friend of Miguel's family asked us to adopt her baby, due in a month. After therapy and much discussion, we said, "Yes, we should do this." Carlos arrived well and happy.

Miguel continued to work on his dissertation while I took care of the four babies, all under three, did some consulting work and kept things going financially. When my mother questioned my load, I answered cheerfully, "Once Miguel finishes his degree, we'll have the life we want."

Meanwhile the pressure of Miguel's research was turning him into a basket case. He began having horrible nightmares and losing momentum.

After each nightmare I said, "You have to finish or you'll always question yourself. I can sacrifice whatever's needed."

For months we went without sex. "I just don't have the desire because I'm so stressed," Miguel explained.

I wasn't concerned. "So what? Life isn't perfect and what a marvelous husband I have!"

When it was time for Miguel's oral examination, I went with him. "This is great," I thought, sitting in the Harvard Yard. "Finally, the eleventh hour! My husband is taking his orals and I'm here to cheer him on and to hold his hand when he gets anxious."

After graduation Miguel became severely ill. He was so sick physically and emotionally that work was impossible for months. Our sex life was still nonexistent. Since he had always been an over-achiever, I figured he was just getting sick to extremes.

Yet his depression scared me to death. With my encouragement, he went into therapy, choosing a psychologist in Boston an hour and a half away. "Why not?" I thought. "Maybe they have professionals of higher quality in Boston."

I also suggested that he think about making friends. "Why not join a men's group of some kind?" I said one day.

Miguel chose a group concerned with men's issues. It turned out that three-fourths of the men were gay, but I encouraged him out of my open-mindedness to continue going to meetings.

Soon Miguel began to stay out until two and three in the morning several evenings a week. When asked about it, he said, "I need some alone time to think."

"Yeah," I answered, "it's hard to think with four kids in the house." I thought, "He needs time to tend to his own needs after these years of struggle." But his absence began to annoy me.

When I brought it up, Miguel said, "Caitlin, I love you. You're wonderful. Just give me time to work things out about myself. Please be patient."

Before long I began to lose sleep, worrying that he would commit suicide from depression. Soon we began arguing about his late hours, we who had always been nice to each other. I finally made an appointment to see his therapist.

"Is Miguel going to get better or have a breakdown or what?"

"I don't think he'll have a breakdown," he said, "but if he does, you must think about your own needs. What if he never changes? Can you live with that? Does the marriage meet your needs?"

"Sure," I thought.

That Easter we were putting the kids to bed when Miguel said that he wanted to talk. Downstairs he handed me a six page letter. I sat down on the sofa, turned on the light, and began to read.

> Please do not hate me, Caitlin. I really do love you. That's why I married you, but it has become obvious that I cannot love a woman the way I love a man and that I am gay.

I drew in a deep breath and kept on reading. As a child he'd felt attracted to other boys but fought the urge. A few homosexual experiences freshman year in college scared him into going to a psychologist who said, "Don't worry. You're eighteen and haven't had sexual experiences with women yet."

"I'm not 'strange' after all!" he told himself and repressed his homosexual feelings. Although he dated girls, he avoided sex by keeping busy with jobs and a full course load. He went with one girl for many years until she mentioned marriage. When the next girl he dated became intimate with him, he ended the relationship.

Then he met me, the epitome of the woman he wanted in his life. "You didn't press me for a physical relationship," Miguel's letter said. "You were nurturing and understanding." As he fell in love with me, he again questioned if he was gay.

The psychiatrist he went to for a year told him, "You're not gay. All you need is a good woman. But don't tell Caitlin."

Somewhat reassured, Miguel subdued his fears by keeping afrenetic schedule, always under pressure from work, school and community activities.

> "My breakdown started," Miguel's letter went on, "when I was staying several weeks at a time at Harvard a year and a half ago. I met a master's student who turned out to be gay and we started an affair. Because of his fast life of bars and parties, I

ended the relationship after a few months. Then I met another person at the university....

I became sick trying to avoid the issue. I knew it was wrong and I still loved you and the children. So I got help from the therapist in Boston (who is gay), the men's group, and a gay advocacy group until the pressure finally broke me."

As I finished reading the letter, not totally surprised yet still in shock, I said, "Well, let's not panic. I can deal with it. Let's figure out what to do. Poor Miguel! Look at all you've gone through. I'm so sorry. Don't worry. I'm not going to hate you."

Miguel came over and we sat together, holding each other and talking. Then he mentioned Ed, his friend who had visited us often. "He's more than just a friend, Caitlin."

Miguel had met Ed in the men's group. When Miguel brought him to our house, I liked him. A good-looking man, he seemed warm and friendly. He came for dinner several times and once we set him up on a blind date with a friend of mine. Recalling this, I couldn't believe what Miguel was telling me.

When he finished, I said, dry-eyed, "This doesn't mean our marriage is over, but I need you to be honest with me. If we're going to make this marriage work, it's got to be based on honesty. I don't want any surprises."

"Sure," he said. "No surprises."

Then I stood up, saying quickly, "I need to take a drive."

Calling my friend, Judy I asked, "Can I come over now?"

Before leaving for Judy's, I telephoned a college friend in Washington. "Can I come for the weekend? I can't tell you why."

"Of course!"

When I arrived at Judy's, I said, "I've got to tell you something." Then I began to cry.

She held me as I talked and sobbed until I was calm enough to go home.

That weekend none of my Washington friends were surprised. "We figured it had to be that. Nothing else would upset you so."

On my return Miguel met me at the airport. As we drove home, he said, "I'm not sure you realize that Ed is still my lover." Then he explained that they had already been sleeping together when I invited

Ed for Thanksgiving and Christmas, thinking he'd like a family dinner since he lived away from home.

"Remember that weekend retreat my therapist recommended?" Miguel continued. "Ed had a job in the area that weekend and stayed with me in the cabin."

"My father's cabin? You two were having sex in my father's cabin?" I cried.

As I was digesting this news, I discovered that in my absence Miguel had hired sitters and gone out after reading to the kids and putting them to bed. Hurt and annoyed, I said, "You can't even give up your social life for the family!"

Two nights later I had Miguel invite Ed over so that I could talk with him. While Miguel stayed upstairs, we talked for four hours. "I'm not going to be ugly about it," I told him. "I'm not against gay people. You're not going to ruin Miguel's life. If it had to happen, I'm glad it's you."

He replied, "I like you, too. I'm not going to be strange or try to take away the kids or ruin your marriage. I told Miguel not to tell you so it wouldn't be ruined."

For the next four months, I kept telling myself, "This is part of my life now. Miguel is gay and has to have time with his lover. I can deal with that. I'm going to be loving, supportive, rational and think about the needs of the family."

For a while our sex life improved. Miguel kept telling me how much he loved me. Soon we worked out a system for him to be with Ed two evenings a week, Friday and one other.

"I'm not ready for you to spend the night with him," I said. As it was I cried every evening he was with Ed.

Next I spent forty dollars on books to read all I could on homosexuality and on marriage. I located a support group of wives of gay men in Boston and met a woman who had been with her gay husband for thirty-five years after he'd come out. They had raised their kids together. She'd become his friend, confidante, and mother protector. She'd made him get one man out of his life because she thought the man was "weird."

As I looked at this overweight chain smoker and apparent alcoholic, I thought, "Wait! I can't let this happen to me."

Going to the support group was like coming home. The other women understood where I was. As I listened to their experiences, some more ugly and painful than mine, it became clear that my increasingly negative feelings were normal.

In the group the image I projected was "We have a wonderful marriage. I'm going to made it work." Everyone was impressed with how positive, cheerful, strong and capable I appeared. Even I believed it. It was true because I'd worked hard at realizing this image I'd always had of myself.

Inside I was thinking, "Something's destroying my life, my marriage and my fantasy."

Finally I agreed to let Miguel spend Friday nights with Ed. Yet I cried when he was gone, despite his saying, "It's a wholesome experience, much like having sex with a woman."

Bit by bit I discovered underwear decorated with cupids in his dresser and cards from gay baths and bookstores in his wallet. Though I knew looking for them wasn't right, the discoveries forced me to finally see reality.

Four months later after I could no longer stand my jealousy which was alien to my nature, I said, "Miguel, I can't think clearly about this. I need space. Please move out."

We told the children, "Daddy needs time out. He's really tired."

I helped Miguel move into an apartment ten minutes away. All six of us spent the first night there. The second night just the kids stayed with him.

Once he was in the apartment, jealousy overwhelmed me. "What's happening to you?" I asked myself between crying bouts. "You're usually such an accepting, supportive woman."

A few weeks later en route from visiting my parents, the children and I stopped by Miguel's apartment. "I need to see him," I thought as I rang the bell. "Ed may be there, but that's okay. The kids should see their father."

When Miguel answered the door, I saw the candlelight dinner the two men were having. They both looked embarrassed. "I don't care how they feel," I thought. "I'm the one who's hurt."

Because Miguel lived so close, we were still a couple, seeing each other every day. We still loved each other tremendously and felt like best friends. I wanted him to share everything he was doing in his life away from me, even intimate details about his sex life. Each time he finished telling me, I thanked him, welcoming the hurt.

Then Miguel received a job offer in Washington. He let me decide whether he should go, as he had with the Ph.D.

"Go," I said. "Take the job." I'd started consulting work again, juggling it with the care of the children and our large house. Having him out of town was what I needed emotionally.

Once he was gone traveling for his job, it was hard handling the kids by myself. With energy only to survive, I didn't realize the trauma his absence was causing me. The pressure of keeping his secret compounded my turmoil. One day, when picking up Felipe at a playmate's house, the mother whom I didn't know well asked how I was.

Without thinking I blurted out, "My husband's gay."

Though she was conservative, she held and comforted me. As I left I thought, "This secret isn't as awful as I'd imagined."

When our anniversary came around in May, we spent it together in New York. For my birthday a week later, we met in New York again.

The following weekend I called him. "Let's try again. Let's see if we can make it work."

"Fine."

"I want the next year to be just us," I continued. "I don't want Ed nearby."

"O.K."

Though I didn't like making all of our decisions, I sold the house, left my job, packed up our belongings and moved the four children and myself to Washington before school started. While house hunting, the children and I stayed in a motel and Miguel remained in the house he rented with several straight men.

Right away Ed moved to Miguel's house. When we found a four-bedroom house for our family, Ed took Miguel's place in his old house. Once again he and Miguel spent Friday nights together. Once again Miguel traveled. Once again I put up with it because we were trying to redefine our marriage.

Miguel's lifestyle made me tense especially when he and Ed went to the baths, even though he said, "We don't do anything with anyone else. It's the only place where we can be together publicly."

I didn't believe him. I couldn't trust him any more. There was no way to know if what he said was true or not.

By then our lovemaking was infrequent. When we made love, it wasn't very good. Miguel was also having work-related stress. To get the bills paid, I took a good-paying job unrelated to my field.

Then our anniversary came around again. I gave Miguel an azalea plant as a sign of growth. He gave me nothing, though we had dinner at a restaurant we found at the last minute. Although I understood that his money was tight, I was disappointed that he hadn't thought ahead. I can't recall whether or not we made love that night. By then I didn't want to anymore because of the possibility of getting a venereal disease.

The next week I vowed, "If this marriage is going to work—and, by God, I'm going to make it work—it will be sexless. I'm going to give up my sex life for this marriage. I'm going to find love in other ways, not necessarily sexual. Lots of friends will nurture me. This is not going to ruin me."

That weekend I told Miguel, "I've given up my fantasy of being Donna Reed in a blissful Hollywood marriage. It's hard to give up so much. I will need support." Tired and weak, feeling physically ill, I counted on his help.

My birthday was the following Saturday. Friday night I was alone since Miguel was with Ed. After I took the kids to stay with relatives, I rented movies and a video machine to binge on something other than alcohol or food. Stretched out on the couch in front of the TV, I watched movie after movie until well past midnight.

The next day Miguel and I went out to lunch and walked among the cherry trees. Before dinner I said, "Please don't drink too much. I'm too tired to drive having watched movies so late last night."

Miguel drank at dinner and then at a show bar we went to afterwards. He slept all the way home while I drove.

When we arrived home he asked, "Are you disappointed?"

"Well, yes. I know money's tight and I appreciate spending the day and evening out, but I didn't get a present or a card from you. Birthdays are important to me. You know that."

Suddenly he screamed, "What more do you want from me? I didn't have time to buy you a card. I didn't even have time to go to the bathroom all week!" Then he stormed out of the house.

I was furious. It was the first time I could remember being angry with him.

The next morning Miguel came home. "Sorry, Caitlin," was all he said.

A few nights later while I was resting on my bed listening to classical music, it suddenly became clear. "Why am I giving up my whole life for this marriage?" I thought. "What do I get out of it? Give me crumbs and I'll stick around? I can't even have sex with anyone else. I can't be an unfaithful wife."

Then my thought switched. "Wait! Miguel's the one who's unfaithful. You don't even have a marriage you morally agree with, Caitlin. It's not based on faith and trust. Your image of right and wrong is screwed up. What Miguel is doing is wrong. Therefore this marriage can't last."

There was nothing more to do. It had taken two and a half years of trying to make the marriage work for me to see that it was over. I'd wanted my fantasy to come true so much that I'd compromised who I was and what I believed to make it real.

Of course my fantasy couldn't come true! Until that was blatantly obvious, I couldn't let it go. Now I could finally let it go and deal with reality.

Reversing The Negative Effects Of Deception

The deception revealed by the partner's coming out presents a painful enigma for the straight spouse to unravel. To some extent the partner's deceit may seem motivated by good intentions such as the belief that love for the spouse will override the partner's sexual orientation, the desire to keep the marriage going and the family together or to not hurt the spouse. Yet to the spouse it can appear as if the partner did it primarily to serve personal interests. While the partner's closet may have provided him or her protection from sexual or moral confusion or anti-gay discrimination, in the marriage it created a false world in which the spouse unwittingly helped carry off the masquerade. With the discovery of the partner's sexual orientation, the spousal role may seem like a charade and the marriage a sham. In the spouse's eyes, the real partner was hidden behind a misleading mask. As a professional woman, formerly married to a gay man, commented, "Our husbands were the best actors!"

For many spouses the deception implies that they have been living a lie without knowledge or consent, through the misleading behavior of the beloved partner they trusted. Discovery of the truth destroys their world as they thought it to be. As sex therapist Sharon Nathan comments, "(It) robs you of some sense of continuity with your own past."[1]

Some spouses, quickly deciding that the partner's betrayal nullifies the marriage contract, divorce at once. A more common reaction is to ignore the deception as too painful to address right away. Divorced or married, it takes months for spouses to sort through the moral issues surrounding the duplicity and to determine a moral compass to guide their lives.

Rebuilding moral integrity involves eight steps:

- Sorting out the truth from lies
- Assessing the power of the lie
- Using anger constructively
- Understanding both sides of the closet
- Rebuilding trust in others and self
- Sharing the secret
- Reconstructing moral values
- Acting with integrity

Sorting Out the Truth from Lies

When spouses finally realize the discrepancy between the truth and what they assumed it to be, their reactions can be explosive. When Herb yelled at Tracey that she was a bad mother, she, unable to reconcile such an unfounded accusation with reality any longer, cried, "It's over! I'm tired," and filed for divorce. Later, when she realized the extent of Herb's duplicity, severe psychosomatic symptoms erupted.

Until the marriage is recast in a framework of honesty, the first task in restoring integrity, the spouse rarely feels certain about anything in her or his life. As one twenty-year-old said, in trying to get her husband to tell her where he'd been overnight, "Everyone needs the truth."

In retrospect, layers of lies are usually found woven into the marriage, often from the beginning and almost always from the time the husband came out to himself. Most lies appear as omission of facts, projected blame, rationalizations or cover-ups—what some wives describe as "mind-bending" by their husbands. Explicit denial occurs rarely and usually in response to a confrontation.

The screen of rationalizations used to hide the secret may have seemed plausible at one time. Being late or absent because of gay encounters at teahouses, bars or designated places in the community can be camouflaged by believable explanations—extra work at the office, heavy traffic, or overtime at a construction site—excuses that any errant partner might offer. Actual events like meetings or choir practice can provide gay contacts. On the other hand, an excuse like, "Let's not go out with the so-and-so's. He's too dull," may turn out to be a smoke screen for the husband's fear that he'll make a pass at the other man, as Tracey's husband did.

Once the truth comes out, it may seem incredible that it could have been hidden and that the spouse didn't suspect. Many spouses wonder if they were accomplices to the deceit through a naivete that made the charade possible or an unconscious wish to deny the truth out of loyalty or fear of being hurt. There may also be nagging guilt, feeling somehow responsible for their partner's life.

Often spouses continue to discount the truth by playing "What if" and "If only" games. For example, wives who have separated and divorced may tell themselves, "If I'd only known, I could have done something to make the marriage work before it was too late." Dwelling on hypotheses that can't be proved isn't constructive. It only perpetuates more self-blame and prolongs the denial of reality.

Some spouses, unable to accept the betrayal, may seek out further proof of the painful truth. The result can be upsetting as Caitlin found when she walked in on the candlelight dinner of Miguel and his lover. Such hurtful encounters help cure disbelief, somewhat like cauterizing a wound. Yet enough is enough on top of the guilt and growing anger of this stage.

Gradually as spouses sort out the truth, they begin to understand more clearly why their partners blamed them for sexual or other marital problems. Whether or not the blame is at all merited, placing all accountability onto the spouse is a way to deny the real cause and to substitute a false culprit. Such psychological projection erases the partner's culpability.

Assessing the Power of the Lie

Assessing the impact of the partner's lie on the spouse's life, the second task of recovery from deception, may be one of the most unsettling parts of the coming out for the spouse. Without knowledge of the sexual incompatibility in the marriage, it is impossible for the spouse, no matter how capable, to resolve sexual and marital problems. If Tracey had known Herb's sexual orientation, she wouldn't have tried to attract him nor suffered the subsequent humiliation. More devastating was the realization that Herb, knowing his sexual orientation, let Tracey continue her futile attempts to seduce him.

Wives whose husbands knew but didn't reveal they were gay or bisexual before marrying, feel doubly hurt because one of the primary factors for deciding to marry was deliberately hidden from them. Although some men marry believing it will help cure or overcome gay inclinations, their wives nevertheless have no say in the decision that affects them as well. One such woman, an intensely sexual "flower child" of the sixties, married a doctor who promptly stopped making love to her and groomed her into a doctor's wife. He made no effort to satisfy her frustrated sexual desire. Finally, thirteen years later, he revealed that he was gay.

When asked why he had married her, he responded," I expected to have a sexless marriage."

"Who are you to tell me," she exploded, "how I'm supposed to live my life?"

Ultimately many wives feel stripped of power over the quality and direction of their lives. As Sissela Bok, Ph.D., explains in her classic study, *Lying*, applicable to straight spouses, "...to be given false information about important choices in their lives is to be rendered powerless. For them, their very autonomy may be at stake."[2]

The negative effects of a partner's deceit can have serious consequences for the spouse beyond psychological problems. Lisa, a twenty-three-year-old mother of a toddler, had her tubes tied because of her husband's anger over her second pregnancy. After the truth came out and they divorced, Lisa had to cope not only with his deceit but with the fact that she couldn't bear any more children should she remarry.

Even after the coming out, many spouses' lives are dominated by deceit as their partners ask them to keep their secret in strict confidence. Many spouses feel powerless and alone in their predicament with no one to turn to. As their partners suffer from the social stigma, so do they.

Some spouses find themselves caught in the cross fire between their partners and a homophobic society. In one extreme case reported in a metropolitan newspaper, a Catholic Archdiocesan Tribunal annulled the marriage of a straight wife on the basis that her ex-husband was actively gay before the marriage and did not tell her. Although he admitted the fact, he sued the ex-wife along with the archdiocese for several million dollars over terms used in the privileged document, such as "personality disorder." Nearly three years later, with the suit still pending and a non-refundable retainer fee spent, the wife feels like a pawn in the larger social-moral controversy.

Feeling victimized by the lie, many spouses struggle for a long time to shake off its negative effects. They feel robbed of their lives and experience intense rage at their partners, the gay world, homophobia and themselves for having been taken.

Using Anger Constructively

Anger at deception can predominate spouses' thinking for months and years, diverting them from regaining control of their lives. Such fury generally stems from expectations about what the partner "should have done," presumptions that Albert Ellis, M.D., founder of the International Institute for Rational-Emotive Therapy, calls "irrational beliefs."[3] Although anger is a normal reaction to feeling duped, it does not change what the partner did or might do in the future. Harboring resentment or hostility tends to color interactions with the partner, preventing constructive resolution of subsequent couple problems.

Spouses can learn how to use their anger as a tool for positive growth, the third step in restoring integrity. This is done, Ellis explains, by perceiving anger as resulting from a specific feeling such as frustration, disappointment, irritation, or pain. Spouses can determine what feeling is actually underlying their rage by asking, "What am I really angry about? Am I mad because things didn't turn out as I expected, I didn't get my way, or my partner's behavior is bothering me?" By handling the specific feeling aroused by the circumstance, the spouse may be able to distance herself somewhat from the debilitating anger and move towards resolution of the problem.

For example, the fury that a wife feels when her husband goes out with his lover can be recognized as disappointment at not having him at home. Rather than rant about his behavior which she cannot control, it's more productive to plan ways to avoid similar disappointment in the future. In this case, the wife may decide to go out or invite a friend over the next time the husband leaves her to be with his lover, thereby replacing the disappointing situation with one that she enjoys.

Constructive use of anger can be practiced on everyday problems such as waiting in line at the bank. Rather than fuming over what the teller should or shouldn't be doing, energy can be used to do something productive like thinking through a problem at work. That task will then get accomplished and the spouse won't be so upset over the inconvenience of waiting in line.

Understanding Both Sides of the Closet

As their anger becomes more controllable, spouses can begin to unravel the perplexities of why their partners hid the truth. The dilemma can be resolved by understanding their partner's motivation and, conversely, helping them to comprehend the spouse's hurt. This twofold task is the fourth strategy in rebuilding integrity.

It is critical to understand what was at stake for the partner to have carried out the deception. The purpose isn't to excuse what was done, but to understand how guilt, fear and other motivating factors can cause homosexual and bisexual persons to deny the truth to themselves and to hide it even in marriage.

In seeking to understand the partner's behavior, it is important that a spouse hear the partner's side of the story without refuting what may sound like rationalizations. Typically gay husbands may say, "I didn't want to face the possibility myself and didn't want to upset you," or, " I'd rather have died than tell you I was gay. I didn't want to lose you and the kids." They may also say that they dated men because cheating with women would have threatened or hurt their wives more.

When listening to such statements, it is more effective to concentrate on the partner's underlying emotions and to resist the temptation to argue. It helps to remember that the aim of this dialogue isn't to "catch" the partner in more lies, but to comprehend his or her motive. Trying to understand feelings shifts the tone of an otherwise adversarial discussion to one that is mutually supportive.

As spouses begin to comprehend the powerful role that guilt and fear play in their partner's lives, incomprehensible actions like husbands leaving telltale clues around can be explained. Often the rationale in that instance is, "I've put out the signs. It's up to her to act upon them." According to Diane Vaughan, Ph.D., this is a common ritual used to break up a relationship without hurting the other person.[4] The irony is that the spouse does get hurt anyway.

Living a false life may hurt the partner as well as the spouse. In prolonged deception, Bok explains, the pattern of covering up becomes hard to reverse. At the same time, living in constant fear of being found out slowly erodes integrity.[5] If the partner has a lover, the need for secrecy becomes even more complex, Vaughan points out, as both the sexual identity and the affair have to be hidden from the spouse.[6]

The partner's deceit—often to him or herself as well as to the spouse—can also lead to severe physical problems or self-destructive behavior such as alcoholism or suicidal feelings. One husband who married thinking his graduate school affairs were behind him suffered severe chest spasms eighteen years later. As he hovered near death, his wife took him to several doctors who were unable to determine the cause. Undergoing further treatment including massage, rolfing and Reichian therapy, he finally revealed what had been buried in his frail chest. After he disclosed his homosexuality, he left the doctor's office pain-free.

When partners finally tell their spouses the secret, they feel tremendous release from guilt and pain. Many are proud of their courage to be honest. Before the impact of the deception hits them, spouses often empathize with their partners. They may even encourage them as one said "to stop hiding behind this facade." Only later do they begin to see how the duplicity has hurt them.

As spouses realize the extensive role that deception has played in their married lives, it is important to express candidly to their partners the harmful effects of the deceit on them. The aim isn't to punish the partner or arouse more guilt, but to raise his or her awareness of the spouse's side of the crisis.

Spouses may find it hard to suppress their resentment or anger when explaining how the deceit has affected them. Yet the surest way to be heard is to communicate negative feelings calmly and directly. For instance, when a husband responds by saying that he didn't want to hurt the wife by telling her, she might reply quietly, "Well, it's really the other way around. Not telling me hurt far more."

In many cases the partner may counterattack, especially if the spouse is agitated. From her counseling of straight spouses, Aurele Samuels describes how a gay husband often reacts to an angry wife. "She is accused of homophobia, being crazy, overreactive, hysterical, and unreasonable. Her dilemma is discounted in preference to his."[7]

Such a response is counterproductive and inaccurate. The wife may be hysterical, but expressing her hurt is not a homophobic attack. The husband has no right to deny the wife her feelings. By listening to her underlying emotions, he may better understand her position and become more sensitive to her concerns. If the couple is unable to discuss their problems constructively, they may need the mediation of a counselor.

To hear each other out requires patience and objectivity on both sides. In particular, understanding the spouse's perspective can help the partner to become less defensive about his or her actions and to be better able to examine the consequences of his or her coming out.

Rebuilding Trust in Others and Self

Having been duped by the most important person in their lives, many spouses experience difficulty in trusting others and themselves after the coming out. The loss of trust is one of the more damaging aspects of the deceit, since trust is fundamental in any healthy relationship. Rebuilding trust in others and self is the fifth task of this stage.

After the disclosure, spouses often begin to distrust everything their partners say or don't say. "He must have other secrets," many think. For example, wives may wonder if their husbands have "quickies" in men's restrooms or how often they make "eye contact" with other men in public places. Worries arise, such as "Does he really practice safe sex elsewhere?" or "Will he tell me if he tests HIV-positive?" Repeated protestations of love, typical of this period, may also become suspect. Many spouses wonder, "How can he love me if he's gay?"

As wives realize the extent of betrayal, their distrust increases. After repeating, "Poor Miguel," with empathy for his pain, Caitlin was horrified to hear that he had used her father's cabin for secret trysts with his lover. Then when Miguel went back on the agreement not to see Ed for awhile, Caitlin's buried suspicions about his reliability surfaced and she stopped trusting him altogether. Honesty was the basis of their marriage after coming out.

Increasingly cynical, many spouses now lose confidence in everyone, including themselves. Straight husbands and wives alike often suffer from the distorted impression that anyone of the opposite sex may be secretly gay. Spouses may also doubt the reliability of their own judgment in having placed such unquestioning trust in their partners. Many wonder why they weren't able to perceive their partner's homosexuality when friends or family were able to.

Recently during a TV talk show on straight wives, an older woman in the audience asked one of the panelists, "Why couldn't you tell, being married for twenty years? I could three months after we married just by the way he talked and walked and dressed. Anyone who stayed in the rest room as long as him had to be gay."

"But my husband didn't look or dress differently from other men I knew," answered the panelist quickly. Afterwards, her confidence vanishing, she said to a friend, "Why didn't I see other clues!"

To lessen what are unnecessary mea culpas, it may help to remember that until recently there was little if any information available on gay-straight marriages. Throughout the seventies, common opinion held that married persons with children couldn't be gay. Although the spate of comings-out in the eighties proved otherwise, many people still assume that marriage and homosexuality are a contradiction of terms.

Moreover, most gay men don't display stereotypical behavior such as effeminacy or flamboyance. Many gay men are indistinguishable from their straight counterparts and are found in all walks of life, just as some straight men who use effeminate mannerisms may appear "gay."

As information about gay-straight marriages becomes more widespread, there will be more likelihood for such marriages to be based on honesty and trust with more chance for success. Yet just as there are progressive centers across the country, there may always be pockets of misinformation in some communities and subcultures since sexual attitudes are partly the product of cultural values. Hispanic groups, for example, who place high value on macho behavior, as well as African-American groups, who adhere to religious sanctions against homosexuality, tend not to recognize the existence of gay men. Recently the blind trust of a widow of a Latino in Dallas turned to agony when the cause of death was listed as "AIDS from multiple partners."

Most spouses eventually decide that in general it was far better for them to have trusted than doubted their partners. Their only regret is not having had the courage to explore issues when the deceit was first suspected.

Another troubling issue is the partner's distrust of the spouse. Many wives, wondering, "Why didn't he trust me enough to tell me?" begin to doubt their own trustworthiness. Dispelling such self-doubt can be a long and painful process.

Spouses can restore confidence in their own trustworthiness by performing a self-trusting activity each day such as fulfilling a promise to call a friend or to help a relative. To reinforce self-trust, it helps to record each accomplished task in a journal.

The process of building trust in others can be reinforced through positive interactions with close friends. Friends can be especially helpful by going out of their way for the spouse. Gradually the spouse will realize that trusting others doesn't always lead to hurt and that her or his own judgment of others is reliable.

Sharing the Secret

Learning to trust is particularly important for spouses who haven't yet shared their partner's secret. Until they tell a trusted friend or relative, many spouses are plagued by such questions as, "Aren't I guilty of deceit too? Whose secret is it? Whose responsibility is it to tell the children, friends, and family? Do they have a right to know?" Spouses who have disclosed the secret to support groups and counselors but not to the key people in their lives often feel similar disquiet. Resolving the dilemma of secrecy is the fifth step toward the reestablishment of integrity.

Keeping the secret isolates spouses from the reality check that outsiders may provide. Consequently, their judgment may become distorted and they may sink into depression. Stuck in the closet, it's common to exaggerate the horror of their situation. For example, when Caitlin blurted out her tale to her conservative acquaintance, the woman expressed empathy instead of repulsion. Caitlin then realized that her secret wasn't as terrible as she'd thought.

"We're only as sick as our secrets," says a character in Libbe S. HaLevy's play, *Shattered Secrets*, about incest.[8] Such stigmatizing secrets have to be destroyed in order for moral healing to begin. Telling others does just that.

Revealing the truth isn't easy. Yet as moral conflict increases, it becomes crucial to tell someone—counselor, support group, trusted friend or family member.

Friends or family who suspect or know the secret can help by gently informing the spouse. However discreetly it is done, however much support is given, the truth will hurt but less so than perpetuating the silence as Tracey's friends and family did.

Each spouse's approach to handling the secret varies according to what is most appropriate for her or his particular circumstances. Some wives, valuing their privacy, never tell. But many eventually find that the tension from leading a double life overcomes the compulsion to protect their partners and themselves from anticipated discrimination or rejection. When they finally share the secret and explore its moral implications, the downward spiral of their lives can be reversed.

Reconstructing Moral Values

Once the secrecy issue has been resolved, spouses can begin to rebuild their own moral code, the seventh step in regaining integrity. This task is complex and demanding but can be accomplished through redefining individual concepts of right and wrong. Eventually spouses will regain the confidence to be true to themselves.

First, moral sensibility needs to be nourished. This can be achieved most effectively in solitude. Simply reflecting upon their moral confusion will allow repressed beliefs to emerge. Further insight can be gained by reading biographies of admired persons which broaden the spouse's moral perspectives or by seeing movies and plays on moral issues. Another helpful exercise is to imagine how the deception might be viewed by people whose values the spouse respects, such as a former teacher, deceased grandparent, ancient philosopher or spiritual leader.

Talking with other spouses who face the same moral questions may help confirm the half-formed concepts that arise in solitude. Writing in a personal journal may help to formulate individual moral values. Some spouses find that listening to music or engaging in creative activities may allow moral sensibilities to emerge. For example, as Caitlin listened to classical music, her true feelings about Miguel's double life became evident to her.

Unexpectedly the spouse may have a glimmer of an opinion about the morality of some incident at home, at work or in the community. This is the first clue that the inner work is bearing fruit. Putting such moral views into words may be hard for the spouse who feels insecure or unaccustomed to asserting his or her opinions. Such a tentative expression, however awkward, is an important step towards regaining a moral sense.

Eventually the spouse will be able to formulate a moral opinion, perhaps in thought, aloud or in a journal. It may be on any everyday problem, a child's prank, a friend's oversight, the generosity of a stranger, a miscalculated grocery bill, crime in the neighborhood, a news story on some ethical issue or the spouse's own accomplishment. This usually comes in the form of a judgment call on some incident like "Good!" "That's not fair!" or "Here's an error!" Making such a statement is a giant stride for the spouse towards regaining control over the moral quality of his or her own life.

The next step is to explore the deeper ethical questions of a problem, such as "Does this action harm anyone? Does it infringe on the rights of others? Is this action a responsible one?" It may be enlightening to discuss such issues with a friend. Finding the answers deepens moral perception.

Those who fear taking a position contrary to another person might try it in a non-threatening situation with a close friend or counselor. Once spouses discover that their friendships aren't affected by expressing differing points of view, they will feel more comfortable asserting their opinions with others. They will also see that their moral views have the power to influence only their own lives, no one else's. Exercising such moral power now seems possible.

Developing moral clarity can take a long time. For example, a housewife in New Orleans married to an HIV-positive man who has been arrested twice in public rest rooms, remains in her caretaker role with him and their children while she awaits the meaning of her suffering to be revealed by inner "voices." Although spouses like her may not feel ready to assert their own moral needs, waiting too long may lead to chronic depression, chemical dependency, or other self-destructive behavior. This can be averted if they keep trusting their own judgment and moral views.

Acting With Integrity

With moral values in place, spouses have a foundation from which to take control of the quality of their lives and to act with integrity. This final stage of recovery involves a two-step process: first, forming a judgement about the moral issues raised by the coming out and second, guided by that moral compass, resolving how to live life with integrity. Spouses need to make major decisions about their positions on homosexuality, rights and responsibilities in the marriage and the ethics of deceit. A realistic resolution of these issues can be attained through decision making that balances moral concerns with compassionate understanding.

A spouse's personal views on homosexuality are fundamental in determining what role their partner will play in their lives. For many spouses, courage may be needed to explore the idea that homosexuality is a natural sexual variation, a position that runs counter to the prevalent view of society and their own moral standards instilled since childhood. A number of spouses are naturally accepting and not bound by tradition. Others, despite strong religious convictions, are curious to know why some religions accept homosexuality and others don't. They begin to wonder, "If gays are rejected only for being sinful, who then is acceptable?" Still others choose to work through stereotypical ideas to look at homosexuality from a fresh perspective.

Challenging long-held moral views can be difficult and threatening to many spouses. However, most gradually transcend earlier ideas and develop a more positive view of homosexuality.

Acceptance of homosexuality is supported by a substantial body of Judeo-Christian biblical and theological research, as reported by evangelical authors Letha Scanzoni and Virginia Ramey Mollenkott. This view holds that accepting gay, bisexual and lesbian persons is as Christian an act as respect for any other human beings. Moreover, loving, caring, committed relationships between people of the same sex are consistent with values about love and relationships found in the Bible and early Christian history.[9]

"Ultimately," says Reverend James DeLange, "the issue is not how do we reconcile homosexuality and homosexual behavior with a few Bible passages that purportedly address the issue, but how do we reconcile the continued exclusion of gay and lesbian people from full participation in the life of the church and society with the gospel of Jesus Christ? I don't think it can be done."[10]

While some accepting spouses go on to take strong positions against anti-gay discrimination, others go the other way to reject the possibility that gay persons are normal or good. In a personally painful situation like a coming-out crisis, it is especially hard to entertain a view that contradicts beliefs upheld by family and religion. Yet Scanzoni and Mollenkott caution, "The refusal even to consider the possibility of such transcendence may well lead to moral rigor mortis."[11]

In many cases the coming out and the partner's new lifestyle raise the moral concern, "What is a just balance of individual rights and joint responsibilities in a mixed-orientation marriage?" Many spouses conclude that the partner has a right to express gayness, but that it must be weighed against family responsibilities. In creating a new lifestyle, the partner is not entitled to deny the spouse and children the right to a stable family based on trust.

Many spouses conclude that homosexuality isn't a matter of choice, but homosexual persons can choose how to handle their lives responsibly.

"If they hurt others by their chosen behavior or lie about it," one straight wife stated, "that is wrong." This is not to say that the partner can't be forgiven for wrongdoings, only that hurtful behavior can't be condoned.

Spouses also need to examine how they are handling their own responsibilities and rights. For instance, spouses who seek an outside affair need to consider how it affects others in their lives.

The AIDS crisis heightens the morality question for mixed-orientation couples. Bonnie Kaye, founder of Spouses of Gays, a national network, reports that over seventy of the two thousand wives she counseled between 1983 and 1985 have contracted AIDS through their husbands. For some, that was how they discovered their husband's secret.[12]

To diminish the chance of infecting their wives, actively gay married men have a moral obligation to tell the truth to their wives. Yet denial and fear remain powerful deterrents even in such grave circumstances. No one knows how many AIDS-infected husbands haven't told their wives. However, a wife on the East Coast reports that four of the five husbands being nursed by their wives in the AIDS ward of a public hospital have not yet disclosed their homosexuality to their spouses.

The final moral question straight wives face is what to do in response to their partner's deceit. While spouses may feel they originally had little choice in marrying their partner, they now can choose how much support to give him or her, how much priority to give their own and their family's needs and which situation—marriage, separation, or divorce—would best serve their own moral imperatives.

No single resolution of the issue is common to all. Most women who have already divorced find that the consequences of the deceit confirm their decision to end the marriage. For many women still married, the extent of the deception or betrayal of the marriage vows influences whether or not they leave the marriage. The longer the deception, the more likely it becomes the major reason to separate or divorce. Only a minority of wives decide that love and marital satisfaction supersede the hurt of deceit. If honesty has been reestablished in the relationship, they are more likely to choose to stay married.

Divorce itself may present a moral dilemma. Though Tracey's reluctance to break up the family vanished when she discovered Herb's deceit, guilt remained until her psychiatrist helped her realize that only divorce could end her misery. Her priest dispelled her lingering feelings of selfishness when he told her, "To take care of others, we must take care of ourselves first."

When spouses finally make a decision based on their own moral values, whether it is to stay married or to divorce, they experience liberation. For the first time in a long time, they are acting without fear or guilt. They are finally in control of their lives.

Part six examines how spouses use their new-found moral strength to break out of old patterns and transform their lives within the marriage or after divorce.

six

BREAKING THE MOLD

TRANSFORMATION OF A
SHATTERED BELIEF SYSTEM

Turning the coming-out crisis into an opportunity to create a new life with new purpose, outside or within the marriage, is the last challenge on the long road to recovery. Even after restoring self-identity and integrity, many spouses find themselves without direction. To find meaning and hope for the future, they are challenged to shift roles from victim to victor and to overcome difficult circumstances in their lives.

For most people, it is easier to cling to a familiar way of life than to plunge toward an unknown future. The spouse needs to make a quantum leap in perception in order to let go of the past as well as transcend any blame, guilt and regret that may linger. This may require forgiving partner, society, oneself and sometimes God for the pain so that energy can be freed up for new growth.

Transformation generally begins during the third year after the coming out, and only after practical and personal issues have been resolved. The first step, abandoning the past, brings grief and emptiness. The second step, typical of anyone in crisis, requires that the spouse come to terms with his or her pain. To achieve this many spouses find it helpful to view their crisis from a larger perspective. In this context the pain no longer seems unique and can be seen as an example of the suffering inherent in the human condition. Spouses are not alone in their hurt. Unrequited love and betrayal fill the pages of history.

The goal is to stop seeing the coming-out trauma as a gay versus straight conflict but rather as a universal paradox. The truth that frees one person may hurt the other. Hurt and love coexist in life.

When this broader philosophy is grounded in the belief that positive values do exist and constructive change is possible, spouses can make a breakthrough in their lives. The recognition of even the slightest glimmer of beauty, joy or love in everyday experience helps create the seeds of a new belief system. Many spouses also seek something beyond themselves to bring meaning into their lives. This can be a sense of nature, the cosmos, a divine being or a deep individual spirituality. Such faith expands the possibility of transformation. Once a belief-centered philosophy is established, hope and purpose return and a new future seems possible.

The following stories depict the transformations of one married and two divorced spouses. The final story recapitulates all of the issues straight spouses typically face in their struggle toward transformation. The concluding analysis examines the crisis of belief spouses face, along with strategies for creating a new belief system through which they can break the mold and transform their lives.

Personal Stories

The Joy Of Openness
Jim

In the old days homosexuals were "fags" and "queers," people you pointed at and made fun of. No way could I connect that image with Janie! She wasn't any of those terrible things. So obviously she wasn't homosexual.

Before we married in the mid-sixties, she'd referred vaguely to intense friendships with women in high school and college. Later she disclosed that some of these had been physical.

"What's she talking about?" I thought. "Girls dance with each other and hold hands and hug and even kiss all the time."

"I'm not out molesting young people, Jim," she said, "doing what the far right portrays gays and lesbians as doing. I don't desire that. So I'm not lesbian. I just love women."

Curious, I began to read everything on homosexuality that I could lay my hands on during my business trips as a fairly high-powered executive on the East Coast.

Most of the considerable amount of literature on homosexuality wasn't very positive. Slowly over a two-year period, I found that most of my knowledge about it was inaccurate, the result of being fearful and ignorant. As I learned more, I kept comparing the information to what I knew about Janie until one day I said to myself, "She *is* a lesbian! The definition we've been using is wrong."

She and I talked about it constantly, though never using the words "lesbian" or "homosexual." Every now and then Janie said "gay," but it was like choking to get it out.

Meanwhile, while we had some lovely sexual experiences in private, whenever I came into the kitchen and started caressing Janie, she moved away. Yet when we went out, she held me and squeezed my hand as the loving wife. Alone with me, she backed off.

For eight years I travelled all over the country very impressed with myself and my company perks. Meanwhile, Janie gave birth to two sons, Jimmy and Chet, went through the seminary and was ordained as a minister. In 1972, I realized something was missing. At that time, middle managers in companies like mine were being jailed for illegal pricing. Two years later, not wanting to be the fall guy for my firm, I left to manage a book company in San Francisco. It was our tenth move since we had married. Once there, Janie looked up an old friend, Jackie, to assist me.

Four years later I became active in our Presbyterian Church at a time when people were confused over what was happening in the gay world. Use of the word "homosexual" had the same effect on the congregation as a four-letter word. The vote of the Presbyterian General Assembly which I attended that year was on whether or not to ordain gays as ministers or to the offices of deacon, elder and teaching elder.

The committee who had investigated the issue for two years had made a majority report approving ordination. The conservative members of the church then successfully organized a lobby to elect people to express *their* point of view. A new majority opinion was drafted stating that practicing homosexuals were ineligible for ordination to any of the offices. This was the issue to be voted on at the assembly.

"You know this violates the church government," I said to Janie as I prepared to go. "The sole authority for ordaining ministers is the local presbytery. The sole authority for ordaining elders and deacons is the church unless two-thirds vote of all the presbyteries in the nation change the rule."

It was late afternoon when I arrived at the assembly. By the door a diminutive man was handing out brochures and all the people recessing to go to supper were giving him a wide berth. "What's going on?" I asked someone.

"Oh, he's the one who wants to be ordained."

Hearing that the Presbyterians for Gay Concerns (PGC) were holding an agape feast in the basement of a nearby church, I joined the group going to it which included the outgoing and incoming moderators of the assembly and a bunch of other powerful folks.

There we were, 120 of us having communion, singing and full of joy, yet on the verge of experiencing a monumental setback. During all this love and singing, I suddenly was overcome by something powerful inside me. "Here are 120 people aligned against 4,000 over there," I thought. "How can they be so thankful they've come this far!" My antennae were tuned to the energy in the room, especially from the people I knew were gay, the closeted ones who were trying to give support but not be found out. I was moved to tears.

Once my eyes were opened to the religious truth of this agape experience, I couldn't close them to it again. "If they can fight, so can I," I said to myself on the way home.

Once home, I started a PGC chapter in our church. We had no real idea of what we wanted to do or how to begin. Though my involvement was sporadic, Jackie, by then financial secretary of the church where Janie was assistant pastor, came down to work regularly in the chapter.

Through my sales visits to libraries up and down the coast, I continued reading about homosexuality. One day I discovered Don Clark's *Loving Someone Gay*, published just after the American Psychiatric Association declared that homosexuality was no longer a psychiatric disease—thus curing it by writ.

"This is the most straight-forward, honest book I've discovered!" I told Janie, handing it to her as I left on another book-selling trip.

When Janie finished reading the book, she went to see Don Clark in Palo Alto. Next, she saw Bill Johnson, a gay minister who, along with a woman, had been ordained in the United Church of Christ.

On the way home from my trip the next day, I stopped at a pay phone to tell Janie when I'd be home. When she answered I heard tears in her voice. "What happened?" I asked.

"I met with Bill Johnson. Jim, I'm definitely a lesbian."

"Oh, Janie!" That was it. I knew that her admitting her homosexuality meant there was no question about it. Every bisexual person I knew was just afraid to be gay. Once gays discovered that they weren't awful people, they gave up masquerading as also being straight.

Back in the car, I drove down the freeway sobbing. "I've finally won the argument," I thought. "Janie agrees that she's gay."

Within days we sat down at the kitchen table with Jimmy, nine, and Chet, seven. "Daddy's heterosexual and Mommy's homosexual," we told them, "and it doesn't work. We've been trying, but it just doesn't work."

Then the four of us sat there and cried.

When we stopped crying, the boys asked, "What does that mean? What are you going to do? Don't you love each other?"

"Yes, we love each other. We don't know what we'll do. Probably we won't stay together."

By the end of the week, we saw divorce as the only thing to do. On our thirteenth wedding anniversary, Janie moved to a condominium she'd bought and I to an apartment I'd rented.

Soon afterwards I said to her, "We can't have an ugly falling out. I love you too much."

"And I love you. I don't want to give up the family."

"Janie," I said, "divorced or not, you're family. And as for the kids, I already lost them for nine years of their lives through mismanaging my time. I'm not going to lose them for their last nine years at home like other divorced men I know. Why don't the boys spend half the time with you and half with me?"

"I'm for it."

My schedule didn't lend itself easily to the arrangement nor did Janie's. Now a minister in a church that served the poor in downtown Oakland, she and her lover moved across the bay and bought a house in the hills.

About that time California State Proposition 13 was passed, killing my business as every library in the state cancelled all orders. I sold the company and got into life insurance, which allowed me to work from home and spend time with my boys.

Since Janie wasn't "out" yet, I couldn't tell people why we'd split. It was hard explaining how we loved and respected each other but were no longer married. Actually, people in our church thought I was the gay one. First, women aren't "queer," only men. Second, it couldn't be Janie, an ordained minister. Third, I'd been up to my ears in all those gay rights activities.

My "coming out" like this was kind of fun at first, finding out what it was like to be in the closet. People crossed the street to avoid meeting me. People I thought loved Janie and me changed their seats when I sat down in a pew. "Who are my friends?" I wondered.

One night I thought, "This hurts, but I have an advantage over gays or lesbians. If I get too scared, I can run away saying, 'O.K., you guys, I'm straight.'"

Yet friends' reactions hurt so much that, in my first love affair, I modified everything I said to my lover in support of gay persons until I wasn't me any more. Realizing that, I ended the relationship, vowing, "I'll never adjust my behavior to fit into somebody else's life again even if it's His Holiness, the Pope!"

About three years after Janie left me, the head of her church telephoned her to say, "We want to talk about your `lifestyle.'"

Telling me about the call, Janie said, "It must relate to my downtown ministry and my house in the hills. It doesn't look good to live in a rich white area and work with poor blacks."

"Naive Janie!" I thought and then said, "No, they want to talk about your lover. The word is out. They're coming after you."

They came and forced her out, the lesbian minister who'd been doing an incredible job for many years. "This is what you do when you hate gays and lesbians," I told myself. "You punish this one woman for no good reason."

It was now 1981. Many gay people were being fired. Most of them went quietly away so that the "sin" of whatever had occurred wouldn't be known. Each time it happened, I said to myself, "Come on, you guys, fight!"

When Janie was fired, she came out of the closet. I took the responsibility for the local news stories on it, especially the article for our county paper assigned to a somewhat homophobic woman reporter.

The night before the article was to appear, the boys were staying with me. Calling them into the living room, I said, "There's going to be a story in tomorrow's paper about Mommy. They may even have her picture."

Jimmy, twelve, sat crying in the corner, still feeling the peer pressure from school where the word was already out.

Chet, barely ten, looked up at me and said, "Hey Dad. Somebody's got to be the first to use the 'Whites Only' fountain and ride in the front of the bus."

Then it was my turn to cry.

In the days that followed, I gave up worrying about what people thought. Remembering the agape feast, I told myself, "If you're going to be friends with gay and lesbian people, you'd better be ready to deal with the negative stuff."

Soon I found my conversations couldn't go on for three minutes without my saying, "gay" or "lesbian." It was now such a part of my life that it just came out.

I became the "gay day parade" type, celebrating the community feeling of the minority, the joy of openness. It did a whole lot for my soul and was an outlet for a lot of poison in my life.

Each time I celebrated that joy in my church by talking about homosexual concerns, it offended half the members. "Who wants to be a trouble maker?" I finally said. "I'm not going there any more."

When straight friends spoke with prejudice about gays, I corrected them until I got tired of both the hurt and the effort to correct them. After I stopped feeling hurt, I thought, "They're dumb when it comes to homosexuality. I don't want to be with such ignorant people." So I dropped most of those friends.

It was different when I met closeted homosexuals. "I'm happy you're gay," I'd say right away.

That mesmerized them. It was often the first time that anyone had said that to them and had identified with them as being truly oppressed. "Don't you see," a gay friend explained. "I've lived all of my life afraid of people. When you treated me with the same respect you'd give any human being, it had a profound impact on me."

The first time I acknowledged a gay person, it was as if a door had been opened. I had a sense that he cared about me too. Over time I found that if you do anything positive such as treating gays and lesbians as being part of God's natural order, they become your friends no matter who you are. Seeing people as human beings who also happened to be gay created a spiritual bond between us.

Gradually I came to live pretty much in the gay world with Janie and Jackie. Jackie was one of the few people who appreciated our relationship. Her friendship with Janie had begun long before I'd met either of them. My coming into the picture, loving and being loved by Janie, hadn't altered their friendship. Jackie had left a twenty-five-year-long marriage. She knew the people she wanted to be with and why.

After the newspaper article appeared, the three of us went around speaking to students at local high schools. We called it "The Jim, Janie, and Jackie Pony Show." At the start of each session, the students expressed great curiosity about seeing a real, honest-to-God lesbian.

They always asked, "What were your kids' reactions?"

"Well," one of us would say, "Jimmy, the older son, is the more open. Janie was assistant pastor at our church when he was growing up and youth minister for a group that included him and all his friends. They loved her, 'queer' or not, giving Jimmy strength not to fear being identified with a gay mother."

"Chet's situation is different," another of us would say next. "He hesitates to be open because of pressure from his friends who were too young to understand why Janie was fired at the time." Then we'd describe Chet's incredible reaction, "Someone has to be first." That always got the students' attention.

Four years after our divorce, I married Jackie. Janie was the one who married us, adding another topic to our pony show. The kids always asked Jackie, "How can you sit beside your husband's ex-wife? Aren't you jealous?"

"We were friends," she said, "before Jim knew either of us."

After our wedding, Jackie became my business partner. We worked out of the house I'd bought. When her father died, her-mother moved from her quiet little town to live with her only daughter, now married to a gay rights activist. Although she had never known a gay person before, she went to functions with us and in the process shared our friends, by then mostly gay. Some became more her friends than ours.

Three years later Janie split with her lover, left their house and came directly to ours. Jackie's mother, the only one home at the time, invited her to live with us. When Jackie and I got home that night, there was my ex-wife with my ex-dog and my mother-in-law having a great time.

Valium kept me going for a week before I could take it all in. When I calmed down a bit, I told myself, "Janie's just a friend. I can give up the past. Everything's going to be normal."

That decision worked with twenty to thirty valium a week plus sitting down for spells. Yet soon I settled down, drug free, to live with my wife and ex-wife.

For two months it was dynamite. The boys lived at our house full time, no more back and forth. Then Janie found another lover and moved out.

About this time, the first diagnosed AIDS patient died and the insurance industry began to wonder about honoring these claims .

The gay community was screaming, "Discrimination. You can't trust an insurance company. They're all crooks."

The insurance companies were screaming, "You can't trust gays!" For the first time, I had an insurance claim rescinded.

In September I read that the Concerned Insurance Professionals for Human Rights were holding a meeting in Los Angeles. I flew down to discover that the group shared my view that an AIDS claim could be honored on legitimate policies.

Although most members weren't life and disability brokers like I was, the group became my beacon. When a question came up, I could call several of them to ask, "Hey, is this homophobic or is it the appropriate thing to do?" Together we explored the larger question, "Is insurance by nature discriminatory since it separates everyone, not just gays, based on criteria?"

We got information as needed out to hundreds of thousands of agents in language their communities could understand. Gradually we made an impact on the industry.

Then my seventy-six-year-old father, a vital man who grew and canned his own vegetables and fruit, made furniture and toys and shoveled everybody's walk, got a melanoma and died. It was my first taste of death.

Though grief counseling helped, I wasn't doing well at all. My panic and fear were channeled into working with the insurance group until September 1985, when I became emotionally paralyzed. By January our business had declined by four million dollars because of AIDS cases. To salvage what we had, I declared bankruptcy and sold our house.

Jackie insisted that we go to counseling. Having been in therapy all my life since my mother was an alcoholic, I fought it. Finally I agreed.

Had we not gone, I couldn't have told this story now. Even so, I was out of business for several months and only medication allowed me to handle the peaks and valleys.

Meanwhile Janie became involved in the Ministry of Light, an outgrowth of the Presbyterians for Gay Concerns. This group became responsible for Birthright, Parents and Friends of Lesbians and Gays, a gay youth program and a county AIDS support network. They also opened up a San Francisco chapter, which has had great impact on the church and our old presbytery. At each monthly meeting, the Ministry of Light gives its report. No one is offended by the word, "homosexual," any more.

What I do now in my life follows my own agenda, not just "the cause." Out of the openness of agape, I now have a string of friends and relationships which will last a lifetime. Doing things for these people I love gives me pleasure.

Yet the sum of all of my efforts is focused on my family. Last Christmas, seated around our dining room table were Jimmy and Chet, Jackie's mother, Jackie's son and his wife, my grandfather, Janie, her mother and father and her lover—all of us getting along fantastically.

No matter what I think or don't think, Janie is always going to be a lesbian and the mother of my two boys. We remain very close friends, arm in arm for such a long time.

We Don't Fit The Script
Barbara

Everyone knew Josh was gay—family, friends and people at work. In fact, few of his friends were straight. He'd been in Manhattan fourteen years when we met at work.

When I first saw this tall blond, my immediate thought was, "This man is gay." If you're a woman living in Manhattan, you learn to recognize gay men and stay away from them unless you have a propensity for suffering, which I didn't. Besides, I was dating lots of other men. My mid-twenties was a time to have fun.

After we met, Josh smiled whenever our paths crossed. One morning, he asked, "Hey, Barbara. What about lunch today?"

"Wait a minute," I thought. "This man's making advances. There's sexual energy here. If a man's gay, he's gay with none of the energy this one gives off."

After lunch at a sandwich place around the corner, he told me he volunteered in a gay rights organization.

"Well," I thought, "that sort of settles it."

Yet he kept flirting with me over the next few weeks, making me wonder, "This is very strange. This is a shy man, not the type who flirts with everyone he knows."

One afternoon a few weeks later, I announced to my co-workers, "I feel like going out for a drink after work. Anyone interested?" Josh, of course, was my target.

"Sure!" he said.

One other person joined us as we left for the bar down the street. Josh and I kept ordering until we drank her under the table. Once she left, it felt as if we were on a first date—awkward with each other—quite out of character for me.

After we finished our drinks, we walked toward my apartment, where I lived with three other women. "Want to come up?" I asked.

"O.K., but why not go to my place? It's closer."

I agreed and that night we made love. Though stilted, it seemed to be a serious thing. It wasn't as if I were an anonymous woman Josh had bumped into, but instead someone he knew and wanted a relationship with. As for him, I didn't know what his gayness meant, whether he'd had sex with a couple of men or with one lover only or many.

During our next night of lovemaking Josh said passionately, "The only time I've ever been this excited is with a man."

The comment stayed in my mind for weeks. "What sparked this passion?" I wondered. "How was our lovemaking like that of men?"

One evening I asked Josh what he'd meant. He couldn't answer. As our relationship continued, I realized he wasn't being evasive. The problem had to do with language, with not being able to describe such a feeling.

By then we were going out a lot and, without much ado, Josh told me about the one long male relationship he'd had and his many "tricks." "But I'm not interested in the gay life any longer," he said. "I got tired of the scene six months ago and had three casual affairs with women. I want a real relationship with a woman," he added, "but not because I want to settle down with a family."

I was dating several other men at the time. When one of them came down with crabs, I was beside myself and called Josh. "Can I come over? I want to talk to you about something."

Once at his apartment, I told him flat out.

Well," he said, "get some Quell and we'll wash. Let me know if it works." All matter of fact. His easygoing attitude about sex attracted me.

At this time, which was a period of experimentation for me, I was also having a relationship with a woman.

When I told Josh, he said, "Well, you know, honey, just because you have sex with a woman doesn't mean you're a lesbian. But if you are, you are. There's nothing you can do about it."

With that reassurance I got the feeling, "No matter what happens, I can talk to this man about it and gain some satisfaction."

This was very different from my first long-term relationship in college, who never let me rest if I did anything with another man. Without let up, he would keep insulting me to remind me of it.

One day Josh said, "I think we're seeing each other too much. Let's cut down to weekends and once during the week."

We followed this schedule until we had a little fight and he walked out. A day later at work he acted furious.

After everybody else went home, I said, "All right, now, what's this?"

"I'm mad at you, Barb, because I went out and tricked. Then I felt guilty for the first time in my life."

I looked at him. "You felt guilty? Why?" We were only dating. The relationship wasn't going to last.

"Because of you."

"Why me?"

"I don't know. I just did. Somehow you're to blame."

I laughed at this comment. Though it didn't make sense, I liked him enough to keep dating. We had fun and were comfortable together, yet he wasn't a man I could commit my life to.

I also kept watching for signs that he was gay. "When is he going to change back? Is he just running away from it like other men I know? But who would he be running from? His parents know. The gay group he's working for knows. Who else?"

For Josh, the issues were settled. No running away. No more questions. His seeking a woman wasn't an accident. One evening he asked, "How would you like to live with me, Barbara?"

"I'll have to think about it." I'd never lived with a man.

As I thought, what struck me the most about Josh was his comfort level with sex, perhaps stemming from having had sex with so many people. He was comfortable being naked and seeing me naked. No big deal.

After two weeks I said, "O.K., I want to live with you."

"Well, if your decision took this long, we shouldn't do it."

Several months later he said he wanted to move back to Chicago where he'd gone to graduate school and where my family lived.

"Well, I'm not ready to."

"O.K." he said.

While he made plans to move over the next year, our relationship continued. Then I got sick of my job. "Josh," I said one night, "I want to go to Chicago too."

"Fine," he said. "We'll move in together."

We arrived in Chicago with only the hope of finding jobs. Josh was hired right away by an architectural firm. It was harder for me to find a job in my field of sociology. Then through Josh's gay friends from prior political activities, we located an apartment in a four-unit building. Gay men occupied the others.

In the late seventies, a gay man living with a woman was enough to intimidate these men as well as his former gay friends. Their reaction to Josh in essence was, "What do we have to talk to you about?" Despite his many calls to them, none kept up the friendships. They didn't like to know about people like Josh, who had broken the unspoken rules. We weren't following the script.

In our new life together, Josh and I didn't talk about marriage but we did discuss children. "I'm too selfish to be a father," he said one day. "I want to be free and independent."

Independence was a problem area for us. Josh had gone from living alone to living with someone else. I'd changed from living with three other people to living with only him. For me, the problem was that I was alone all day. When Josh came home I would lunge at him. But he needed space and time for himself.

In our second year in Chicago an agency job opened up for me. The personnel officer there suggested that I go to graduate school to be assured of continued employment through funded grants. About a week before Northwestern was due to send out letters of acceptance or rejection, my doctor told me I was pregnant.

Telling Josh that night, I said, "I just know it's going to be a girl, but I'm not sure I want to keep it." It was a big issue for me, a pro-choice person.

I thought about it for a long time, but not about the moral issue about whether or not to have a child. I wanted the baby, but not to carry it by myself. My question was, "Does Josh want to be a father?" If he didn't want to share parenting, I'd decide to have an abortion.

For days Josh thought about why he didn't want to be a father. After he thought, we talked and then he thought again and we talked some more. By the end of the month he said, "I'd like to be a father after all, Barb. I love you and we've been together almost two years."

Keeping the baby meant that marriage was a strong possibility. That raised the gay issue again in my consciousness. The question sent me to Gladys, a marriage counselor who'd been my mentor from college days.

After telling her the details, I asked, "So, what do you think? Should I marry the guy with his history?"

"Well," she said in her no-nonsense way, "if you're concerned about him cheating on you, straight men cheat on their wives too—fifty percent of them, one study shows. If it's a question of whether or not it will work, you can never can tell. The oddest people who shouldn't be together stay together. Relationships which seem made in heaven, aren't. Do you love him?"

"Yes."

"Do you get along with him?"

"Yes."

"Then go for it."

Yet the gay issue stayed in my mind. "How can he be gay and want to marry?" I kept asking myself. "If he does, can it work?"

I discussed each question with Josh, bringing his gayness back into his mind. One night while we did the dishes, I asked, "Don't you ever think about going out with men?"

"No. I don't want to."

"Why not?"

"It makes me feel too guilty, Barb. I'm with you. I'm in love with you. I'm involved with you."

I kept on reading all the books and research articles in the graduate school library, comparing that information to my experiences with Josh and wondering, "How can he be a legitimate gay man if he doesn't fit any of these things?"

One night I asked, "How come you don't go to the baths?"

"I don't want to go."

Another time I asked, "What do you fantasize about?"

"Barb," he said, "I really don't like being your guinea pig."

"I know. I'm sorry. I just want to sort it all out."

"Well, sometimes I fantasize about men and sometimes women."

Then rereading the books and articles, I'd think, "Wait! This doesn't apply to Josh." It got to the point where I asked myself, "Why am I plying this theme? Do I want him to go out to seek a relationship with a man just so he'll fit in with the scene? He's decided to live a straight life. What am I doing?"

That was the end of that, but the question of marriage remained. "The outside world won't consider our relationship valid, married or not," I told Josh one weekend. "It doesn't match their expectations about gay men. Also, the research says marriages between straight women and gay men are doomed to fail in several years."

At that time our sex wasn't as frequent as we wanted and sometimes our interest in making love didn't coincide any more. When I was interested during semester breaks, he wasn't. Other times when he was interested, I wasn't.

One day I suggested we both see Gladys about the gay-straight issue. "With her experience with couples, she might have some answers. Our sex life's been a bit unsettled lately anyway."

"Sure. Let's go."

Once we were in Gladys' office, I told her our concerns about getting married.

"Well, I can't help you with that, but let's work on the things I know," she said quietly, "the relationship issues." So we talked about Josh's wanting independence, my loneliness and our unsettled sex. Gladys pointed out how our different work schedules might be affecting our sexual drives. Then she said, "Barbara, your loneliness probably comes from your dependency on Josh, which in turn affects his need for independence."

That helped, but it didn't answer my questions. My girl friends couldn't answer them either. They knew less than I did about how gay-straight marriages work. So Josh and I talked again.

"I don't know, Barb. I love you. I want to be with you and marry you and don't want sex with men. That's all I can say. I can't give you any definitive answers to refute the research."

So simple and clear. Our relationship had internal validity regardless of outside standards. I knew it would be long-term too in view of Josh's long, monogamous relationship with his lover before. "That's his nature," I thought.

Our wedding was a small gathering. It including my parents, who didn't know about Josh's past lifestyle.

"Why must they know?" I commented. "It would only be a reason to object." Then I chuckled. "It would certainly shake them up!"

Once we were married, it suddenly hit me that Josh wasn't going to wake up some morning and say, "By the way, Barb, this has been fun, but I'm a homosexual. See you later." I was in the bedroom looking in the mirror at the time. I just sat there, brown eyes twinkling as I thought, "This is going to be an enduring relationship!"

Later that day I reflected, "Gayness is part of Josh, but it's part of his history. Right now he's heterosexual. His straight lifestyle is his identity. Just because I've had sex with two women," I smiled, "I don't perceive myself as lesbian."

That convinced me to stop prodding Josh about his gay lifestyle. Then I wondered, "Did my probing encourage him to act on what isn't his style any more?"

Once Josh mentioned a married gay man that he'd met. "Do you know he has sex with boys, brings them home, and has them there for breakfast with the wife and child?"

"Good Lord! That would go against my grain too much. He'd be out on his ear," I said.

"I couldn't tolerate it either," Josh said in his quiet way.

Rachel was born that spring. We found a house to rent in a working class neighborhood and began a new life. Josh helped take care of the baby along with housework and laundry, as he'd always done. If anything, he did more housekeeping than I did because he was the neat one. Comparing notes with my girl friends about who did domestic chores in their households, I saw we had more equality than any of them.

When Rachel was two I returned to graduate school. If anything can kill your sexual desire it's graduate work. Constantly exhausted and preoccupied, I sometimes found myself finishing a term paper in my head as we made love. "Now that paper on...if I just added a quotation from...." Afterward I felt horrible about it. Then there were the surprises when sex improved during semester breaks.

Other times Josh rebuffed me because he was tired. If this happened three times in a row, the gay issue popped up again in my head, "That's why he doesn't desire me any more."

Then I'd quickly ask, "Is it because you're homosexual?"

"Of course not." It wasn't his nature to question why he thought or did what he did.

Whatever Josh answered gave me more to think about. Then I talked with him some more and thought some more. It was tough exploring the gray areas in what seemed like a very black and white issue. Yet each time we did, we worked through our problems a little more and made further resolutions about our relationship.

Nobody else knew as much about us as we did. The support group I tried was of no help. Since most of the women had just found out that their husbands were gay, their issue was betrayal, which didn't apply to me. "They're angry too," I thought, "something I don't feel at all."

Josh was unhappy with his career at that time, while I was going through the ups and downs of graduate school. We were both taking care of Rachel and getting her to child care while working on housekeeping and cooking issues, as well as worrying about our sex life. For months there was never a stable period.

Every now and then on a Saturday night, I went out with my girl friends while Josh stayed with Rachel. He didn't like that much. Not that he wanted to go with me. He just wasn't having fun at the same time.

Then four years after we married, I dated another man. He was aggressive and married. One night as we kissed and embraced, I remarked, "Josh doesn't react to me this passionately!"

"I can't believe anybody wouldn't desire you the way I do," he said in his baritone voice.

Flattered as that made me feel, we didn't have intercourse. Back home as I lay in bed with Josh about to make love, guilt and thoughts of the other man's desire and his flattery obsessed me.

"Am I attracted to him because Josh isn't that passionate?" I wondered. "Does the fact that Josh doesn't act as delighted with me as this man mean that he's gay after all? If I had an affair, would that make Josh go out and have sex with other men?"

As old doubts were triggered, I sat up in bed and cried, "Josh, I can't make love till I tell you about tonight."

When I finished, Josh said, "I know the man and don't like the idea that you went out with him, Barb. Are you going to again?"

"Oh, no! I don't have any desire for him."

For two hours we talked it out, how I felt, how he felt, and how an outside relationship couldn't be kept going without affecting ours.

By the time we finished talking, I thought, "Why would I pursue a relationship with this other man when I have intimacy with Josh? If his wife had done what I did, he wouldn't have dealt with it as casually as Josh did. What I have here is more precious than sex with that man. Here's trust, perhaps more so than in any straight relationship I know."

Yet the gay issue lurked below the surface. Whenever anything went wrong in our lovemaking, it was so easy to say, "See, it's him!" It became a defense by making Josh the issue rather than the relationship.

Occasionally I compared married sex to my fervent experiences as a single woman. The contrast was hard to accept until I remembered that I had been in my twenties, without a child or the responsibilities of married life. "Besides," I thought, "I don't masturbate that often any more either."

Over the next two years, Rachel started school, I finished my doctorate and Josh developed his own architectural project which he pursued more aggressively than anything before. Sex remained an important part of our life, something neither of us could live without.

Gradually the challenge became, "How intimate can I get with Josh?" It's much more difficult to have both an emotional and an erotic relationship than it is to have just casual intercourse. Since I had experienced both, there was no need to see if sex might be different elsewhere.

"I want to be the one bringing my husband to orgasm," I said to myself one night. "I want him to think about me when he thinks about sex because I'm the one who can please him. If he slept with a walrus," I thought, grinning, "I'd be jealous because he'd be reaching heights of intimacy without me."

It took a while for us to write this script for ourselves. We've survived seven years of marriage by tolerating the ambivalence of what we are and the uncertainty of what could happen. It has always come back to our ability to communicate expectations and what our relationship means to us. When I have doubts or fears, I just tell Josh with no assumptions, no judgments, only the belief that he'll help. In turn, he has become less shy about sharing his fears and thoughts.

If Josh came to me now and said, "I've decided I want to have sex with a man," would that mean the end of the relationship? No. In addition to a nice life and all of the reasons anyone would stay in a marriage, I love him. He's the one I like to be with and want to be married to. Besides, I don't think that sex with a man would be a meaningful emotional experience for him now.

If Josh decides some day that he doesn't want to be married, would I say that I made a foolish error? No. We have a life together. He's the father of my child. My time with him is now.

❦   ❦   ❦   ❦   ❦

Two years later Josh and Barbara decided that they wanted a second child and Barbara began to study Josh's religion, Judaism, to provide deeper roots for her family.

Coming Of Age
Kirstin

Friends called us a "storybook family." Living in our old-fashioned house outside of Houston, Paul and I and our children, Karl and Heidi, did everything together, home projects, city explorations, weekend excursions and vacations.

Paul and I met at a party in the fifties. When a friend introduced me to this chestnut-haired man, his lively conversation impressed me. He was thirty, four years older than I, and he'd just moved to Houston to work for the state. I'd left Minneapolis several years before to be an assistant editor in a publishing house.

Several weeks after the party, I called him on an impulse. "I remember you," he said. "How about meeting for a drink?"

Our drink extended to dinner and an evening of intense conversation and much laughter. From then on for two months, we saw each other as often as possible to picnic on the Gulf, dine and dance, go to films and galleries and hold deep discussions about many topics, especially our shared liberal political views. Yet coming from conservative families, we had an unspoken agreement to forego premarital sex.

Despite my sexual reserve, I was prone to outbursts of hugging and kissing, to which Paul, like previous boyfriends, responded in kind.

When my company transferred me back to Minneapolis, I thought constantly of Paul but heard nothing from him. After three months I began to date. That fall, two men proposed. One was a charming man with a history of depressions for which he'd been hospitalized. I told him, "No." Marriage alone was challenge enough without possible depressive behavior.

When my doctor friend proposed, I said, "Yes." He seemed perfect, intelligent, passionate, desirous of having many children, supportive of my career and part of a large circle of friends. But after one too many arguments with him over my belief in spiritual values, I broke the engagement.

"I love you," I said, "but marriage shouldn't start with disagreement on basics."

My mother, concerned that I wasn't married yet, suggested writing Paul about the breakup.

He telephoned at once. "I'd heard you were engaged, but I knew it wouldn't last," he said. "I knew you'd marry me."

"So how come you didn't write?"

"I thought you knew how I felt," he explained. "Anyway, let's pick up where we left off."

For months Paul courted me by letter and phone, sent tokens of his affection and then invited me to Houston for the Fourth of July weekend. When I saw him at the gate, his face hidden behind a bouquet of yellow chrysanthemums, I threw my arms around him saying, "Yes!"—without realizing he hadn't asked the question that was between the lines of his letters. "I mean," I stammered, nodding my blond head, "Of course I'll marry you."

The next three days together were nonstop activities, dancing, dining, a picnic, galleries and walking everywhere. The few hours left of the last night were spent in his apartment rather than at my friend's place where I was staying. Exhausted, we slept side by side fully clothed. More ardor would have been welcome, but Paul's reserve was a relief. I was determined to wait for sex until marriage.

The wedding was in Minneapolis that winter in the church where I'd gone as a child. A church ceremony was important to me, symbolizing my belief that marriage was a spiritual as well as a physical commitment.

On our wedding night, undressing for bed, I was somewhat nervous until Paul said, "Come on in! The water's fine!"

Laughing, I slipped into bed with him and let myself go at last! It was wonderful being spontaneously responsive and expressive, skin touching skin. Making love was even more exciting.

Once in Houston again, I volunteered in community organizations and took some classes. At home Paul and I shared everything from his career problems to joint investment projects. We had luncheon dates, went to cultural events, partied with friends and traveled in the States and Latin America. Our friends were mostly my old friends, now married—his were still single—and new ones made through my volunteer work. As we circulated together at gatherings, Paul would say, "There's no one here as interesting as you."

After two years, my optimism about getting pregnant began to wane. We'd been trying from the start. My irregular periods didn't allow conception to be planned with any certainty despite faithful charting of my cycle. Then one day out of the blue, the doctor said I was two months pregnant.

After a shaky first trimester, I blossomed. "Oh, Paul!" I said one day with a radiant smile from the sensual pleasure I felt as the baby grew, "This is so great!"

Heidi was born in December. Nursing, not a common practice at the time, was a delight. As the baby grew, Paul and I kept exchanging astonished glances each time she did anything remarkable, like learning to sit up.

A year later we moved to the suburbs. When Heidi was three, I discovered to my surprise that I was pregnant again. Karl arrived that summer. For two more years, except for community work, motherly duties and pleasures absorbed my hours.

One night Paul said, "Why don't you go back to work, Kirstin? It's more rewarding, dear, than volunteer activities."

The publishing house rehired me for a different department. Whenever work made me late, Paul made dinner. Otherwise, while I cooked, he read to Heidi and Karl. On weekends we four went to parks, museums, the movies, or our favorite corners of the city.

One night Paul brought up the idea of not having more children. "I don't have enough emotional energy," he said.

Never having thought of limiting our family, I spent weeks mulling over what that would mean. Our children gave me tremendous pleasure, yet Paul had a point.

"He's over forty and I'm in my late thirties," I thought. "We'll be in our fifties and sixties when any new children would be teenagers! Could we give them the same level of support we give these two?"

I finally agreed reluctantly. The next question was how to achieve our objective of no more children. Paul didn't approve of vasectomy and my doctor had cautioned me, "The birth-control pill or any mechanical or surgical contraceptive method is too risky for you, Kirstin."

After two other doctors confirmed his judgment, our old "taking my temperature" method seemed to be the only option.

When I told Paul, he said, "Charting didn't work when we were trying to have children. It won't be reliable to prevent it."

The ultimate choice therefore was either no sex or taking a chance on having more children.

Whether or not to stop our sex life during my childbearing years preoccupied me for weeks. "Paul shows his love in so many other ways!" I argued with myself. "He hugs and kisses me whenever I want. He's always saying how much he loves me and what a wonderful wife and mother I am. What would it be like without the most intimate aspect of marriage?"

I went back and forth in my mind with the problem. "I'd hate not having sex!" I told myself, thinking of our warm moments together. "But I don't want Paul to get angry if I get pregnant either. Besides it's only a postponement of pleasure till menopause." A Depression child, I knew how to "make do."

Eventually I agreed to give up sex in order not to have any more children. It was back to premarital days, waiting to make love again. Menopause became the light at the end of the tunnel.

Then I thought, "Paul will have a harder time with this since men have the more powerful sex drive. I don't want to tempt him any more than necessary." So I stopped wearing perfume to bed and rarely undressed in front of him.

For a number of years, Paul stayed as demonstrative as ever. We hugged and kissed every chance we got. In the meantime, art projects, guitar, tennis and my now full-time job diverted my sexual energy.

During this time Paul was promoted and the children did well in school. As our investments grew, we moved to a bigger house where we continued to entertain. Family trips took us to Latin America and we each traveled for our jobs. Paul seemed to thrive on travel, saying it made him feel like a different person, "almost flamboyant!" Our life was wonderful and friends accused me of wearing rose-colored glasses.

As Heidi entered her teenage years, a crack appeared in my rosy outlook. One vacation when I had to handle some business by phone, Paul said, "We might just as well have stayed home."

"Oh," I thought. "Doesn't he understand that work isn't on my mind except for this call that so much depends on?"

Several months after I stopped working during vacations, Paul said, "Kirstin, your job makes me jealous."

Even when I cut back overtime hours and forbade home calls from clients, something still felt amiss. Then as Heidi began coming home late and going to wild parties—no longer our exemplary daughter—Paul stopped doing chores around the house and suggested that we stop giving our annual fall party.

One Saturday as I was mending socks, Paul came into the bedroom. Startled to see this grim man seating himself on our lounge chair, I put down my darning to give him full attention.

"Kirstin," he said, his face colorless, "I've changed as much as I can. All I want now is peace."

My insides froze. "He wants a divorce!" flashed across my mind. Suspecting that he was referring to the family stress that Heidi's new behavior had caused, I thought, "This is another of his one-liners, said after exhausting all other solutions. It sounds like an ultimatum."

After a minute I said, "All right, Paul. I'll take care of keeping the peace."

From then on the children's problems and disruptive behavior became my concern. Karl, who was entering his preadolescent identity struggle, contributed to family changes as his grades began to fall. Week after week I resolved potential catastrophes before they reached Paul's notice. Playing the go-between, I explained the children's moods to him and Paul's needs to them, hoping that their mutual understanding might lend some peace to the household.

Then all of a sudden, anger seemed to be brewing just below Paul's control. I heard him shout angrily at others in business dealings and I didn't want the children or me to be his target. Once, trying to diffuse his potential fury after Karl had done something annoying, I said, "Karl's just trying to figure out who he is, Paul. It's typical. He'll grow out of this phase."

"You sound like a tigress protecting her young!" Paul snapped at me. He no longer said, "You're such a wonderful mother."

Before long there were no more surprise gifts, no more luncheon dates and only a rare "I love you!" My emotions were called superficial. When Paul began to eat dinner before I came home, many of my evenings were spent alone in front of the television experiencing unexpected bursts of pleasure from paltry love scenes.

I kept checking with my doctor, knowing that some women in their late forties get pregnant when they think childbearing is over. When he finally said, "No way can you can get pregnant now," I could hardly wait to tell Paul. Sex at last!

When Paul heard the news, he looked across the table at me and shook his head. "I don't think I can," he said.

I was speechless. Days passed before his statement sank in. Eventually I decided, "If he can't or thinks he can't, then he can't. It would be fruitless to try to persuade him."

When I confided what had happened to a professional friend one day, she said, "Well, take a lover."

"Oh, no!" I said. "I'm not about to commit adultery!"

Over the next months the friendly hugs of male friends and colleagues sustained me, though they were unaware of how much their male responses meant to me.

A year or so later, browsing in a city gallery, I came upon etchings from Picasso's *Erotica*. I returned again and again to see them, so often that a curator approached me one afternoon convinced that I was a serious buyer.

Heidi was off at college by then and Karl was struggling through his junior year of high school. That spring, one Saturday after our twenty-first anniversary, Paul and I were lingering with our wine after lunch. For a brief moment his green eyes twinkled, a look which, though rare now, always prompted a surge of love. As I rushed to hug him, he turned away as he'd done for some time.

"Paul, why do you duck when I kiss you?"

His answer came quickly. "Oh," he said in a calm tone, "I'm not into marriage any longer."

At that my world fell apart. All the negatives of the preceding three years tumbled into my lap. Since Paul never wasted words, I knew the truth was out there on the table and I'd have to deal with it.

As we talked into the late afternoon, I cried often into my wine, which I kept replenishing. At one point I said, "I'd like more affection, something physical between us."

"There are other couples our age who don't have sex," Paul replied. "It isn't unusual."

"But, we're not 'other couples'!" I said and then asked, "Am I a burden to you, Paul? Do I keep you from expanding?"

"No." After a pause he asked, "Do you want a divorce?"

"We can't decide that now. That takes time."

As I arose, weak and nauseous, Paul came over, arms outstretched to embrace me. "Kirstin, you're still the most wonderful person I've ever known," he said, holding me. "I'm just complicated." Then he went upstairs.

I stood there dumbstruck and confused. Here was my husband no longer "into" marriage, yet saying that I was still the most wonderful person in the world. He'd just mentioned divorce and then hugged me as never before. I was too exhausted to figure out what had happened or what it meant. It took another three years to do so.

Over the next few weeks, I took down all photographs of myself from the family room, put away mementos of our trips and slept as far over on my side of the bed as I could.

Next I invited old friends to lunch or for a glass of wine after work, both women and men. Many I hadn't seen for years. I needed them to affirm me, whoever I was. I no longer knew.

Both at home and while commuting to work, I reviewed the preceding twenty-one years to see what I'd done to make Paul feel he was out of the marriage. Wine became a way to relieve tension and deaden sensitivity. With a glass by my side, whether I was in the kitchen or in hotel lounges after meetings, I jotted down all aspects of our marriage and ways to improve our relationship. To understand why I'd married Paul, I listed his best qualities. To figure out who I was, I listed my strengths and failings, likes and dislikes, as well as goals.

Reading books on psychology and marriage, often devoured on the run in city or airport bookstores, my goals shifted from trying to prove I was right to trying to work it out.

After six months of this turmoil, I was down to ninety-two pounds, "looking like an old lady of 110!" a friend said later. I couldn't talk to friends without bursting into tears.

One friend insisted that I see her therapist, Frances. At the end of the first session in which I did all of the talking, Frances commented, "You're an articulate, intelligent professional, but you don't seem to have any idea of what your feelings are."

For months Frances listened and clarified, helping me identify my feelings. At home I tried out the new skills I'd learned from her. One Saturday morning as I was about to drive Karl to some project he was starting, Paul said, "Let him take the bus. You spoil him!"

"That hurts, Paul!" I said and as he kept implying that I was a bad parent, I repeated it over and over.

"But I'm right, aren't I? That isn't the thing to do."

"That's not the point," I insisted. "What you said hurts."

Later that month Paul tripped on an oriental rug in the hall. Running out from the kitchen, I found him sprawled on the floor and took him in my arms for the first time in years. When he came to, he pushed me aside and stumbled away. I didn't move from where he left me, unable to express so deep a hurt.

Then I discovered *Love is Letting Go of Fear*, by Gerald Jampolsky. "Aha!" I thought, reading it, "Personal attacks are signs of the attacker's inner pain, not an actual assault."

Trying to figure out what was bothering him, I asked Paul one night, "What are your plans when you stop working?"

"To find happiness. I didn't find it in marriage or the family."

I gasped silently. "But Paul," I continued, remembering Jampolsky's theory, "you're not going to find happiness outside of yourself. It's *within you*."

That fall Paul took a leave of absence and began to explore sports activities he'd missed as a boy. Then a freak accident to his lower back made him stop all of them. Five different specialists, varied exercises, exotic medicines and a cumbersome brace did not ease the pain.

Each night when I came home, he was bundled up in a wool jacket reading in his den. Before eating my dinner, I played the therapist, listening hard to discover a clue to his misery. Night after night he aged before my eyes.

Like a yo-yo, I alternated between being my spontaneous self, who wanted to share my natural euphoria with Paul, and being a submissive woman who expected to be rejected. Holding myself back to avoid rejection made me feel deprived. But if my *joie de vivre* bubbled over, it turned to pain when he didn't respond.

Trying to get through to him, I used his favorite perfume once again and wore sexy clothes around the house. While he read in the bedroom, I undressed in front of him. He never noticed.

As the aura of rejection pervaded the house, I realized that the Kirstin whom Paul had chosen to marry had disappeared under layers of accommodation. "Is there anything left to change?" I thought.

To keep my sanity, I played my guitar, worked in the garden and bought a bound journal for composing my thoughts. Reading it regularly like a book, I saw that my feelings were beginning to focus on what I wanted rather than on what I didn't have.

One night after musing about how much happier he was before marriage, Paul commented, "I feel imprisoned by responsibility."

All of a sudden a way to free him flashed in my head. "Why not take a trip, Paul?" I suggested, remembering how he thrived on travel. "Stay as long as you want. We'll be here when you get back." My thought was, "He'll come home his ebullient self. We'll have fun again and stay together as a family."

That weekend Paul said, "All right, Kirstin. I'll leave. But I'll wait till Karl takes off for college."

"I didn't say 'Leave'!" I shouted in alarm.

When my emotions settled down, I wrote Paul a note explaining that a trip would be a chance for him to be happy. To make sure my words wouldn't be twisted again, I added, "Whatever you decide, do it on the basis of what you want for yourself not on what you think I want."

Nothing more was said on either side.

For the next three months, I went on with work and family life like a perfect wife, ignoring the possibility that Paul would actually leave. I tried to be the perfect parent too, telling Paul and the children to work out their persistent animosity themselves. "I'm not going to be the go-between any longer," I told each of them.

One day after Paul had ignored Heidi when she came home from college, making her cry bitterly, I decided that he had to know that she felt hurt. As we talked about it, remembering his negative feelings toward his mother, I said, "You know, I think you hate women!"

Paul said nothing.

Our twenty-third anniversary came the next week. After thanking me in the morning for the hanging I'd made for his den, Paul didn't mention the anniversary again.

That night I thought, "I can't take this slap in the face silently, even if speaking up means the end of the marriage."

The next night I forced myself to enter the den where Paul was writing letters. "Paul, I want to talk about something."

Sitting down, I began what I'd rehearsed all day. "I noticed you didn't say anything about our anniversary yesterday other than 'Thank you.'"

"Why celebrate a marriage that doesn't exist?"

"Oh!" I said, startled. For several moments I said nothing, formulating what I needed to express out of my pain of the preceding five years. "Well," I continued in a quiet voice, "I can't go on any longer without any emotional or physical interaction."

Another long pause.

"I'll be moving out," Paul finally said.

"I could go back to the city," I said. "I wouldn't mind."

"No, the husband always moves."

We stayed where we were in silence for several minutes as twilight darkened the room. Even now I can see Paul sitting in the shadows, motionless. He didn't say that he'd try to be more responsive. I didn't say, "Don't go." In that silence the final decision was made.

In the emotional vacuum of the next few months, Paul and I play-acted at being married. I hated it and didn't want to feel that hatred. It wasn't part of the Kirstin I knew.

While I was deciding when we'd discuss how to tell the children he was leaving, Paul told Karl who told Heidi. Home for mid-semester break, she came to me very upset. "Why didn't you tell me? Is it because of me?"

"Of course it isn't because of you!" I said, putting my arms around her. "It's a matter between Dad and me." I didn't tell her I was flabbergasted that for the first time, Paul and I hadn't jointly decided a family affair.

Paul moved out in June. As I left for work I kissed him good-bye, saying, "I hope you find the happiness you want." Then I went out to the car knowing that he and whatever furniture he'd chosen would be gone when I returned that evening.

There was a sense of peace without Paul in the house that night. There was also a sense of new life which contrasted with the morgue-like emptiness that had pervaded the house when he had been there. Over the following weeks, I opened the blinds to the trees and blue sky, put a bright-colored comforter on the bed and bought more lamps. The photographs of me went back into the family room.

For the next five months, Paul and I did things together in Houston, often at his apartment complex where he introduced me as his wife. Although he no longer wore his wedding ring, I still wore mine.

"He looks so much happier and younger!" I told a friend one evening. "His pain has disappeared!"

"Kirstin," she asked, "Why are you doing so much with Paul? What about your own life?"

Realizing that my involvement with him used up time I should be spending on my life, I took Paul out to lunch at our favorite spot the following Sunday to suggest that we see less of each other.

Tears ran down his cheeks. "You mean you're going to take away my best friend on top of making me leave!"

I couldn't believe my ears. "That's not true," I said. "I didn't make you leave. I suggested that you take a trip."

Then the conversation somehow turned to the end of our sex life years before. "Oh," Paul said, "I suggested it because you were frigid."

"Frigid!" I exploded. "You said it was because you didn't want any more children. You mean you covered up your real reason?" Clear white anger filled my being. I was ready to scream, to throttle him in front of the other patrons.

He continued, "I didn't know what else to do and you didn't like sex anyway."

"I loved sex! Why didn't you check it out with me?"

I was seething that he had deceived me about a major decision in my life. Not wanting to make a scene in public, I called for the check and invited myself back to his apartment.

For five hours I screamed and yelled. "How dare you assume what I think? What else have you assumed? What else haven't you checked out with me? I feel so betrayed!"...and on and on.

As my fury abated I said, "Intimacy meant so much to me! I looked forward so much to having sex again."

"I don't know, Kirstin," Paul said. "Maybe I just burned out. I did all I could."

Then I described my deep sexual feelings and how men had found me sexually attractive over the years, although nothing had ever come of it.

"They didn't have to live with you," Paul replied.

I couldn't take any more. Driving home, my anger spent, I wondered what Paul thought of my outburst. Shortly before we separated he'd said, "Kirstin, it's so frustrating the way you don't ever get angry!"

The impact of the episode diminished over the months as I struggled to survive each day and keep family communication going. I was waffling between hating Paul's behavior and wanting to save our marriage. Then Paul had minor surgery. The day after the operation, I visited him in the hospital with some investment papers to be signed, a bouquet of flowers and a bottle of wine.

He was sitting up in a chair, dressed in his lounging robe and still under medication. Once the papers were signed, we chatted about mutual friends as he drank a soft drink and I some wine.

After half an hour he said, "I've got something to tell you."

"I think I know what it is," I murmured without thinking, somehow wanting to make it easier for him to tell me whatever it was and to prepare myself for something I suspected he might say. A hunch about his lack of responsiveness had floated briefly across my mind a year before we separated.

"You do?"

I nodded.

"I'm gay!"

I smiled slightly.

"How did you know?"

"I didn't, really," I said. "But as you became more withdrawn and unhappy and didn't respond to my wiles, it seemed possible that you might be a latent homosexual and not know it."

It was more than that. For an hour Paul described his first explosive homosexual experience before he'd met me, his lover before our marriage and his gay lifestyle since our separation. "I was never active," he reassured me, "while we lived together."

As Paul recounted each detail, his medication acting like truth serum, his words transported me into an unreal world. At times we both broke into laughter, saying, "It's better than a soap opera!"

Astonished at the revealed chapters of his life, I thought, "This is the man I lived with for over twenty-three years, the man I tried to re-attract for so long!"

"My love for you was so strong," Paul went on, "that I thought that although it wouldn't change me, it would overcome the homosexual drive. I often wanted to be killed in a crash so I'd never have to tell you."

I sat mesmerized. "This man sitting here, presumably my husband but now a stranger, held this secret inside him all this time, a secret which profoundly affected me," I thought. "He's still the same person I laugh and talk with, but in a new body unknown to me, in a world completely separate from mine."

At the same time I felt a new closeness to Paul since I now shared his secret self. All of him was available to me for the first time. "Here's the vibrant man I married," I thought, "plus a new joy of his own that is no longer repressed."

Sitting in shock, I seemed to be acting out a part someone else had written for this ludicrous scene, Paul in his robe and me in my tailored dress, the sterile hospital room serving as backdrop for the climactic moment.

That night I wrote in my journal:

All has fallen into place. Now I must absorb this new side of him, though he's still the same Paul. But my struggle is over. So is my slim hope that we could reunite. Yet who knows? I can't give us up especially since he's more expressive now.

My struggle was nowhere near over. I didn't give up hope for over a year. It took fifteen months to admit that there was a wall between us, impossible to penetrate, to scale or to break.

The morning after Paul told me the truth, I went off to work carrying his secret which I'd agreed not to tell to our mutual friends. Since my close colleague didn't fit that category, I told her.

"So what else is new?" she said.

I gulped.

"My husband picked it up when they met that one time."

Her words made me blush. I felt foolish that her husband, a stranger, had figured it out while I hadn't.

For weeks my emotions contradicted one another as I immersed myself in Paul's new life and went on with my own. From moment to moment, I felt relieved or sad, happy or hurt, amazed or angry.

Tremendous relief came from knowing the real reason why Paul had changed so drastically during our last years together. "Now I have the key to what locked him away from me," I thought. "It wasn't anything I or the children did or didn't do."

When I told Frances that Paul had come out, I smiled wistfully at having continued to try to attract him and sighed, "How ironic!"

"Poignant," she said.

"Well, it certainly explains why he found me frigid."

I was also deeply sad about how Paul had suffered from hiding his gayness. "It nearly crucified me, Kirstin," he commented a few days after he came out.

Then I read *Now That You Know*, written by parents of gays and lesbians, which made me view Paul as a parent might. My sorrow about his prior suffering turned to joy that, "complete" at last, he could be who he really was and express his true nature.

Reading everything available on married gay men, I became an instant expert. As the bias of other people's opinions became more evident, I decided it was more reliable and more fun to do things with Paul in his gay world and find out for myself what gay men were like.

Paul was eager to have me meet his friends. "After all," he chuckled, "you like men."

His friends were of all ages and physiques, some previously married, others single, some with their lovers. They included a travel agent, a computer programmer, an architect, an investment broker, a former athlete, an ex-priest. Some were attractive, some not. They were open, sensitive, and knowledgeable in many areas.

In contrast to the last cold years Paul and I had lived together, he was now openly affectionate with me.

"Why couldn't you have just hugged and kissed me like this?" I asked him one evening. "That would have been enough."

"It would have been misleading."

"No it wouldn't," I thought. "We could have set limits."

Sometimes we went out with his preferred friend at the time. Walking down the street between two handsome, attentive men, I fantasized about the three of us living together.

Despite such delightful times with the revived Paul and his friends, I felt empty and alone once I returned home. I was "in the closet" now, forced by Paul's secret to deal with my sorrow without support from friends who had helped me before.

Fortunately I had a network of professional friends across the country. On my first business trip after Paul told me his secret, I dragged my closest colleague to a private spot on the conference grounds. As I told her, deep sobs shook my body. For the first time I felt like the victim of a long cruel plot.

When I mentioned my fantasy of a *menage a trois* with Paul and his friend, she queried, "How would you like to have Paul making love with a man upstairs in your house?"

"Oh-h-h," I groaned, "I hadn't thought of that."

Back in Houston the negative aspects of a threesome were forgotten as I continued to search for a way to live happily ever after with Paul. "What about a *menage a trois*?" I asked him.

"No," he said emphatically, "I'm too monogamous."

That night I wrote in my journal, "Literal monogamy is more important to him than acting like a real monogamous husband who cherishes his wife."

The next day I thought, "But I'm no longer his real wife!" Off went my wedding band for good.

Soon I noticed that each time we dined in a gay restaurant, Paul would look around to spot attractive men —he who had always found me the most interesting person in a room. Besides feeling horribly insulted, I felt defeated. "By competing with these strangers for his sexual attention, I'm the loser," I thought. "With women I'd have a fighting chance."

It also hurt to see Paul glow when he looked at gay friends. To watch him embrace them with obvious pleasure became torture even though I knew it was important for gays, as "misunderstood people," to demonstrate mutual support.

Yet he kept embracing me, too. One night I wrote:

> Irony! He wants to kiss, hug, express love for me as a 'total person' but not as a man to woman. And I can't respond to him sexually, knowing it can't be consummated. I yearn for a man who loves me as a woman.

A few months later I realized that Paul's world was as separate from me as mine was from him. "He's in good company," I thought, "but it's a dead end for me in the romance department."

Yet I couldn't envision life without Paul. It would have no meaning. Even as the reality of his gayness poked holes in my fantasy of living happily ever after, I wondered, "Could we resurrect our marital bond as it was, outside of his gay world?" The idea went in and out of my journal ad nauseam.

> He acts so much like the man I first fell in love with, the person who was lost for so long!

Then a few days later:

> I have to remind myself of how awful it was before he came out, when he was miserable in his prison.

Paul didn't remember his withdrawn state before he'd come out. "Everything was fine," he said one day. "I could have gone on forever like that. You're the one who broke the marriage vows."

I broke the marriage vows? My rage boiled up. "What vows?" I thought, feeling too weak to confront him directly. "Vows not to have sex? By imprisoning himself from men, he'd locked me out too. Didn't that break the vows?"

For months when least expected, Paul made digs at me mid-conversation. One night he said, "You made me go out into the world I didn't want."

Anger rose up on the back of my neck. "Now he's blaming me for living a gay lifestyle," I thought bitterly. Taking a deep breath, I repeated what I'd said so often. "I didn't make you go. I suggested that you take a trip."

Eventually I blotted out Paul's accusations, thinking, "How pained he must still feel to be doing this!"

By this time I'd started to go to a spouses of gays support group suggested by Paul. Most of the other women were attractive and articulate, between twenty-five to fifty years old, and still lived with their husbands. They were models of how we too might work it out. They also helped me face my growing awareness of hurt and anger.

When they heard how Paul had said that I'd made him leave, one woman made a fist, shouting, "I'd like to sock him in the nose!"

Then the group leader said, "People with low self-esteem tend not to own up to what they've done. Instead they blame others."

"Aha!," I thought. "Another reason for Paul's blaming!"

Spurred on by my reading and my support group, I finally asked Paul directly if he thought we could get back together.

He shook his head. "No, I'd probably end up the same way as before."

That was when I saw the bittersweet paradox: his coming out released the man I wanted to find again but made him unavailable as a husband. With that loss of hope came great sorrow.

There was also deep anger. Most of my rage had been spent over Paul's accusation that I was frigid, the unspoken reason why he'd suggested we end our sex life. My anger now was at another level. Out there in the world were gay men for me and other women to fall in love with unknowingly and with expectations that could never be met.

Yet I still felt compassion for the agony Paul had felt from repressing his homosexuality in order to live in a society which said he didn't belong if he were gay.

"It's tragic!" I said to a former colleague. "Paul believed he'd find happiness by doing 'the right thing.'"

She nodded. "Yes, I've seen you support people at work like this, people who have hurt you gravely. It's a bit unreal, you know."

Many friends felt uncomfortable with my compassion as if it invalidated their anger. Some of them had figured out what had happened. Others I'd told after Paul had come out publicly. Several pressed me, hoping to rouse some rage.

"Of course I'm angry at what Paul did," I explained, "but not at him! He thought that he was making the right decision in marrying me. I resent not being part of a decision which determined my life for twenty-four years and I'm furious at being deprived of sex for so long. But he didn't hurt me on purpose. His own pain blinded him to mine."

That fall I went to Brazil for a conference and decided to stay longer. Sitting on the beach or in cafes, reminiscing about visits there with Paul, I began to wonder what I could have done differently so that things wouldn't have turned out as they did.

Gradually my sanity seemed to slip away. I couldn't buy a railway ticket without anxiety. Finally solace came in old churches, where their coolness refreshed me in the heat of Rio. As I prayed I felt that God understood what was going on in my life. I wasn't absolutely alone. I wasn't crazy.

Back home I reflected in my journal:

> I cry easily and can't rejoice about my superb vacation. Aloneness is so overpowering that I can't be assertive. I don't care about anything enough to have a preference. I'm stuck in a place I thought I'd left behind. My past is a distant motion picture. I feel empty, a non-woman. Can I resume response to anyone?

A year after Paul had come out, I finally said to myself, "Cut the shackles. Stop using your energy on the relationship." Yet I clung to it as a drowning person grabs a splinter to keep afloat.

Then one day I realized, "Paul is having his cake and eating it too. I have neither a sex life nor him as a husband."

Something had to be done, but I was too weak to do anything beyond surviving in my hectic work schedule. One morning, weeping, I telephoned an old friend in Minneapolis. "My dream is dead," I mourned, seeking sympathy.

"Well, create another!" he replied simply and sharply.

There it was. It was pointless to think any more about whether or not I'd failed in my marriage or given up the fight to save it. It was time to work on a new life. Known for creative problem-solving, I knew I could do it.

Yet starting a new dream required many risks for a woman in her mid-fifties. Although half our assets and my salary would provide enough financial support, could lost time be made up by forming relationships with straight men? I prayed for insight to figure out what to do and the courage to do it.

It was clear that only divorce would reflect the reality of our relationship. It was a matter of integrity. The following Saturday I told Paul my decision.

Once I had decided, the need to "get on with it" drove me forward. Friends encouraged me, saying, "Leave Paul to his life and start the rest of yours." Yet cutting our bond was hard.

I don't like the tension that accompanies the drive toward the divorce. This isn't Kirstin, the person who cares and listens and reflects. Will I surrender to the uncried tears, the unscreamed anger, the stiffened muscles, the barren heart?

Breaking what was by now a twenty-five-year habit, I no longer referred to "us." Paul was no longer "my husband." I called him less often and turned down joint activities that I'd have enjoyed. When he brought up gay topics, I changed the subject.

Then Paul began to give me surprise presents as he had early on in our marriage. They didn't dissuade me from moving on. "Doors are ajar," I wrote. "I have the choice to close them."

In May I saw a divorce lawyer although Paul and I planned to work out our own terms. Propelled by a sense of adventure, I travelled more in my job, changed my hairstyle, bought some new clothes, negotiated with Paul and went out with male friends.

Soon I realized that my men friends weren't romantic prospects. "I've got to do something to find real dates," I decided. "Men aren't going to come looking for me."

After finding no prospects in the several night classes I was taking or the political group I'd joined, I placed a "personal" ad in a metropolitan weekly. This and later ads opened up a treasure chest of men of all ages, occupations, and objectives for this inexperienced, fifty-five-year-old woman.

One of the first persons to answer was a younger man, an artist and ex-military psychiatric social worker. His invitation to make love a few weekends after we met startled and scared me.

"Give me a minute to think about it," I said. In that minute I said to myself, "Kirstin, if you don't do it now, you never will. You'll always have an excuse."

I said, "Why not?" Holding my breath, I led the way to the bedroom with an armful of candles he had me gather. After lighting them all and placing them around the room, we proceeded to make love.

Gently and patiently he introduced me step by step to basic sexual experiences to arouse me. "You're like a seventeen-year-old virgin," he whispered with a smile.

I smiled too, thinking, "I'm not frigid at all. Inexperienced, yes, but clearly responsive."

On the second evening at my house, he remarked, "You're so playful and giving!"

Astounded to find out that partners need to help each other in order for lovemaking to give pleasure to both, I saw how my ignorance and Paul's silence had worked together to deprive me.

That concern went out the window in my delight with my lover-teacher-healer, who introduced me to a realm I hadn't known. Then he left for Mexico to paint for an unspecified time.

I contacted Frances, my counselor, to help me handle the turbulent feelings unleashed with my sexuality. My opening-up revealed the weak, vulnerable faults that I'd carefully controlled over the years in order to be "perfect" and avoid criticism, my own as well as others', especially Paul's. A whole, imperfect Kirstin faced me for the first time. I didn't want to see her.

Listening to my sobs alternated with laughter, Frances said quietly, "You're experiencing a rebirth of Kirstin!"

As I talked with her over the next weeks, I remembered the waves of attraction I'd felt toward Paul, but no particular passion from him toward me. "I never felt desired as a woman with Paul," I said with some bitterness. "I never heard 'I love your body.'"

Before long a sense of betrayal inflamed me. "My God! My sexuality was sacrificed for Paul's secret!" I told a friend.

A broken wrist and sprained knee indicated that I should slow down and use my limited strength wisely. Something had to be done about the scraps of the old dream which kept floating in and out of my consciousness and distracting me from my resolve.

> I must use all available energies to get on with my own life and to become the person I'm supposed to be. It's self-defeating to spend it on a story that's over.

Soon after my home reflected a new lightheartedness as I entertained more and rediscovered the nesting instinct, adding pillows, an easy chair, more lamps and plants. Karl and Heidi remarked on my new strength. At work I held my own in a beleaguered situation. New men came and went, some from ads, others from organizations I joined. I took an AIDS test to allay any fears men might have, even though there was no possibility I'd been infected. I expected the new men to take AIDS tests also, for both our protection. I was on my own, not having sought Frances' counsel for some time.

That fall I planned a two-day "transition" rite. It was to take place at an inn on the Gulf, where I'd sit before a fire all night to let thoughts and emotions freely flow to create a new perception of me and my life and to leave the old one in the ashes.

Instead the ritual took place in a hospital, where I was taken with a severe case of pneumonia brought on by exhaustion. During the months of recovery at home, I read voraciously. Several men I'd dated had introduced me to writers of non-Western spiritual philosophies I didn't know, like Hesse and Gurdjieff. These readings led to others, rekindling a dormant interest in the spiritual realm.

As I was unable to work, I had hours to reflect upon and incorporate many of these ideas into my view of life. By the time I returned to my job, part time, "living" and "loving" meant something broader and deeper than achievement and romance. A new Kirstin had been molded, no longer connected with Paul.

When the divorce became final that summer, I didn't cry much although I wrote in my journal, "I'm sad that my former life is over."

A year later, the family gathered for Christmas as usual—Paul from the city and Heidi and Karl from inland towns where they worked and lived. After gift-opening, we laughed over family stories as we enjoyed a leisurely feast in the house we'd once shared.

As Paul left he hugged me, saying, "The children become nicer every year. You were a wonderful mother!" We had come full circle to years before as if nothing had happened in between.

I responded to his embrace as a "family" gesture, not a sexual experience. Only the bonds of shared history and parenthood remained for me. The passage of time had created a healing distance from the hurt and left but a sad reflection of what we'd endured.

While I was still anxious that too much time had been lost in my sexual life for any straight male to want me as a lifelong mate, a new bond was developing with a caring, accepting, spiritual lover who made me feel fulfilled as a complete woman, faults and all.

That Christmas night, I wrote in my journal:

> Whatever uncertainties of life lie ahead for me in the New Year, I feel confident that I can meet and overcome any obstacle or challenge in my path.

> In my fifty-seventh year I had come of age.

Creating A New Belief System

Breaking loose from timeworn patterns to form a new life is the final hurdle for the straight spouse. Shattered beliefs and assumptions must be incorporated into a new belief system. Then spouses can move forward into what is for many the most rewarding period of their lives, with or without their partners.

Examples of such transformations appear throughout this book: Jane regained her womanhood and entered the ministry; Rita created an independent life during and after her marriage; Grant became an active, caring father for Heather; Cliff created a fearless, confident identity; Tracey moved forward as a guilt-free divorcee; and Kirstin fulfilled her potential sexually, psychologically and spiritually.

Dramatic and profound change cannot be realized through impulsive decisions made out of shock or anger felt in the early months. True transformation comes only after all issues have been resolved: damaged sexuality, altered relationship, conflicting parental-spousal concerns, destroyed identity, confused morality and fragmented belief system.

Once autonomy and integrity have been restored a sense of restlessness or dissatisfaction often begins the spouse's transformation. Almost overnight there is a subtle shift in how everything is viewed— partner or ex-partner, family, job, present circumstances. Reality no longer seems so fearsome or overwhelming. Threats to autonomy can be countered. The spouse no longer feels so vulnerable to other people's actions.

While natural regeneration and the passage of time assist the process of change, there also needs to be an explicit affirmation on the part of the spouse that change is possible. Yet for the spouse whose former beliefs lie in fragments, the mere thought of moving into a new realm can be terrifying.

Many spouses have overcome such fear to create a new life. Through will power, inner work, persistence and sometimes prayer, they have broken the bonds to their past to effect change. Seven strategies enable transformation to occur.

- Letting go of the past
- Learning to forgive
- Coming to terms with loss
- Reformulating a philosophy of life
- Reestablishing a belief system
- Creating a new dream
- Taking the first step as a new person

The more focused the process of transformation is, the more assured the progress will be. For this reason, it is vital to have a confidante, professional counselor or journal for reflecting upon the journey.

Letting Go of the Past

Before change can begin, the spouse needs to clear away any leftover feelings that could impede growth. If any denial of pain, dependency, residual anger or self-pity remains, chances for a breakthrough are diminished. Feelings of insecurity, such as "You can't do it. You'll fail again" need to be left behind. Letting go of such impediments from the past is the first and possibly most difficult challenge of transformation.

Yet endings are part of the natural cycle of life. As William Bridges, Ph.D., explains, "New growth cannot take root on ground still covered with the old, and endings are the clearing process."[1] Yet just because something ceases to exist doesn't mean that it has ended. The spouse's shattered life cannot be resuscitated but it can be recast.

It requires a conscious decision to leave the past behind but it can be and has been done.

It also takes time for spouses to break free from their former lives, which may or may not include their partners. Jim was prepared intellectually for Janie's coming out and consequent ending of the marriage. Yet until she actually did, he put off dealing with the emotional loss involved. When she finally came out, he broke into sobs. He then carefully organized equal parenting time and mediated Janie's public coming out. He didn't acknowledge the "end" of their life together until he remarried a few years later.

Although the passage of time weakens past ties, the deliberate act of cutting them, like pruning, hastens regrowth. Talking about what it meant to be the ex-spouse of a lesbian to high school students helped Jim give up the "wife" image of Janie and form a "family" connection with her.

It is common for spouses to hang onto the old relationship for months even if separated or divorced. Often a wife clings to her husband for security. Admitting that the bond has ended would mean being cut adrift. She may wonder, "What would I have left? What would give meaning to my life?" Kirstin, for instance, while knowing her storybook dream was dead, still couldn't cut the connection to Paul.

Then something happens to impel the spouse to finally break the ties. A friend may say out of exasperation, "It's over! Cut bait!" Or the partner may do something that excludes the spouse from his or her gay world. At that moment the ending is crystal clear. It can seem like awakening from a prolonged nightmare to find that one is really alive and the sun is out.

Learning to Forgive

Despite the sense of liberation the spouse feels, anger towards the partner may linger. Anger is as much a bond as love and must also be left behind. While it is a normal reaction, it can drag a person down in its whirlpool of negativity.

The most effective resolution of anger is forgiveness. This enables the spouse to switch roles from that of judge to disengaged observer. To forgive the partner for all of the pain suffered from the coming out is one of the hardest but most powerful turning points of the transformation process. The aim of this second task of establishing a new belief system is to replace emotional turmoil with peace of mind.

In this stage anger is often expressed as general negativity about the entire situation and the partner is cast in the role of "the enemy." Such an adversarial view is counterproductive. Angry thoughts reinforce the bond to the partner and limit the expression of more positive emotions, such as compassion, needed for transformation.

Perpetuating an adversarial relationship makes reconciliation increasingly difficult. After Patty heard that Frank had AIDS, in "I Love You, Jeff and Peggy" of part three, she telephoned him, whispering, "I wish I could be there to hold you." But by the next day her anger had resurfaced.

Persistent resentment may blind the spouse to aspects of the situation that could be changed for the better, such as her or his own fear, vindictiveness or dependency. Focusing on what can't be changed, such as the partner's sexual orientation, goes against the guiding principles of the most effective recovery programs.

Anger comes from judging the partner as uncaring, deceitful or hurtful because of the painful consequences of the coming out. Yet who has the right to judge another? Who knows the myraid motives of others? The complexity of the partner's motives cannot be reduced to one single reason. Many factors that even the partner may not be aware of operate in the coming-out process.

The act of forgiving the partner frees the spouse from judging and from feeling responsible for the partner's actions. Forgiveness allows the spouse to cease struggling to change the unchangeable. Forgiveness reopens the door to the partner's side of the closet. The spouse can then accept the partner as a fellow human rather than as the oppressor.

For forgiveness to be a sincere rather than a mechanical exercise, spouses need to consider all aspects of the harm they feel their partners have done, deliberate or not, and then forgive them. Spouses may need to forgive themselves too for whatever role they may have played in the situation.

It isn't easy to surrender the false sense of power that comes from judging. Tremendous humility is needed to give up the right to "pardon." Remembering that the goal is peace of mind will lessen the urge to punish or get even.

Forgiveness may be done anywhere and in any way as long as there is sufficient time to do it. Walking in the park, sitting on the beach or lying in bed; anywhere is fine provided there are no distractions. It helps to write down what needs to be forgiven in a journal or talk with a close friend, counselor or spiritual advisor. By discussing forgiveness with someone else, troublesome feelings that arise, such as the natural urge to vindicate oneself, can be put into perspective.

The act of forgiving is simple. The spouse simply acknowledges what was done and then, no matter how horrendous or painful, lets go of it. While the statement of forgiveness may be made in any form, it needs to be deliberate, explicit and heartfelt. It doesn't even have to be said face-to-face to the partner. A simple, "I forgive him (or her) for what was done," will suffice. The sole aim is to accept and forgive.

Some spouses forgive through prayer, turning over painful memories to God or some other spiritual being to be healed.[2]

The rewards of forgiving compensate for the pain it evokes. A middle-aged professional in San Diego, for instance, guided through the forgiving process by her parish priest, remarked, "As I forgave Ron unconditionally, I was in tears, exhausted but cleansed."

Forgiving doesn't mean forgetting what happened nor the lessons learned from it. To maintain a sense of self and to revive purpose in life, it is critical to maintain continuity with the past. True forgiveness brings a balanced picture of the marriage into focus, which includes the partner's admirable qualities and happy times together.

Three years after Moira's story, "Brainwashed" in part one was told, she was able to write, "The anger that engulfed me is no longer there. I am grateful for that new peace as I can now really enjoy family events with Tim. I realize that to get on with my life I have to release the past."

Coming to Terms with Loss

Cutting the last ties to the past causes a profound sense of loss. This act is the reprise of all the phases of the coming-out struggle. Though similar to the loss of a husband or wife by death or divorce, the loss felt by spouses of gay or lesbian partners is unique. Widows and widowers mourn grievously, but don't have the tangible presence of their partners to fan passion and remind them of their pain. Straight spouses often remain vulnerable to powerful feelings through continued contact with their partners, such as Jim who had to take Valium to cope when Janie moved in with him and his new wife. In contrast to divorced heterosexuals, where the possibility may exist of rekindling a sexual response from the ex-partner should they desire it, most straight spouses of gays and lesbians know that their sexual relationship with their partner is over forever.

This sense of loss is probably the most profound feeling of the coming-out crisis. Recently a multiracial group of wives and former wives, ranging in age from early twenties to late fifties and coping at different stages of recovery, all agreed that loss—whether of their partner, marriage, personal identity, or hope—was the cause of their greatest pain.

This overpowering grief can be turned around by viewing the loss as a doorway into a new life. Some spouses find it beneficial to mark the ending of the past with a formal "commencement" celebration. Cutting the cord thereby becomes a rite of growth, unleashing energy for new life.

Such a ritual can be done in many ways, but most spouses do it alone. Methods vary from removing all traces of past pain from the home to reflecting upon the end in a private hideaway. The rite can be conducted in nature, in one's bedroom or at a retreat house. Although Kirstin's illness kept her from performing a transition rite in the inn as planned, her hospital stay turned out to be an appropriate place and time. Wherever it happens and whatever the ritual, the culminating effect for many spouses is a feeling of empowerment.

When the past is finally released, there is often a sense of disorientation, but it differs from the confusion felt after the coming out. Although the spouse is still on unfamiliar ground, he or she now has a stronger sense of self and of personal values. The idea of forging a path through the unknown doesn't seem so daunting.

Some spouses may not have sufficient physical or emotional strength to take immediate action. There may be only enough energy to reaffirm the desire for change. Current circumstances such as children to be nurtured, work to be done or bills to be paid may also pose a barrier too strong to overcome. Yet as spouses cope with these problems, the seeds of the next step are germinating.

Reformulating a Philosophy of Life

To forge a new path, spouses need to have a clear vision of the direction in which they want to go. To achieve this goal, their views of life, in many cases turned upside down by the coming out, need to be reformulated. Creating a new philosophy, the fourth task of this stage of recovery, begins with reflection upon the larger meaning of the coming-out trauma.

Until this point spouses tend to see their devastation as unique, crying, "No one who hasn't been here can understand!" With their self-confidence restored and no longer controlled by the past, they can now begin to view their individual crises from a broader perspective. To do so, they might ask themselves, for example, "Can I get anything positive out of my experience? What would Shakespeare say? How would a TV sitcom handle it, or a documentary? What can my experience teach me?"

It is hard for many spouses to look at the crisis from a different perspective because of the intense suffering it engendered. They typically wonder, "How come this happened to me?" as if the trauma were an unmerited punishment. This feeling comes from viewing suffering, which is an inherent condition of life, as something voluntary.

Professor Elaine Pagels, Ph.D., explains that because people think suffering is related to voluntary behavior, they see it as a sign that they have lost control of the moral quality of their lives. Consequently, they feel guilty about feeling such pain. Believing that "This is punishment for doing something wrong," makes them feel in control.[3] In reality, no one decides when or if he or she will experience suffering. It is involuntary and a necessary part of the human condition.

By reflecting on their pain, many spouses eventually come to understand the universality of suffering despite unique circumstances. Sooner or later everyone suffers pain and dies. No one is exempt. The only choice is in how to handle it.

Another pitfall of the coming-out crisis is the temptation to view everything in either straight or gay terms. Transcending such polarized ways of thinking enables the spouse to formulate a more encompassing viewpoint on the situation. Developing a broader view is fundamental in creating a new philosophy of life.

An effective strategy for overcoming straight-or-gay thinking is to see human sexuality as a continually shifting spectrum. Few people are totally "straight" or "gay" in all thoughts, fantasies and behavior throughout their lives no matter where their basic orientation falls on the scale. Does having the occasional same-sex fantasy, desires, one or two random gay experiences make a person a dyed-in-the-wool homosexual or bisexual? These are the questions Barbara asked at first. The more significant question to consider is the quality of the total person, not his or her sexual orientation.

Many aspects of homosexuality are also presented in either-or terms such as the debate over whether homosexuality is the result of choice or destiny, biology or environment. It is far more enlightening to consider such issues from the viewpoint of a both-and relationship. Both free will *and* destiny operate in life. Prenatal *and* environmental factors exert a major influence on how all people turn out. Through both-and thinking, what may have seemed like a divisive issue can be seen as reflecting the puzzling nature of the human condition in general.

Unifying concepts underlie many of the paradoxes of the coming out. By reflecting on the contradictory aspects of their situation, spouses may be enlightened about life in general. For example:

- The partner's deceit, originating from a wish to avoid hurting the spouse, hurts her or him.
- The coming out of the closet for the partner is often the going into the closet for the spouse.
- The partner's liberation is the spouse's devastation.

All three paradoxes illustrate a universal fact of life: In any situation, what's good for one person may be bad for another. The question is, "Is there a middle ground or a long-range good for both?"

In examining the love-hurt dilemma in the coming out, spouses may reflect upon the fact that love and hurt coexist in all aspects of life. Life is neither all happy nor all hurtful, but a mixture. The essential point is what can be learned from it. As a monk advised one spouse, "Ask, 'For what aspect of this painful experience will I be grateful some day?'"

As spouses become aware of the universal meaning in their individual crises, their trauma no longer seems so unique or overwhelming. The devastation can now be viewed with some dispassion. For example, a wife's futile attempts to seduce her husband may take on a bittersweet irony. Such a woman in Indiana, three years after her husband came out, shared the following vignette with her support group:

Wife: (sighing, after months of rejection and trying to entice her husband) "Well, is there another woman?"

Husband: "No, dear. I never look at other women."

She might not have been able to tell the story earlier without blame and self-pity. Now it's an inside joke, a sign that she's left the gay-straight closet. Having transcended the pain, the spouse may be able to laugh at the incongruities in life, to see that the world is a funny as well as a serious place. With this view, a new philosophy emerges.

Reestablishing a Belief System

For transformation to take place, the spouse's philosophy of life needs to be grounded in belief. This is the fifth task of this stage of recovery. The most valuable of the spouse's shattered beliefs need to be regenerated, new ones discovered and both sets integrated into a cohesive blueprint for living.

The spouse may need to do some soul searching in order to find old beliefs that still seem valid. Discoveries can be made through talking with others whose points of view are respected, reading meaningful literature, writing in a journal or observing what others learn from crises. Sometimes simply focusing inwardly on the self alone in a private place will help a great deal.[4]

In this search for new meaning, insights may seem to come out of nowhere. Realizations may pop up amidst everyday events: a cloud over a sunset, the look on a child's face, a phrase in a book, a theme in some music, a prayer in a church service, a scene on television, the comment of a friend, an image while jogging. According to an ancient Sufi teacher, "For him who has perception, a mere sign is enough. For him who does not really heed, a thousand explanations are not enough."[5]

However small, the insight or revelation may fill the void in the spouse's life. Kirstin, feeling abandoned, found a whisper of faith in the empty church she entered to cool off on a hot afternoon in Brazil. In the emptiness, she sensed that someone was aware of her pain. That someone was God. Just as instantaneous was Jim's experience at the Presbyterian assembly before Janie came out. Participating with the supporters of gay deacons in an agape celebration being held despite the expectation of being outvoted, he felt a rush of joy.

Such glimmers of meaning are the seeds of a new belief system. Many spouses do not see the meaning in their lives until the emptiness and hunger characteristic of this period impel them to look for it.

Forming a personal connection to some intangible being or force beyond themselves provides an anchor for many spouses. The spiritual dimension has been a critical part of transformation for a number of spouses studied for this book. Kirstin, for example, introduced to spiritual philosophies by men she dated, devoured metaphysical books during her hospital stay. Others have increased their spiritual awareness through retreats, workshops, nature walks or meditation.

The reflective process cannot be hurried. It requires patience on the part of friends and family who may be exasperated by the spouse's seeming lack of progress. They may need to be reminded that the spouse's confusion or indecision hides considerable internal activity that will eventually produce profound change.

Slowly but surely through many possible avenues, a belief-centered philosophy can be formed. Then spouses may at last feel that their lives have meaning and purpose. Jim's spontaneous experience of agape, love that gives more than receives, became his keystone for life, empowering him to be open to gays.

Lynn Conley, founder of the National Support Organization for Spouses of Gays and Lesbians, who stayed in constant dialogue with a higher being while recovering from her coming-out crisis, said, "I never thought the pain would go. Now I'm glad I went through it. It taught me a lot. I'm very different. I'm sure of myself and love myself."[6] Such assuredness is the mark of a strong belief system. With it returns the hope that was missing for so long. Now nothing seems impossible.

Creating a New Dream

When Kirstin wept that her dream was dead, a friend said, "Well, dream another." There are always new dreams to be dreamed. This time around the spouse can base these dreams on reality. Creating a new dream may be the boldest decision of the spouse's life as she or he must break out of a lifelong mold of habits. In fashioning a new dream, the sixth task of transformation, the focus shifts from the present to the future.

Through the processes of releasing the past and creating a new belief system, the spouse has already broken down many former patterns of thinking about the world, marriage, partner and self. For some spouses, such changes provide sufficient peace of mind.

Others feel compelled to make radical changes in their behavior or environment. Their goals are to pursue individual convictions and passions, to ensure continued individual growth, as well as to challenge their potential to reach its full realization.

The dream can be realized inside the marriage as well as after separation or divorce. Spouses still married need to take into account whether their partners respect their beliefs and goals. A compromise may have to be reached so that the dream will not be negated by opposing factors or lack of support.

If the positive factors in the marriage such as love, security and emotional satisfaction outweigh sexual frustration or destructive relationship patterns, the spouse's dream may be to create a more recip-rocal relationship. However, the partner's cooperation has to be ensured in order for such a plan to be realistic. As the stories illus-trate, only a minority of spouses feel that the marriage is an integral part of their growth. Barbara is among them, having chosen life with Josh as part of her dream.

The more common situation is that the gay-related goals of the partner run counter to the imperatives of the spouse's new belief sys-tem. Once the spouse is confident that all has been done to keep the marriage going, she or he may have to stop trying to make the mar-riage work and instead concentrate on making her or his own life work. Typically the decision is to divorce or separate.

In envisioning separation, spouses need to be aware that parts of their new lives will be linked to their old lives. Resuming old habits may become tempting. Therefore they need to examine carefully any aspect of separation which might keep them from being consistent with their new belief systems.

The vision of a new life separate from the partner differs from individual to individual. Jim sought the joy of openness and passion for gay advocacy, while Kirstin wanted fulfillment of her psychologi-cal, spiritual and sexual identity.

Many spouses are already divorced when they reach this stage. Though being unattached is lonely and painful, divorced spouses have endless possibilities to envision. One woman in her twenties, Anne, realizing that family tradition and stereotypes about women's roles had kept her from pursuing a childhood dream to be a business woman, made that her new goal.

Dreaming and actually making it come true require different skills. Waffling over what to do or hesitating from fear of failure won't bring the new dream to life. Such delays are unnecessary because there's really nothing to fear. With everything in place for a new life to begin, a great leap forward is possible.

Taking the First Step as a New Person

Bolstered by courage and faith, the spouse is now ready to take the first step toward the new goal. A sense of adventure and mystery impels many spouses forward. Nothing can block the way to making the dream a reality. Though the path may not be smooth, each step will take the spouse further ahead in the chosen direction.

The journey will not be as difficult if some of its pitfalls are anticipated. With each new step, the spouse will experience some feelings of insecurity. Echoes of fear, self-pity, frustration, blame, and guilt may be heard, requiring will power to ignore them. Such emotional changes can make each step feel like a giant leap upward, requiring rest and reflection to absorb the significance of it. Energy may slacken and spirits falter, making it crucial to call upon partner, friends, family, therapist, and support groups for help.

Spouses who choose transformation within the marriage find it a harder task than expected. Those who succeed discover that individual goals need not be sacrificed for the couple bond to grow stronger. The two aren't at cross purposes but complementary if beliefs are constantly reinforced and not abandoned for the sake of the relationship. This is why Barbara continually questioned and talked with Josh as they rewrote their script.

Most spouses who stay married, usually straight wives, find a way to maintain the relationship without compromising beliefs. Along with the personal qualities defined in part two, flexibility, openness, honesty and humor; commitment to something beyond themselves seems to help many spouses resolve problems. Barbara focused on positive qualities in the relationship and on Josh as a total person rather than on personal concerns regarding the gay issue. Eventually rising above the gay-straight dilemma, she reached a deeper level of understanding. To strengthen her belief in family values, she decided to adopt the Jewish faith.

It is crucial that partners support their spouses in their transformation. Josh's willingness to listen to Barbara's concerns and to express his own was critical in shaping her development from a twenty-five year old who saw gay men and marriage as mutually exclusive to a non-judgmental, loving and autonomous wife of thirty-five.

Other resources are available to help wives change themselves within the marriage including psychotherapy, marriage counseling, sex therapy, communication workshops and self-help books such as those listed in appendix A.

The majority of spouses achieve transformation through separation or divorce. For each spouse the breakthrough is different and occurs at different rates. Divorce results in the most abrupt transformation yet the pain from it compels many spouses to move ahead. For example, the breakup of Jim's marriage, along with the joy from his agape experience, propelled him to create a new life. Once remarried he included his sons, mother and mother-in-law, Janie and Janie's lover, and even the dog into one big family. His work, social life and family activities revolved around issues of oppressed gays. The transformation of this corporate businessman into a gay advocate was strikingly different from Janie's reluctant coming out.

Similarly, Anne, the spouse who decided to become a businesswoman, was driven by the devastation of cutting ties with her husband she had depended upon for everything. She entered the business world, in her words, "like a steam roller", opened a service shop and in a few years expanded to a second location.

Whether divorced, separated or married, each spouse must forge his or her own path from trauma to transformation. Though none can be duplicated and each has its unique lesson, there is a typical process that spouses undergo that can serve as a guideline for others. Kirstin's story recapitulates the common sequence:

- Paul withdraws and Kirstin suffers an identity crisis.
- When Paul moves out, Kirstin feels new life enter their home.
- Kirstin becomes angry when Paul says she was frigid.
- Paul comes out and Kirstin, though relieved, is in shock.
- Feeling closer to Paul, Kirstin supports his gay activities.
- Feeling excluded from Paul's gay world, she becomes enraged both at his deception and the homophobia in society.
- She rebuilds her self-concept and no longer sees herself as a wife.
- She falls into severe depression and finds spiritual support.
- She clings to the relationship.
- She finally decides that getting a divorce will best reflect the reality of her situation.
- She begins a frantic schedule of work and social activities.
- Through dating she discovers that she's a fully sexual woman after all.

- She explores new spiritual theories while ill.
- She remains friends with Paul and holds family gatherings.
- She is promoted at work and enters into a heterosexual relationship.
- Her divorce final, she believes she can overcome any challenge.

As in real life, Kirstin's transformation does not follow a logical order. Yet there is an overall forward thrust to her journey. Other spouses tell of similar crisscrossings through darkness to final breakthrough. Although the path is uphill, all spouses can reach the summit given courage, awareness and faith in their capabilities.

The journey of transformation is never finished. There is a human need to continue to explore and expand one's potential. Although the devastation that precipitates the straight spouse's recovery isn't to be wished on anyone, the process of resolving it mirrors the struggles of many heroes and heroines in myth and history.

The journey of transformation is ultimately a quest for meaning and transcendence. As psychiatrist Jean Shinoda Bolen comments, in a statement applicable to anyone—man and woman alike—"Traveling this path, the heroine may find, lose and rediscover what has meaning to her until she holds on to these values in all kinds of circumstances that test her...until finally the danger of losing her selfhood is over."[6]

BEYOND THE CLOSET

Like parables, the straight spouses' stories reveal larger meanings in life. Collectively they depict the emotional suffering that results when rights and responsibilities are abrogated. They caution about people who feel forced to be less than they are and people who are hurt without knowing it. They warn about a society which is deprived of the contribution of all its members. Encapsulated in these stories is the universal dilemma of individual freedom versus social accountability.

The straight spouses' experiences afford us a look behind the headlines that too often present gay rights issues in pro- or anti-gay extremes. As members of the mainstream who are also intimately involved with gay, lesbian or bisexual partners, spouses know firsthand both sides of the controversy, from militant gay activism to oppressive homophobia. In coping with the problems posed by a mixed-orientation relationship, spouses forge a middle ground between the two extremes. Their intimate understanding of the sexuality issue provides a unique perspective for comprehending what may be one of the most significant societal-political-moral changes of this century.

As the partner's disclosed sexual orientation threatens the stability of the family, the straight spouse is forced to examine nearly every issue our society faces from privacy to prejudice. Major questions include "What is the full range of human sexuality? Who is my husband or wife as a total person? What are a parent's socio-moral responsibilities to ensure the children's security in the family? What are my rights to fulfill my own needs and potential?" Exploration of this wide range of profound questions results in a comprehensive view of homosexual behavior in relation to the total dynamic of both the family and the community.

In contrast, public discourse most often approaches gay-straight affairs as either-or issues. This position is either pro-gay or pro-straight. A person's sexual orientation determines whether his or her actions are applauded or denigrated regardless of the consequences. Harm inflicted on homosexual and bisexual persons solely because they differ from the norm impels many of them to hide, flaunt or fight for their freedom to be who they are. A vicious cycle of attack and counterattack is thereby perpetuated.

Having created such conditions of fear and hate, our society can reverse them by ceasing to view homosexual behavior in stereotypical terms of abnormality or immorality. A realistic view of homosexuality and bisexuality as natural variations of sexual orientation that have existed throughout history needs to be formulated.

Just as the heterosexual majority needs to look beyond homophobic labels, so homosexual and bisexual individuals need to look beyond their closet. Many tend to view all straight persons through heterophobic lenses without seeing them as individuals with specific needs. A seemingly anti-gay viewpoint may, with closer scrutiny, turn out to be a legitimate concern about a specific hurt to someone or a thoughtful question about broader principles of which the gay issue is but one part.

In seeking civil rights, gay and lesbian groups have a responsibility to respect the rights of others and to consider the possible consequences of their actions on all concerned. Although it is tempting to ignore the needs of others when fighting for freedoms denied by years of oppression, liberation won't be complete until other people's concerns are honored as well.

As we move ahead in the last decade before a new century facing the complex demands of an increasingly diverse society, a comprehensive view of the polarized gay-straight controversy is sorely needed to heal the wounds and to integrate the two camps into a complementary relationship. All sides of the issue need to be considered in the media, research, social theory, and religious thought. Only then can equitable solutions be found for a problem societies have grappled with for thousands of years.

As in most controversies, the more realistic and constructive solutions to the gay-straight dilemma will be found between the extreme positions. To formulate public policy that ensures an equitable balance between civil rights and conventional precedents, we need: social realists to affirm society's need for stability by exploring alternative marriage and family arrangements and sexual realists to point out the diversity of sexual orientations as part of the natural order and but one aspect of the individuals who make up society.

Through a balanced approach to the gay-straight conflict, sexual orientation will no longer be used as a measure of personal worth. Individual character will replace irrelevant labels. No one will be prevented from contributing his or her gifts to society. Homosexual and bisexual men and women will no longer be unjustly deprived of their rights and in turn will feel less pressure to hide or to fight back.

To implement such a transformation, we need leaders, legislators and jurists who will consider the full range of concerns intrinsic to gay-straight issues including legitimate rationales at both extremes. We need communities and schools to take concrete steps towards ending ignorance and prejudice. We need individuals who can see beyond personal interest to determine the common good.

Respect for individual differences and rights, as well as the espousal of social responsibility by all members of society—gay, lesbian, bisexual, and straight—is the ultimate goal. Honesty can become the cornerstone of social relations. Social justice can prevail. Liberation and responsibility can go hand in hand. With the elimination of divisive labels, we may move beyond a closet mentality to enter the new century, the new millennium, as an inclusive society of fully contributing members.

ENDNOTES

Introduction: Coming Out In Marriage

1. This is a modest estimate, based on the 1987 United States
    Census figures of 85,850,000 men 18 and over and 93,773,000
    women 18 and over and the commonly accepted research figures
    for the incidence of homosexuality and the percentage of married
    gay men. If one includes the estimated incidence of homosexual-
    ity among women (half as many as gay men), of lesbians who
    marry (18 to 35% according to Alan P. Bell and Martin Weinberg
    in *Homosexualities: A Study of Diversity Among Men and Women*,
    New York: Simon & Schuster, 1978), of bisexual men and women
    (twice as many as homosexuals) and the percentage of married
    bisexual persons (undetermined) —the actual number of straight
    spouses may exceed four million.

2. Alfred C. Kinsey et al, *Sexual Behavior in the Human Male*
    (Philadelphia: W. B. Saunders, 1948) and *Sexual Behavior in the
    Human Female* (Philadelphia: W. B. Saunders, 1953). Charles F.

Turner, primary author of *AIDS, Sexual Behavior, and Intravenous Drugs* (Washington, DC: National Academy of Sciences Press, 1989) for the National Academy of Sciences, based on a study of 1450 men in 1970 and 638 in 1988, confirms Kinsey's four percent figure but suggests slightly lower percentages for adult males reporting occasional or frequent homosexual conatact leading to orgasm. This difference may be explained by the reluctance of men to reveal homosexuality.

3. Judd Marmor, M.D., in *The Bisexual Spouse*, edited by Ivan Hill (McLean, VA: Barlina Books, Inc., 1987). Figures vary with subgroups, research method, and indicators of homosexuality. See, for example, Bell and Weinberg, *op. cit.*

4. Figures vary. The most thorough study is Michael Ross, *The Married Homosexual Man* (Boston: Routledge and Kegan Paul, 1983).

5. *Ibid.*, pp. 142-51.

6. *Tearoom Trade: Impersonal Sex in Public Places* (New York: Aldine Publishing Company, 1975).

Part One: Sexual Mismatch

1. See Sandra Auerback and Charles Moser, "Groups for the Wives of Gays and Bisexual Men," *Social Work*, 1987, pp. 321-25, and Jean Schaar Gochros, *When Husbands Come Out of the Closet*, (New York: Harrington Park Press, 1989). These findings along with those of the author contradict earlier descriptions, such as the five neurotic wives of husbands in therapy to change their homosexuality reported by Myra Hatterer, "Problems of Women Married to Homosexual Men," *American Journal of Psychiatry*, 131(3), 1974, pp. 275-58 and descriptions of wives in Brenda Maddox, *Married and Gay*, (New York: Harcort Brace Jovanovich, Publishers, 1982).

2. Unpublished essay on spouses' sexuality, May 2, 1986, p. 2.

3. Interview, May 23, l986.

4. Dorothea Hays and Aurele Samuels, Abstract of "Grief Reactions of Heterosexual Wives Who Have Learned That Their Husbands are Homosexually Active," paper presented at symposium on unsanctioned and unrecognized grief, sponsored by Foundation of Thanatology and Columbia University, April 1987. See also Hays and Samuels, "Heterosexual Women's Perceptions of Their Marriages to Homosexual or Bisexual Men," *Journal of Homosexuality*, 17 (3/4) 1989, pp. 81-100.

5. "Abstract" cited in Note 4.

6. *Op cit.*, Chs. 5 and 10. Other chapters present current theories and specific help.

7. (New York: Dutton, 1990), Chs. 6-8 and pp. 161-70.

7. *A Gourmet Guide to Love Making*, (New York: Crown Publishers, Inc., 1972).

8. (Minneapolis: Winston Press, Inc., 1984).

Part Two: Trial And Error

1. *Op. cit.*, p, 323.

2. Pp. 193-216.

3. Brian Miller, "Women Who Marry Gay Men," *The Advocate*, (April 25, 1989), pp. 22-30.

4. (New York: Random House, 1986).

5. "An Investigation of Sexual Behaviors in Mixed Sexual Orientation Couples: Gay Husband and Straight Wife," Institute for The Advanced Study of Human Sexuality, San Francisco, June l987, pp. 31, 39-40.

6. See David R. Matteson, "Married and Gay," *Changing Men*, Spring-Summer 1988, p. 14-16, 45.

7. *Op. cit.*

8. Susan Gerrard and James Halpin, "The Risky Business of Bisexual Love," *Cosmopolitan*, (September 1989), p. 204.

9. *Op. cit.*, p. 40.

10. See Melodie Beatty, *Codependent No More*, (New York: Harper and Row, 1987), pp. 89-100.

11. Interview, October 10, 1990.

12. See Dennis Wholey, *The Courage To Change* (Boston: Warner Books Edition Houghton Miflin Company, 1984), pp. 138-151.

13. Unpublished essay on gay-straight couples, April 5, 1990, p. 2.

14. *Ibid.*

15. Barry Kohn and Alice Matusow, *Portrait of a Bisexual Marriage* (Englewood Cliffs, New Jersey: Prentice Hall, Inc., 1980).

16. *Women and Gay Men* (New York: Seaview Books, 1979).

17. *Gay Men and Straight Women* (New York: New American Library, 1990).

18. Nahos and Turley, p. 12.

19. *The Road Less Traveled*, (New York: Simon and Schuster, 1978).

20. *Op. cit.*, pp. 41-42.

21. *The Art of Intimacy* (New York: Prentice-Hall Press, 1987), p. 73. See also "Participation," p. 269.

Part Three: Growing Pains

1. Full Frame Products, San Francisco.

2. "Growing Up With a Gay, Lesbian, or Bisexual Parent: An Exploratory Study of Experiences and Perceptions," Unpublished Dissertation, University of California, Berkeley, 1986.

3. (New York: Harrington Park Press, 1990).

4. Written with Joan Berlin Kelly, *Surviving the Breakup: How Children and Parents Cope with Divorce* (New York: BasicBooks, Inc, Publishers, 1980).

5. *Op. cit.*, p. 77.

6. Janet Ghent, "When Mom or Dad is Gay," Oakland (CA) *Tribune*, January 29, 1987, p. C-2.

7. *Op. cit.*, p. 93.

8. Paul, *op. cit.*, p. 89.

9. *Ibid.*, p. 80. Sons' concerns may relate to the "fragility of the masculine role" in our society, in contrast to the strong feminist model to which daughters are currently exposed.

10. Peck, *op. cit.*, pp. 120-130.

11. *Mothers and Divorce: Legal, Economic, and Social Dilemmas.* (Berkeley, CA: University of California Press, 1986), p. 100.

12. *Op. cit.*, p. 93.

13. Unpublished "Letter to the Editor," January 14, 1987.

14. Written with Sandra Blakeslee, *Men, Women and Childrena Decade After Divorce; Who Wins, Who Loses—and Why,* (New York: Ticknor and Fields, 1989).

15. *Op. cit.*, p. 92.

Part Four: What About Me?

1. Unpublished commentary, February 7, 1990.

2. Translated by Eknath Easwaran (Petaluma, California: Nilgiri Press, 1985).

3. Suggested readings include Indries Shah, *The Way of The Sufi* (New York: E. P. Dutton, 1970); *The Song of God: Bhagavad-Gita*, transl. by Swami Prabhavananda and Christopher Isherwood (New York: The New American Library, Mentor, 1951); Gerald Hausman, *Meditations with the Navajo* (Santa Fe: Bear and Co., 1987); and *The Old Testament, The New English Bible with the Aprocrypha*, Oxford Study Edition (New York: Oxford University Press, 1976), pp. 569-674.

4. *The Message of the Psalms: A Theological Commentary* (Minneapolis: Augsburg Publishing House, 1984), p. 54.

5. Interview, February 23, 1990.

6. *Op. cit.*, p. 232.

7. *Talking to Yourself: Learning the Language of Self-Support*, (New York: Harper & Row, Publishers, 1981), p. 1.

8. Melba Colgrove, Ph.D., Harold H. Bloomfield, M.D., and Peter McWilliams (New York: Bantam Books, 1977).

9. Timothy Wolfe, "Selected Psychological and Sociological Aspects of Male Homo-sexual Behavior in Marriage," Graduate Faculty, School of Human Behavior, U. S. International University, San Diego, CA., 1982, (University Microfilms International No. DA 83131477) p. 109-10.

10. *Love is Letting Go of Fear* (New York: Bantam Books, 1970).

Part Five: The Power Of The Lie

1. Interview, May 28, 1986.

2. *Moral Choice in Public and Private Life*, (New York: Pantheon Press, 1978), p. xvii.

3. See *Anger: How to Live With and Without It*, (Secaucus, New Jersey: Citadel Press, 1977).

4. *Uncoupling: Turning Points in Intimate Relationships* (New York: Oxford University Press, 1986), p. 193.

5. *Op. cit.*, p. 74

6. *Op. cit.*, p. 26.

7. Unpublished essay on deception, November 16, 1987, p. 4.

8. (Los Angeles: Libbe HaLevy, 1990).

9. *Is The Homosexual My Neighbor? Another Christian View* (San Francisco: Harper & Row, Publishers, 1978), p. 121.

10. Interview, January 9, 1991.

11. *Ibid.*, p. 12.

12. "An Open Letter to Gay and Bi-sexual Men," (P.O. Box 6692, Philadelphia, PA 19149, 1985).

Part Six: Breaking The Mold

1. *Transitions* (Menlo Park, CA: Addison Wesley, 1980,) p. 91.

2. See, for example, Linn Matthew L. and D. Linn, *The Healing of Memories: Prayers and Confession—Steps to Inner Healing.* Mahwah, NJ: Paulist Press, 1974.

3. *Adam, Eve, and the Serpent* (New York: Random House, 1988), p. 18.

4. "When I go down into myself, I discover the universalities." "Conversations with Howard Thurman," video series for private home use only, (San Francisco: Howard Thurman Educational Trust, Inc., 1987).

5. Idries Shah, *op. cit.*, p. 222.

6. Interview, January 15, 1990.

7. *Goddesses in Every Woman: A New Psychology of Women* (San Francisco: Harper and Row, 1984), p. 293.

appendix a

SUGGESTED READINGS

Understanding Homosexuality And Bisexuality

Altman, Dennis. *The Homosexualization of America, the Americanization of the Homosexual.* New York: St. Martin's Press, 1982.

Barrett, Martha Barro. *Invisible Lives: The Truth About Millions of Women Loving Women.* New York: William Morrow and Company, 1989.

Bell, Alan P., Martin Weinberg, and Sue Kiefer. *Sexual Preference and Its Development in Men and Women.* Bloomington, Indiana: Indiana University, 1981.

Bisexuality: A Reader and Sourcebook, edit. by Thomas Geller. Ojai, CA: Times Change Press, 1990. (Publishers Services, P.O. Box 2510, Novato, CA 04048).

Bode, Janet. *View From Another Closet: Exploring Bisexuality in Women.* New York: Pocket Books, 1977.

Brown, Howard. *Familiar Faces, Hidden Lives.* New York: Harcourt, Brace, Jovnovich.

Clark, Donald Henry. *The New Loving Someone Gay,* revised and updated. Berkeley, CA: Celestial Arts, 1987.

Fairchild, Betty and Nancy Hayward. *Now That You Know: What Every Parent Should Know About Homosexuality.* New York: Harcourt Brace, Jovanovich, 1979.

Gay Fathers of Toronto. *Gay Fathers: Some of Their Stories, Experience, and Advice.* Toronto, Canada: Gay Fathers of Toronto, 1981. (Box F, 730 Bathurst St. M552R4).

Jones, Clinton, R. *Understanding Gay Relatives and Friends.* New York: The Seabury Press, 1978.

Klein, Fritz. *The Bisexual Option: A Concept of 100% Intimacy.* New York: Arbor House, 1976.

Marmor, Judd. *Gay, Straight, and In-Between: the Sexology of Erotic Orientation.* New York: Oxford University Press, 1988.

Martin, Del and Phyllis Lyon. *Lesbian Women.* New York: Bantam Books, 1972.

McWhirter, David P. and Andrew M. Mattison. *The Male Couple: How Relationships Develop.* Englewood Cliffs, New Jersey: Prentice-Hall, 1984.

Wolff, Charlotte. *Bisexuality: Theory and Research.* New York: Quartet Books, 1979.

Sexual Healing

Barbach, Lonnie. *For Yourself.* Garden City, New York: Anchor Books, 1975.

_____. *For each other: Sharing Sexual Intimacy.* Garden City, New York: Anchor Books, 1982.

Gochros, Harvey and J. Fischer. *Treat Yourself To A Better Sex Life.* Englewood Cliffs, New Jersey: Prentice-Hall, 1980.

The Complete Guide to Safe Sex, edit. by Ted McIlvenna. San Francisco: Institute for the Advanced Study of Human Sexuality, 1987.

Kitzinger, Sheila. *Woman's Experience of Sex.* New York: G. P. Putnam's Sons, 1983 (reprint, Penguin Books, 1985).

Money, John and Patricia Tucker. *Sexual Signatures on Being a Man or Woman.* Boston: Little Brown, and Company, 1975.

Spong, John Shelby. *Living in Sin: A Bishop Rethinks Human Sexuality.* San Francisco: Harper & Row, Publishers, 1990.

Strong, Bryan and Rebecca Reynolds. *Understanding Our Sexuality.* New York: West Publishing Company, 1982.

Coping With Spousal Issues

(Article reprints and taped presentations are also available from the Task Force of Spouses of Gays and Lesbians, Parents FLAG, listed in Appendix B)

AIDS: A Self-Care Manual: AIDS Project Los Angeles, edit. by BettyClare Moffatt, M.A., Judith Spiegel, Steve Parrish, and Michael Helquist. Santa Monica, CA: IBS Press, Inc., 1989.

Higham, Charles. *Charles Laughton.* London: W. H. Allen and Co., 1976.

Malone, John. *Straight Women/Gay Men.* New York: Dial Press, 1980.

Nicolson, Nigel. *Portrait of a Marriage.* New York: Atheneum, 1973.

Rubin, Lillian B. *Just Friends: The Role of Friendship in Our Lives.* New York: Harper and Row, Publishers, 1985.

Handling Children's Issues

Bozzet, Frederick W. "Social Control of Identity by Children of Gay Fathers," *Western Journal of Nursing Research*, 10, 1988, pp. 550-65.

Gay and Lesbian Parents, edit. by Frederick W. Bozzett. New York: Praeger, 1987.

Gantz, Joe. *Whose Child Cries: Children of Gay Parents Talk About Their Lives.* Rolling Hills Estates, CA: Jalmar Press, 1983.

Rebuilding Identity

Beesing, Maria O.P., Robert J. Nogosek, C.S. C., and Patrick H. O'Leary, S.J. *The Enneagram: A Journey of Self Discovery.* Denville, New Jersey: Dimension Books, Inc., 1984.

Butler, Pamela. *Self-Assertion for Women.* San Francisco: Harper & Row, Publishers, 1976.

Gawan, Shakti. *Creative Visualization.* New York: Bantam Books, 1978.

Johnson, Robert A. *Inner Work: Using Dreams and Active Imagination for Personal Growth.* San Francisco: Harper and Row, Publishers, 1986.

Keirsey, David and Marilyn Bates. *Please Understand Me: Character and Temperament Types.* Gnosology Books, 1984. (Distributor, Prometheus Nemisis Book Company, Box 2082, Del Mar, CA., (92014).

Norwood, Robin. *Women Who Love Too Much: When You Keep Wishing and Hoping He'll Change.* Los Angeles: Jeremy P. Tarcher, Inc., 1985.

St. Teresa of Avila. *Interior Castle*, transl. and edit. by E. Allison Peers. New York: Doubleday (Image), 1989.

Schaef, Anne Wilson. *Codependence: Misunderstood —Mistreated*. San Francisco: Harper and Row Publishers, 1986.

Resolving Moral Issues

Boswell, John. *Christianity, Social Tolerance and Homosexuality*. Chicago: The University of Chicago Press, 1980.

Fortunato, John. *AIDS: The Spiritual Dilemma*. San Francisco: Harper & Row, Publishers, 1987.

Katz, Johathan. *Gay American History: Lesbians and Gay Men in the USA*. New York: Thomas Y. Crowell Company, 1976.

McNeill, John J. *The Church and The Homosexual*. Kansas City: Sheed, Andrews, and McMeel, 1976.

Pennington, Sylvia. *But Lord, They're Gay*. Lambda Christian Fellowship, 1982.

Tripp, C. A. *The Homosexual Matrix*. New York: Mcgraw-Hill Book Co., 1975.

Personal Transformation

An Interrupted Life: The Diaries of Etty Hillesum 1941-43. New York: Pocket Books, 1981.

Campbell, Joseph. *Myths to Live By*. New York: Bantam Books, 1973.

Eisler, Riane. *The Chalice and the Blade: Our History, Our Future*. San Francisco: Harper & Row, Publishers, 1988.

Hesse, Herman. *Siddhartha*, transl. by Holda Rosner. New York: New Directions Publishing Corporation, 1951.

Huxley, Aldous. *The Perennial Philosophy*. New York: Harper and Row, Publishers, 1944.

Krantzler, Mel. *Creative Divorce: A New Opportunity for Personal Growth*. Philadelphia: J. B. Lippincott, Co., 1973.

Smith, Huston. *The Religions of Man*. New York: Harper and Row, Publishers, 1958.

The Choice is Always Ours, edit. by Dorothy Berkley Phillips. Wheaton, IL: Re-Quest Books, 1975.

appendix b

RESOURCES

Bisexual Counseling Services, 1478 Page Street, San Francisco, CA, 94117.

Bisexual Information and Counseling Services, 599 West End, New York, NY, 10024.

Chicago Bi-ways, P.O. Box A3330, Chicago, IL 60690.

Federation of Parents and Friends of Lesbians and Gays, Inc., P.O. Box 27605, Washington D.C., 20038-7605 (202) 638-4200.
    (Names of current regional contact persons for the following task forces which have information about therapists, support groups, bibliographies, and networks: Task Force on Spouses of Gays and Lesbians, Task Force on Children Who Love Someone Gay)

Gay and Married Men's Association (GAMMA), P.O. Box 28317, Washington, D.C., 20038, or P.O. Box 4324, N. Hollywood, CA 91607.
    (Information about groups such as "Straight Partners" and LAMMA—lesbian wives and their families)

Gay and Lesbian Parents Coalition International, P.O. Box 50360, Washington, D.C., 20091 (202)583-8029.
    (Information on Gay Fathers' and Lesbian mothers' organizations, some of which include children's support groups)

Institute for Advanced Study of Human Sexuality, 1523 Franklin Street, San Francisco, California, 94109.

Institute of Sexual Behavior, 4545 Park Blvd., Suite 207, San Diego, California, 92116.

Married Gay Men's Group, Charles Piersol, 59 Hartsen, Rochester, NY 14610.
  (Information on support groups)

National AIDS Information Hot Line 1-(800) 342-AIDS
  (National Gay and Lesbian Task Force information)

The National Support Organization for Spouses of Gays and Lesbians, P.O. Box 772, Salt Lake City, Utah, 84110-0772.
  (Newsletter and information)

Not Alone - A Support Group for Wives and Ex-wives of Gay and Bisexual Men, c/o Metropolitan Community Church, 204 16th Avenue, N.W., Calgary, Alberta, Canada, AB T2M OH4.

Gay and Lesbian Switchboards

Gay Switchboard is in most large cities (see below).

If not available, contact:
National Gay and Lesbian Task Force Information Line
(202) 332-6483

Atlanta
Gay Helpline - (404) 892-0661

Baltimore
Gay and Lesbian Switchboard - (301) 837-8888

Boston
Gay and Lesbian Helpline - (617) 267-9001

Chicago
Gay and Lesbian Information Line - (312) 975-1212

Cincinnati
Gay and Lesbian Community Switchboard - (513) 221-7800
Lesbian Line - (513) 381-5610

Cleveland
Lesbian and Gay Hotline - (216) 781-6736

Columbus
Stonewall Union - (614) 299-7764

Dallas/Ft. Worth
Gayline - (214) 368-6283

Denver
Gay and Lesbian Community Center - (303) 831-6268

Detroit
Gay and Lesbian Community Information Center - (313) 398-4297

Houston
Gay and Lesbian Switchboard - (713) 529-3211

Indianapolis
Gay and Lesbian Switchboard - (317) 253-4297

Kansas City, Mo.
Gay Talk - (816) 931-4470

Los Angeles/Long Beach
Gay and Lesbian Community Services Center - (213) 464-7400

Miami/Ft. Lauderdale
Gay Community Hotline - (305) 759-3661

Milwaukee
Gay People's Union Hotline - (414) 562-7010

Minneapolis/St. Paul
Gay & Lesbian Community Action Helpline - (612) 379-6390

New York City
Gay Switchboard - (212) 777-1800
Lesbian Switchboard - (212) 741-2610

Norfolk/Virginia Beach
Gay Information Line - (804) 423-0933

Philadelphia
Gay Switchboard - (215) 546-7100
Lesbian Switchboard - (215) 222-5110

Phoenix
Lesbian/Gay Community Switchboard - (602) 234-2752

Pittsburgh
Gay and Lesbian Community Center - (412) 431-5422

Sacramento
Lambda Community Center (916) 442-0185

San Diego
Lesbian & Gay Community Information Line - (619) 692-4297

San Francisco/Oakland
Gay and Lesbian Switchboard - (415) 841-6224

Seattle
No hotline. *The Gay News* - (206) 324-4297
Will make referrals and answer questions about gay and lesbian businesses and services in Seattle.

St. Louis
Gay and Lesbian Hotline - (314) 367-0084

St. Petersburg
The Line - (813) 586-4297

Tampa
The Line - (813) 229-8839

appendix c

DESCRIPTION OF RESEARCH

Prompted by the positive response given to a presentation made to the San Francisco Gay Fathers, the author undertook the present study of the effects a married partner's coming out has on his or her straight spouse. Between 1986 through 1990, hundreds of straight spouses and mixed-orientation couples were interviewed coast to coast, located via therapists, researchers, a television panel featuring the author, a newspaper ad, support groups, Gay Fathers, Parents-FLAG, and word of mouth. Research into the literature and discussion with therapists added further insights.

From the interviews, twenty-nine straight spouses and two homosexual partners from nine states agreed to tell their stories for the core of the study. They ranged in age (25-65), in education completed (high school through graduate school), in occupation (wife/mother to administrator), and in length of marriage (from five to twenty-six years).

Using a phenomenological approach,* rather than work from a priori hypotheses, the author analyzed the stories to discern what the coming out meant for each spouse. Repeated analyses from varied perspectives—other spouses, therapists, and research—revealed common issues and reactions among straight spouses as well as typical coping and recovery strategies.

*See Patricia F. Carini, Observation and Description: An Alternative Methodology for the Investigation of Human Phenomena (North Forks, ND: University of North Dakota, 1975).

about the author

Amity Pierce Buxton grew up on the East Coast, where she earned her Ph.D. from Columbia University. For twenty-four years she has taught and consulted in the area of professional and personal growth for educators in the San Francisco Bay Area and nationally. While working in the multiethnic schools of San Francisco and Oakland, California, she has conducted research and published many articles on developmental issues in education and language in the United States, Europe and Asia. She is listed in *Who's Who in the West*.

The discovery in 1983 that her husband of twenty-five years was gay led to a nationwide study from 1986 to 1990 of the effects of the coming out of gay, bisexual and lesbian partners on their straight spouses. She has conducted a support group for ex-husbands and husbands and their spouses for the Gay Fathers of San Francisco, served as their Wives Hot Line, participated in several spouse-run support groups in Bay Area counties, organized a support group for Parents and Friends of Lesbians and Gays (P-FLAG) in Berkeley, California, and counseled spouses across the country. Currently, Dr. Buxton counsels spouses as the Pacific Southwest contact for the Spouses of Lesbians and Gays Task Force of the national P-FLAG organization. Now in a longterm heterosexual relationship, she resides in the San Francisco Bay Area, her grown children nearby.

The Other Side Of The Closet is her first book.

O R D E R   F O R M

☐ *PLEASE SEND ME A FREE CATALOG*

Name_____

Address_____

City_____State_____Zip_____

Quantity	Book Title and Author	Price	Total
	The Other Side of the Closet: The Coming-Out Crisis for Straight Spouses by Amity Pierce Buxton, Ph.D.	$ 14.95	
	When Someone You Love Has Cancer by Dana Rae Pomeroy	9.95	
	When Women Choose to be Single by Rita Robinson	9.95	
	When Your Parents Need You: A Caregiver's Guide by Rita Robinson	9.95	
	Survivors of Suicide by Rita Robinson	9.95	
	Good People: The Whole Self Integration Guide by Ruth Cherry, Ph.D.	12.95	
	Master Meditations: A Spiritual Daybook by Dr. Donald Curtis	12.95	
	The Book of Rituals: Personal and Planetary Transformation by Rev. Carol Parrish-Harra	14.95	
	The New Age Handbook on Death and Dying by Rev. Carol Parrish-Harra	8.95	
	The Law of Mind in Action by Dr. Fenwicke Lindsay Holmes	10.95	
	Axioms for Survivors: A Caregivers Guide by Lon Nungesser, M.A.	6.95	
	Being Human in the Face of Death edited by Deborah Roth, MSC & Emily LeVier, MSC	9.95	
	Stepping Stones to Grief Recovery edited by Deborah Roth, MSC	8.95	
	AIDS: A Self-Care Manual (Third Edition) by AIDS Project Los Angeles	14.95	
	When Someone You Love Has AIDS by BettyClare Moffatt, MA	8.95	
	Gifts for the Living: Conversations with Caregivers on Death and Dying by BettyClare Moffatt, MA	9.95	

Please send check or money order to:

IBS Press, Inc.
744 Pier Avenue
Santa Monica, CA 90405
(213)450-6485
(213)314-8268 (FAX)

SUBTOTAL	
SALES TAX 6.5% (California Only)	
SHIPPING/HANDLING ($2.00 per book)	
TOTAL DUE	

ORDERS   1-800-234-6485
VISA & MASTERCARD ACCEPTED
Weekdays, 9:00 am - 5:00 pm PST

PLACE
STAMP
HERE

IBS PRESS, Inc
744 Pier Avenue
Santa Monica, CA 90405